Vegetarian Cooking
AT • THE • ACADEMY

SUSAN WALTER
Writer

JILL FOX
Editor

PATRICIAN BRABANT
Photographer

ROBERT LAMBERT
Food Stylist

MARIA WINSTON
Photographic Stylist

CALIFORNIA CULINARY ACADEMY

Susan Walter began her culinary career while working for a caterer during college. She has studied cooking in the United States and at Le Cordon Bleu in France, and has traveled extensively in Europe and Latin America studying the cuisines. She owns Susan Walter Catering and is the Catering Director at the Queen Anne Hotel in San Francisco, as well as a cooking teacher, event organizer, and author. She serves as the Immediate Past President of the San Francisco Professional Food Society and as Treasurer of the Northern California chapter of the American Institute of Wine and Food, and is a member of the International Association of Food Professionals. A native of Michigan, Ms. Walter lives in San Francisco.

The California Culinary Academy In the forefront of American institutions leading the culinary renaissance in this country, the California Culinary Academy in San Francisco has gained a reputation as one of the most outstanding professional chef training schools in the world. With a teaching staff recruited from the best restaurants of Western Europe, the Academy educates students from around the globe in the preparation of classical cuisine. The recipes in this book were created in consultation with the chefs of the Academy. For information about the Academy, write the Office of the Dean, California Culinary Academy, 625 Polk St., San Francisco, CA 94102.

Front Cover
For a light menu, try replacing a heavy main course with two side dishes that complement one another in color, texture, and flavor. Thai Eggplant (page 85) and Harvest Stir-Fry (page 86) make a light but satisfying supper.

Title Page
Toast rounds spread with mixture of red bell pepper and almonds float atop a fragrant Sweet Garlic Soup (page 97) in this savory first course.

Back Cover
Upper: One variation of Chicago-Style Pizza (page 79) features escarole, tomato, garlic, and a duet of mozzarella and dry Monterey jack cheese. Cornmeal is the secret ingredient in the crust.

Lower: Beans, tortillas, and eggs are the mainstay of Huevos Rancheros. Guacamole makes a delicious topping for this traditional cowboy dish (page 113).

Special thanks to Mark Felton, Joseph Feuling, Rebecca Johnson, Mark Osborn, Patricia Reuter, and Charles Walter. Ames Gallery (Bonnie Grossman), Cookin' (Judy Kaminsky), Shreve & Co. (Barbara Linklater), and Wedgwood San Francisco.

Contributors
Calligraphers
Keith Carlson, Chuck Wertman

Nutritional Consultant
Marlyn Hanson

Concept Consultant
Tina Salter

Seasonal Charts Compiler
Karen Kimberlain

Seasonal Charts Editor
Andrea Y. Connolly

Additional Photographers
Alan Copeland, Academy students
Marshall Gordon, pages 30, 66, and 80
Kit Morris, author and chefs, at left

Photographer's Assistant
Louis Bloch

Additional Stylist
Doug Warne, pages 30, 66, and 80

Copyeditor
Judith Dunham

Proofreaders
Toni Murray, Leslie Tilley

Indexer
Elinor Lindheimer

Printed in Hong Kong through Mandarin Offset.

The California Culinary Academy series is published by the staff of Cole Group.
Publisher
Brete C. Harrison

Associate Publisher
James Connolly

VP and Director of Operations
Linda Hauck

VP Marketing and Business Development
John A. Morris

Director of Production
Steve Lux

Senior Editor
Annette Gooch

Production Assistant
Dotti Hydue

B C D E F G H
4 5 6 7 8 9 0

ISBN 1-56426-038-0
CIP 92-30275

Address all inquiries to
Cole Group
4415 Sonoma Highway/ PO Box 4089
Santa Rosa, CA 95402-4089
(800) 959-2717   (707) 538-0492
FAX (707) 538-0497

Distributed to the book trade by
Publishers Group West

*Keep the pantry full of root
vegetables, grains, legumes, and
nuts as the starting point for
vegetarian cooking. A good diet
requires a mix of many foods.*

Enjoying Vegetarian Cooking

With healthy meals becoming
a top priority in many homes,
vegetarian cooking deserves
a closer look. Legumes, grains, nuts, fresh
fruits, and vegetables all add variety
and nutrients to our daily diets. When dining
according to the seasons, the cook can
enjoy the best of nature, not only in flavor
and food value but in quality and economy.
Enjoy these recipes whether you are a
vegetarian or an omnivore experimenting
with delicious, wholesome foods.

GOOD EATING

From a nutritional standpoint, fruits, vegetables, nuts, grains, and legumes are primarily composed of complex carbohydrates, making them the ideal fuel for the body. Shifting to a vegetarian diet can reduce the amount of fat consumed while increasing the fiber, vitamins, and minerals. When properly balanced in a diet, grains, legumes, and vegetables also provide adequate amounts of protein.

HEALTH BENEFITS

In a short time, the change to a vegetarian diet may result in better weight control, healthier blood pressure, lower blood fat levels (cholesterol and triglycerides), and a more functional digestive tract.

In the long run, a diet high in fiber and low in fat may help prevent such degenerative disorders as cancers of the colon and breast, coronary heart disease, stroke, and diverticulitis (inflammation of the colon).

The Pregnant Vegetarian

A female vegetarian who becomes pregnant and continues a wise lacto-ovo-vegetarian diet will provide excellent nutrition for both herself and her baby. Pregnant women who wish to continue a vegetarian diet should carefully read the information about protein below. Four servings of dairy products, four small servings of protein-rich foods (eggs, legumes, cheeses), and four servings of whole grains should be eaten daily to provide a recommended prenatal diet. Legumes furnish protein and high levels of minerals, such as folic acid and zinc, both of which are important in prenatal nutrition. Four daily servings of fruits and vegetables supply many of the vitamins and minerals recommended in a prenatal diet. For extra insurance, most childbirth practitioners prescribe a prenatal supplement whether or not the diet includes meat.

Infant and Child Feeding

Although there are numerous considerations to take into account, nutritionists agree that the breast milk of a healthy, well-nourished mother commonly is the best and most complete food for her infant, at least during the first six months of life. With some modification, a vegetarian diet provides a woman with adequate nutrition to support breast-feeding and maintain her own health. Breast-feeding depletes about 600 calories per day. A woman's diet must provide the extra energy to pass on to her child. As a child grows, thoughtfully planned vegetarian meals can continue to provide necessary nutrition.

NUTRIENT NEEDS

Since the link between nutrition and health has begun to be actively explored, much research has been done on the nutrient needs of individuals. The consensus is that most of us eat too much protein, especially animal protein, which is high in fat. An average North American consumes about 100 grams of protein daily, nearly twice the actual requirement. Conversely at least seven other nutrients tend to be low in almost everyone's diet, so it would be helpful for all of us to know more about each of these vital elements.

Protein

One reason a well-balanced vegetarian diet is so healthy is that it provides high-quality, low-fat protein. Grains and legumes—mainstays of a vegetarian diet—are good examples of low-fat protein sources. The lacto-vegetarian can also include protein from animal sources by choosing low-fat or nonfat dairy products. Men typically need 55 grams of protein daily; women about 46 grams.

Protein consists primarily of amino acids, the building blocks of the body. The body uses 22 different amino acids to build cells. Amino acids are simply carbon, hydrogen, oxygen, and nitrogen arranged in different positions on a chain. Think of them as ballet dancers set in various postures by a choreographer who wants to create a certain effect.

Of the 22 different amino acids required for protein structure, nine cannot be synthesized by the body. The nine amino acids that must be obtained from the diet are called *essential amino acids.* Individual sources of vegetable protein lack adequate amounts of at least one of the essential amino acids. This missing amino acid is called the *limiting amino acid.*

Vegetarians, especially those who rely on vegetables for protein, must combine protein sources in order to obtain all nine essential amino acids.

Protein combining is not as difficult as it sounds. Enough high-quality protein can be obtained from all types of vegetarian diets. One way is to combine animal sources of protein—eggs and dairy products—with vegetable sources of protein; for example, to eat cottage cheese and vegetable salad in the same meal.

A vegetarian who excludes animal proteins from the diet must combine vegetable protein sources with complementary limiting amino acids. The three limiting amino acids in vegetable protein are *methionine* (usually low in legumes), *lysine* (usually low in grains), and *tryptophan* (usually low in vegetables and some legumes). A couple of basic protein-balanced food combinations are rice and beans or tofu and vegetables with rice.

Calcium

Calcium is a mineral best known for its role in the prevention of bone disease, such as osteoporosis. Calcium is also important in the regulation of bodily fluids. It is required for the transmission of nerve impulses and for the contraction of muscles, including the heart. A body deficient in calcium borrows it from the supply in the bones to keep vital body functions operating normally. Health experts suggest that adequate calcium also helps protect against high blood pressure and colon cancer.

The Recommended Daily Allowance (RDA) of calcium is 1,000 milligrams, increasing to 1,400 to 1,600 milligrams after menopause. Good sources (and the milligrams of calcium per typical serving) are nonfat milk (300), whole milk (350), collard greens (360), yogurt (270), cheese (225), bok choy (250), and broccoli (200).

Zinc

Ensuring adequate zinc in a meatless diet requires special attention. A zinc deficiency can dramatically impair the immune system and wound healing mechanisms. Zinc is even more important during periods of growth and pregnancy. Athletes who may lose significant amounts of zinc in perspiration also need to be conscious of zinc intake.

The RDA for zinc is 15 milligrams. Vegetables and fruits are generally poor sources of zinc. If you are cutting down on meat, be sure to include some of these foods (the milligrams of zinc per typical serving are listed after each) in the diet every day: black-eyed peas (3.0); garbanzo, pinto, lentil, and lima beans (2.0); brown rice (1.2); wheat germ (3.2); and whole wheat bread (1.0).

Iron

The body only absorbs about 10 percent of the iron taken in through the diet, but it is very efficient at conserving and recycling this important mineral. Bleeding is the most common way of losing iron from the body's iron stores.

The RDA for iron is 18 milligrams for women of childbearing age, but only 10 milligrams for postmenopausal women and men of all ages.

Iron is more difficult to absorb from vegetable sources than from meat, due to the different structure of the iron compounds in these foods. A vegetarian should pay special attention to ensuring adequate iron intake. To increase iron absorption, consume iron-rich foods with acidic foods like citrus fruits, tomatoes, or wine. Cook-

ing with iron utensils when possible can also add iron to the diet. Good vegetarian sources of iron (and the milligrams per typical serving) are prune juice (10.5), black beans (7.9), garbanzo beans (6.9), pinto beans (6.1), and spinach (4.0).

B₆ (Pyridoxine)

This vitamin plays an important role in the use of protein. The exact amount needed depends on the amount of protein consumed. Nutritionists feel that most North Americans get less B_6 than is needed for well-being. This is particularly true in a diet of processed foods, since milling or heating can drastically reduce the B_6 content of a specific food. One example is white flour, which contains only 25 percent of the original B_6 levels in whole wheat.

The current RDA for adults is 2.0 to 2.2 milligrams. Good sources of B_6 (and the milligrams of B_6 per typical serving) are soybeans (.85); spinach (.64); bananas (.61); and navy, pinto, and lima beans (.50 each).

Folic Acid

Most North Americans have a folic-acid intake of less than 50 percent of the recommended amount. Folic acid is required for cell division and reproduction. When a folic-acid deficiency occurs, rapidly dividing cells, such as blood cells and cells in the digestive tract, are especially affected.

Folic-acid levels are high in dark green leafy vegetables, fresh oranges, and whole wheat products. Cooking can destroy over half the folic-acid content in food, and storage for three or four days at room temperature can reduce folic-acid content by 75 percent. The RDA for folic acid is 400 milligrams. Good sources (and the milligrams of folic acid per typical serving) include soybeans (290), orange juice (164), garbanzo beans (125), kidney beans (100), spinach (460), and broccoli (75).

DEFINING VEGETARIANS

Vegetarians come in all sorts and intensities. You may choose to make vegetarian cooking only a part of your repertoire or prefer a constant vegetarian diet for health, religious, or economic reasons. Whatever the philosophy, vegetarianism has become the preferred diet of many people. There are three general categories of non-meat eaters.

Vegan This strict vegetarian consumes only nuts, grains, legumes, fruits, and vegetables. Vitamin B₁₂, necessary for cell development and functioning of the nervous system, is found in milk products. When these products are excluded from the diet, then yeast, fermented soy products, or supplements must be included. Because B₁₂ is stored in the body, it may be years before a deficiency is noted. Children and pregnant women may have special requirements that necessitate additions to the vegan diet.

Lacto-vegetarian This vegetarian eats nuts, grains, legumes, fruits, vegetables, and dairy products. Cheeses, milk, cream, buttermilk, and sour cream increase the variety of available dishes and add necessary animal protein. Dairy products also contain tryptophan, which seems to promote sleep. The old-fashioned glass of warm milk at bedtime may have scientific basis.

Ovo-lacto-vegetarian For this vegetarian, eggs augment an already bountiful diet of dairy products, nuts, grains, legumes, fruits, and vegetables. The use of eggs in the vegetarian diet adds a multitude of possibilities for the cook. Although eggs should be consumed in moderation—usually no more than three per week—many dishes benefit from the addition of an egg.

Although this book primarily addresses the diet of the ovo-lacto-vegetarian, it has dishes for every type of vegetarian.

B$_{12}$ (Cobalamin)

A vegan diet that excludes *all* animal products probably needs to be supplemented with vitamin B$_{12}$, which is the one nutrient necessary for health that generally cannot be provided by plant foods. This is an important consideration when selecting your vegetarian diet; the dairy products and eggs included in a lacto-ovo-vegetarian diet do provide substantial amounts of vitamin B$_{12}$.

Vitamin B$_{12}$ is essential for the functioning of most body cells. Like folic acid, it plays a role in the synthesis of DNA and RNA, the materials that make it possible for cells to divide and regenerate. B$_{12}$ deficiency shows up first in tissues that multiply rapidly, such as red blood cells. Anemia is a primary result, but irreversible nerve damage can occur after a prolonged lack of B$_{12}$.

Good sources in the lacto-ovo-vegetarian diet (and milligrams of B$_{12}$ per typical serving) are cottage cheese (1.2), milk (1.0), buttermilk (.54), Swiss and Cheddar cheese (.28), and yogurt (.28).

Vitamin B$_2$ (Riboflavin)

For both vegetarians and nonvegetarians, dairy products probably provide most of the riboflavin in the diet. This vitamin plays a major role in energy release throughout the body. A vegan who does not eat dairy products should pay special attention to the vegetarian sources of riboflavin.

Neither dairy nor vegetable sources of this nutrient should be stored in containers where light can reach them, since riboflavin is destroyed by light in just a few hours. The refrigerator is an ideal place for keeping these foods.

For adults the RDA for B$_2$ is 1.2 to 1.6 milligrams. Good sources (and the milligrams of B$_2$ per typical serving) are cottage cheese (.61), low-fat milk (.51), low-fat yogurt (.44), collard greens (.38), broccoli (.36), mushrooms (.32), and Cheddar cheese (.26).

Complex Carbohydrates

Complex carbohydrates consist of the starches that, when broken down into simpler forms, provide the body with the energy to function. They are found in unrefined grains, beans, vegetables, and fruit. A complex carbohydrate differs from a simple carbohydrate such as sugar, which can raise the blood sugar too rapidly and let it fall equally dramatically, creating peaks and valleys of energy. Complex carbohydrates allow the energy level to rise gradually, stay at a moderate level, and only gradually taper off. As a bonus carbohydrates seem to burn more calories than protein, long considered essential to weight-loss diets.

Basing a diet on immaculately fresh, complex carbohydrates is a healthy approach to eating. Up to 80 percent of the calories consumed in the diet could be from foods in this category, in a raw or unrefined state. Balance the remainder of the diet with the vitamins, minerals, protein, and fatty acids found in other foods. Foods with more complex carbohydrates usually are lower in fat, which contains more calories than any other component of food. High concentrations of protein in the diet contribute to low energy and sluggishness. Complex carbohydrates supply long-term energy for healthy physical and mental activity.

Fiber

Although fiber is not really a nutrient, it has been the focus of many articles and discussions on nutrition. Health experts believe that fiber, which passes through the digestive system largely intact, plays an important role in maintaining health.

Fiber is found only in the structure of plants. This means that decreasing consumption of meat and increasing that of vegetables promotes optimum fiber intake.

The health value of different fibers varies widely, and the diet should include grains, vegetables, and fruits as sources of fiber. Don't just sprinkle bran on highly processed foods, following an assumption that it will provide adequate fiber. For instance, bran does not affect fats in the blood, but pectins—found in apples and the fiber in oats and carrots—can cause a decrease in blood cholesterol levels.

Since foods that are high in fiber are also low in calories, a diet high in fiber makes weight control easier. Also, because the bulk in these foods is filling and chewing fibrous foods takes a long time, satiety is reached by consuming much fewer calories.

Intake of fibrous foods should be increased slowly to give the digestive tract time to adjust. The body needs a chance to build up its enzyme production so that it can handle a vegetarian diet easily.

NUTRIENT BREAKDOWN

Eight complete menus are provided in this book to acquaint cooks with vegetarian meal planning. Family meals for breakfast, brunch, and dinner are included, as well as special meals for entertaining and party ideas for groups of non-meat eaters. Each menu (except the cocktail party) includes a nutrient-breakdown chart listing the calorie, protein, fiber, cholesterol, vitamin C, calcium, and sodium content of the whole meal, per person. Use these as guides for preparing well-rounded meals for yourself, your family, and friends.

SEASONAL CHARTS

A guide to specific purchasing and storage needs for various produce available on a year-round basis begins on page 9. Guides to seasonal produce appear in each chapter (see page 28 for spring, 46 for summer, 72 for autumn, 97 for winter).

ALL SEASONS FRESH PRODUCE

FRUITS	Purchase	Storage	Special Notes
Apples	For eating fresh use Golden Delicious, Jonathan (brilliant red), McIntosh (red to green), Stayman (red), Red Delicious, or Winesap (red). For making pies and applesauce, use tart or slightly acidic varieties: Gravenstein (green with red strips), Grimes Golden, Jonathan, and Newtown pippin (green to red). For baking, use firmer-fleshed varieties: Northern Spy (red), Rhode Island Greening (green), Rome Beauty (red), Winesap, and York Imperial (greenish yellow) preferably over 3 in. in dia. Look for color and firmness (particularly with large sizes, which tend to mature faster than smaller apples that are often priced more economically, making them more available for cooking). Avoid bruised or immature apples with lack of good color, and overripe apples that yield to slight pressure and are soft and mealy. Scald (irregularly shaped tan or brown area) has tougher texture than skin but does not seriously affect eating quality.	Wash and dry; will keep one week in fruit and vegetable drawer of refrigerator.	Major apple-producing states are Wash., N.Y., Mich., Va., Calif., and Pa.; others include W.Va., Mass., N.J., Mo., Kans., Ill., N.C., and Oreg. Rich in fiber, water, and pectin, which helps lower cholesterol level. Adds bulks and volume to diet, helps prevent overeating.
Avocados	Varieties. Fuerte: produced mainly in Calif., green, pear shaped, thin skinned; Hass: skin is medium thick, leathery and somewhat rough, green at maturity but black when avocado is ready to be eaten; Lula: produced mainly in Fla., medium sized, pear shaped, greenish rind flecked with yellow, greenish yellow flesh. Wide variation in weight, texture, and skin thickness. Color ranges from green to black. Look for slightly soft avocados that yield to gentle pressure (for immediate use) or firmer fruits (for later use). Irregular light-brown markings sometimes found on skin have no effect on flesh. Avoid dark, soft, sunken spots; bruised, cracked, or broken surfaces.	Should be ripened at room temperature, preferably in a dark place; ripening takes from 3 to 5 days; refrigeration will slow process. Fully ripened avocados will have soft, oily-textured flesh and rich flavor; skin color usually green but some varieties turn maroon, brown, or purplish black when ripe. A toothpick that can be easily inserted at stem end also indicates ripeness. Do not cut until ripe. Refrigerate when ripe.	Introduced into U.S. in the late 1800s by Henry Perrine, who sent trees from Mexico to Miami, Fla. Rich in vitamin C: half a moderately sized one provides almost 50 percent of normal daily requirement. Has been a staple for many centuries in Latin American countries.
Bananas	Look for firmness and full yellow color. Ripe when solid yellow skin color is specked with brown; green tips or lack of yellow color indicate immaturity. Avoid bruised or discolored skin (indicates decay) or dull, grayish, aged appearance (indicates exposure to cold).	Ripening continues at room temperature, between 60° and 70° F. Temperatures below 55° F injurious; higher temperatures cause too rapid ripening.	Entire supply imported from Central and South America. Good sources of vitamins A, B_1, B_2, B_6, and C; niacin, and potassium. No cholesterol, 0.2 percent fat, low sodium content.
Kiwifruit	Look for light brown, furry-appearing, oval-shaped fruit about 2½ in. long, with tender, soft skin. Interior texture similar to American gooseberry.	Keep at room temperature.	The fruit of a Chinese gooseberry named after the tiny kiwi bird of New Zealand, where grown.
Lemons	Look for rich yellow color; smooth-textured, slightly glossy skin, firmness and heaviness (indicate juiciness), medium size (all-purpose). Avoid dark yellow or dull color, hardened or shriveled skin (indicates aging), soft spots, mold on surface, skin punctures (indicate decay).	Wash to remove mold and dirt; keep at 50° F, 85 percent relative humidity. If lemons shrivel in storage, immerse in hot water for half an hour to restore freshness and increase amount of juice extract.	Primarily from Ariz. and Calif. Provides some vitamin C; lemon in water improves elimination; adds flavor to salt-free diets.
Oranges	Varieties. Valencia: Apr.–Oct., excellent for juicing, or slicing for adding to salads; Washington Navel: Nov.–May, thicker skin that is more pebbled and easily removed, segments separate readily; ideal for eating as a whole fruit or as segments in salad. Look for firmness, heaviness, smooth and bright-looking skin. Rich orange skin color is not a reliable quality indicator because skin is frequently treated with vegetable dye. Fully mature oranges, particularly Valencia, will often regreen, turning greenish, late in season. Russeting, a brownish roughened area over skin, often found on Fla. and Tex. oranges, has no effect on eating quality and often occurs on oranges with thin skin and superior eating quality. Avoid light-weight oranges, very rough skin texture (indicates abnormally thick skin and less flesh); dull, dry skin with spongy texture (indicates aging and deteriorated quality); cuts or punctures, soft spots on the surface (indicate decay), and discolored, weakened areas of skin around stem end.	Wash and dry; keep at 32° F, 90 percent relative humidity.	From Calif., Tex., Fla., and Ariz. Excellent source of vitamin C. Eating skinned fruit preferred to drinking a cup of juice for benefit of fiber and bulk; whole fruit provides body with fuel for energy over a longer period of time than juice.
Plantains	May be purchased in unripe green state or in ripened golden state. *See Bananas.*	Keep at room temperature.	Always cook before eating: green ones are usually fried with garlic; yellow used in baking; golden included in custards, compotes, and cakes.
Prunes	Look for blue-black, oval, firm-fleshed prunes representing late plum crop. Avoid broken skin, hardness, and poor color.	Keep at 32° F, 90 percent relative humidity.	Excellent source of vitamin A and minerals; contain some vitamin C. High-fiber fruit that improves elimination. Fiber-rich foods reduce chances of heart and intestinal diseases as well as cancer of colon and rectum. Comparison: 1 cup cornflakes=0.3 g. fiber, ½ grapefruit=0.6 g. fiber, Danish pastry=0.8 g. fiber, small apple=3.0 g. fiber, 4 pitted prunes=3.0 g. fiber, ⅓ cup bran cereal=8.9 grams fiber.

ALL SEASONS FRESH PRODUCE (continued)

VEGETABLES Purchase		Storage	Special Notes
Beans			
Fava Beans	Flat, kidney-shaped beans. Look for long, rounded, green, velvety-podded variety. Avoid flabby pods, bruises, or cracks.	Wash and dry; will keep well for 2 to 3 days at 45° to 50° F, relative humidity 85 percent, if well ventilated.	Also known as broad beans, horse beans, and Windsors. Almost all beans, especially green, are an excellent source of vitamin A. A half cup has one third RDA.
Green Beans	Types are bush and pole. Look for string or stringless beans with long straight pods that snap easily, green or waxy yellow (wax beans), flat or round. Avoid ridges and bulges (indicate pods are old, tough, and leathery).	*See Fava Beans.*	The immature pods of an older variety of kidney bean, picked when seeds are tiny. Also called snap beans, garden beans, and string beans.
Lima Beans	Varieties: butter limas (smaller), potato limas (larger). Flat and kidney-shaped beans smaller than favas. Look for clean, dark green, well-filled pods; plump with a tender green or greenish white skin.	*See Fava Beans.*	
Soybeans	A small, fuzzy, pea-shaped Asian legume with richer flavor and more nutrition than common beans. Look for green color, plump pods.	*See Fava Beans.*	Raw soybeans high in vitamin B_1 and moderate in vitamin A.
Beets	Look for globular shape and smooth, firm flesh. Avoid large sizes and soft flesh. Young beet leaves sold as salad greens should be green, tender, thin ribbed, and not wilted or slimy (beet tops deteriorate quickly and do not affect quality of beet).	Wash and dry; will keep briefly at 32° F, 95 percent relative humidity.	Beet leaves are an excellent source of vitamin A; beets contain moderate amounts of sugar and vitamins A and C.
Cabbage	Varieties: bok choy and celery (Chinese): long, oval-shaped, pale green; red: purplish, compact; savoy: yellowish, crimped leaves, head not much harder than iceburg lettuce. Look for well-trimmed, solid heads. Early or new cabbage is less firm than fall and winter strains. Avoid discolored veins, light weight for size, loose leaves throughout.	Wash; keep at 32° F, 90 percent relative humidity, if well ventilated. Wilts quickly in storage.	Common varieties have small amounts of vitamins A and C. Cooked bok choy is an excellent source of vitamin A. Savoy is an excellent source of vitamins B_1 and C. A cruciferous family member, cabbage may reduce risk of colon cancer and provides fiber and minerals.
Carrots	Look for bright orange color, spindle shape, firm flesh. Avoid straggling rootlets, rough surfaces, pliability, or carrots with tops, which draw moisture and freshness from roots.	Wash; will keep well several mo. at 32° F, 95 percent relative humidity.	Excellent source of vitamin A; ¾ cup (raw) provides an adult over twice the RDA.
Celery	Varieties: golden (white), Pascal (dark or light green). Look for stalks that will snap easily, smooth insides of stems, good heart formation.	Wash; keep at 32° F, 90 to 95 percent relative humidity.	Moderate source of vitamin A and minerals.
Garlic	Look for firm and white or light-purple heads, depending on variety, with pungent odor. Avoid browning or softness.	Will keep for several weeks in a dry, cool, dark place.	Used for centuries like an antibiotic.
Lettuce	Summer varieties. Bibb: small, cup shaped, dark green, crisp; butterhead: softer, lighter, and less crisp than iceberg, medium sized, light-green outer leaves, light-yellow inner leaves; leaf lettuce: crisp leaves branch loosely from stalk, color varies from light-green to brownish red. Winter varieties. Belgian endive: compact, cigar shaped, and creamy white from blanching, grown in complete darkness; chicory or curly endive: large, curly, feathery leaves and bitter taste; escarole: broader, paler, less crimped and less bitter than endive; iceberg: tightly headed, heavy, medium green on outside, pale green at heart, should be clean and free from burned or rusty-looking tips; romaine: green, elongated, moderately firm, coarser leaf and stronger flavor than iceberg.	Keep at 32° F, 90 percent relative humidity. Later washing in cool water will restore crispness.	Good sources of vitamin A.
Onions	Varieties: chives: tiny onions, both roots and tops used; large yellow: all purpose; medium: good for chopping, boiling, stuffing; pearl: less than 1 in. dia., fairly mild, good pickled, or creamed; shallots: small, cloved, dried, reddish skin, purplish white flesh; small white boilers: good in stews and casseroles; sweet Spanish: may be yellow or white, round to slightly oval. Look for shapeliness, dryness (enough to crackle, excepting leeks, green onions, chives), thin necks, bright and hard bulbs. Avoid wet, soggy necks.	Keep in dry area with 70 to 75 percent relative humidity; at higher humidities onions may decay and eventually grow roots. Never store with potatoes; onions will absorb moisture and decay quickly.	Peak seasons are spring and summer. Moderate sources of potassium, protein, and fiber.
Parsley	Varieties: curly leaf, flat leaf (Italian parsley). Look for bright green leaves. Avoid wilted, wet, or blackened leaves.	Keep at low temperature, 32° F (preferably in crushed ice), high humidity. Chopped parsley should be folded into a towel and wrung out thoroughly so it dries quickly.	Good source of vitamins A and C.
Potatoes	Varieties: long white group, round red group, round white group, rural or round russet group, long russet group (russet Burbank). "New" potatoes are younger and frequently smaller sized. Look for firmness, relatively smooth and clean surface, reasonable shape. Avoid cuts, bruises, wilting, sprouting, sun or light burn. Size does not affect quality.	Keep in cool, dry, dark area to avoid greening (when potatoes are exposed to artificial light for an extended time), which causes a bitter flavor. New potatoes can be stored for only a few days.	Trace amounts of vitamin C. The potato alone is not high in calories.
Turnips	White, yellow, red, or gray; long, round, or flat. Commonly have white or yellow flesh, with a green or purple band across top of skin. Can be very sweet. Look for crisp green tops, firm roots.	Refrigerate.	There is little nutritional value in the root; the greens are rich in vitamins and minerals.
Watercress	Look for rich green leaves free of dirt. Only one variety of watercress, but wild cresses and land cresses exist. Avoid wilted or discolored leaves (indicate aging).	Highly perishable; will keep briefly in refrigerator if enclosed with ice in plastic. Do not soak in water.	Rich in vitamins A and C; good source of calcium.

ALL SEASONS FRESH PRODUCE (continued)

NUTS & SEEDS	Purchase	Storage	Special Notes
Shelled Nuts **Unshelled Nuts**	Nuts can be purchased unshelled or shelled, roasted, salted, or raw; unprocessed nuts and seeds can be found at natural-food stores. Most nuts last longer in shells. Look for nuts that are uniformly colored and sized, crisp, and fresh smelling. Avoid rubbery or rancid nuts. Unshelled nuts (the least processed excepting peanuts, pistachios, and chestnuts) should be clean, undamaged, and heavy for size. Avoid nuts with splits, cracks, stains, or holes, or that rattle (indicates dryness, possible staleness). Do not buy or eat nuts with any signs of mold; they may be toxic.	Store nuts and seeds in tightly covered containers or airtight plastic bags in refrigerator or, if purchased in cans or vacuum-packed jars, on a cool, dry shelf 12 to 18 mo. or until opened. Opened cans and jars will keep up to 1 week on shelf or up to several mo. in refrigerator if tightly covered. Keep jars out of direct sunlight. Keep opened cans and jars of shelled nuts in tightly covered container in refrigerator to avoid rancidity. Shelled nuts can be frozen if in an airtight container, but they tend to lose flavor and crispness after thawing.	Aflatoxins are natural poisons caused by certain molds during harvesting, shipment, or storage of some foods, particularly nuts, grains, and seeds. The U.S. Department of Health and Human Services has determined through laboratory studies that these aflatoxins cause liver cancer in animals and may be linked to cancers of the stomach, liver, or kidney in humans. Exposure to the molds is reduced by keeping nuts, grains, and seeds in dry, sealed containers and heating for 10 minutes at 350° F before consuming. Discard such foods if moldy. In the United States, commercially sold nuts, grains, seeds, and any food products containing them are monitored for safety and quality by the Food and Drug Administration and by industry. Generally, nuts are a good source of phosphorus and potassium. Sesame seeds are an excellent source of calcium.

GRAINS

	Purchase	Storage	Special Notes
	To ensure quality, purchase packaged grains from a reputable store; grains can harbor molds.	Store whole grains—whole groats, cracked or ground—in tightly lidded containers or sealed plastic bags in refrigerator up to 4 to 5 mo. Will keep up to 1 mo. at room temperature, although pearl barley and hominy will keep up to 1 year on a cool, dry shelf. To protect grains from insects, add bay leaves.	
Barley	Available as groats (whole, husked kernels consisting of bran, starchy endosperm, and germ), as pearls (called soup barley, the bran has been removed), or as grits (coarsely ground pearl barley).	Will keep in pantry up to 1 mo. or in refrigerator or freezer 2 to 3 mo.	
Bran	Is the outermost part of seed. Wheat bran is most common, although oat bran provides an alternative for those allergic to wheat.	Will keep in pantry 1 mo. or in refrigerator or freezer 2 to 3 mo.	Rich in fiber and the mineral ash.
Brown Rice	When cooked, long grained is dry and fluffy, with each grain separate; short grained looks plump, sometimes almost round, and is creamier and stickier than long grained. Brown rice is usually light-brown and still has the bran coating on each grain. Look for dry and clean rice in a busy store with a high turnover of goods. Avoid any hint of rancid odor.	Keep brown rice, which contains natural oils that can go rancid, in an airtight container in refrigerator up to 6 mo. Cooked rice will keep up to 7 days if covered with plastic wrap or stored in tightly sealed container and refrigerated. (Keep white and wild rices in an airtight canister to keep out dust, moisture, and insects. Both will keep indefinitely at room temperature with no loss of nutrients or eating quality.)	
Buckwheat	Groats may be raw or toasted (often called kasha when roasted and ground into grits).	Keep on shelf up to 1 mo. or in refrigerator up to 4 or 5 mo.	Since not in grass family, good for those allergic to wheat. Excellent source of protein. Flour has high fat content and no gluten.
Bulgur	To ensure freshness, purchase prepackaged from reputable dealer. Avoid black specks, a sign of spores.	Will keep on shelf 1 mo. or in refrigerator 3 to 6 mo.	Bulgur is wheat that has been boiled, then dried; a small amount of the outer bran is removed, then wheat is cracked. Cracked wheat is a coarse meal, cut rather than ground from the whole wheat kernel, which is cooked for a cereal or side dish, or added to homemade bread for nutty flavor and crunchy texture.
Cornmeal	Varieties: white, yellow. For cooking they are virtually the same. *Enriched* or *degerminated* means germ has been removed and lost nutrients replaced; stone-ground has had the larger bran particles removed through milling.	Keep degerminated in pantry up to 6 to 12 mo. or in refrigerator or freezer up to 1 year. Keep stone-ground up to 1 mo. in pantry or in refrigerator or freezer up to 1 year.	
Cornstarch	Silky, white powder often used as thickening agent for sauces, puddings, and fruit-pie fillings.	Look for dating code on box to determine a reasonable storage time.	
Kasha	*See Buckwheat.*		
Millet	Comes as tiny yellow whole kernels, produced from a grass.	Will keep on shelf 3 to 6 mo.	A useful grain for people who are unable to digest wheat and other gluten-containing grains. Good source of protein.

ALL SEASONS FRESH PRODUCE (continued)

GRAINS	Purchase	Storage	Special Notes
Oats	Available as whole kernels but more commonly processed for rolled oats. Most of germ and bran remain after processing, so higher in fat than most grains.	*See Bulgur.*	Good source of thiamin and other B vitamins and iron.
Potato Starch	Used as thickening agent.		
Rice Flour	Ground from white or brown rice; white has almost no fat, brown has considerable amount of fat. Sweet rice flour, a type of white, can be used only as a thickening agent.	White will keep on shelf 6 to 12 mo. or in refrigerator or freezer up to 1 year. Brown will keep on shelf 1 mo. or in refrigerator or freezer up to 2 or 3 mo.	
Rye Flour	A nonwheat grain that yields a heavy, pungent bread. Dark and light varieties interchangeable in recipes, although dark has stronger flavor.	Will keep on shelf 1 mo. or in refrigerator or freezer 2 to 3 mo.	
Soy Flour	Ground from whole soybeans. Also called soya or soy powder.	Will keep on cool, dry shelf up to 1 mo. or in refrigerator up to 4 mo.	Very nutritious. If added to whole wheat flour when baking, breads and cakes will be moist, fine grained, and high in iron, calcium, and protein. Also used as thickening agent. Very high in fat content (defatted variety is available), has no gluten or starch.
Unbleached Flour	Contains no chemicals to artificially whiten or age flour. Has creamy, off-white color.	Will keep on shelf 6 to 12 mo. or in refrigerator or freezer 1 year.	
Wheat Germ	The heart of the wheat kernel. Available flaked or as a coarse meal, raw or toasted. Minerals increase protein when added to baked goods. Look for refrigeration when purchasing unless in vacuum-packed jar, which must be refrigerated after opening.	Will keep in refrigerator 2 to 3 mo.	High fat content, so is most perishable of the wheat kernel. Increases protein when added to baked goods.
Whole Wheat Flour	Also called graham flour. Contains all parts of kernel—bran, germ, and endosperm. Varieties differ in coarseness. Stone-ground has more vitamins than steel-milled. Look for sharp, fresh scent.	Will keep on shelf 1 mo. or in refrigerator or freezer up to 1 year.	

LEGUMES

	Purchase	Storage	Special Notes
	Look for brightness, uniform size (mixed sizes require different cooking times). The longer a legume is stored, the more it fades and the longer it needs to be cooked.	Store in sealed plastic bags purchased in or preferably in glass. Will keep 1 year on dry, cool shelf.	Legumes are high in fiber and contain moderate amounts of minerals. Generally, complemented with an equally sized portion of rice, legumes make complete proteins.
Black Beans	Small, black skinned; used in Mexican and South American cuisines. Relatively strongly flavored.		
Black-eyed Peas	Small cream-colored ovals with a black or yellow spot; a favorite in the South.		Good source of potassium and fiber.
Fava Beans	Large, brown, shape similar to limas.		
Garbanzos	Also called chick-peas; tan, round, firm textured, with a nutty flavor; popular in East Indian, Latin American, and Middle Eastern cuisines.		
Kidney Beans	Varieties: light red, dark red. Oval pink or red, large, kidney-shaped beans. Tougher skinned and stronger flavored than pintos or whites.		Good in soups, stews, and chiles. Light-red kidneys cook faster than dark red.
Lentils	Varieties: red, green, brown, yellow. Available whole or split. Small, flat disks. Usually brown, greenish tan, or reddish orange.		Often used in casseroles and salads. Cooking time is much less than peas or beans.
Lima Beans	Pale green, kidney-shaped beans, big or small. Taste is a cross between white beans and fresh green beans. Buttery texture.		Also available fresh, canned, or frozen.
Pinto Beans	Pale pink and patterned with brown or beige flecks; slightly nutty flavor, mealy texture.		
Soybeans	Small, light-tan, pea-shaped Asian legume that has richer flavor and more nutrition than common beans.		Excellent source of protein. Are 18 percent fat (1½ percent fat common in other large legumes) and 34 percent carbohydrate (other beans higher in carbohydrates than in protein). In dried form may be sprouted for use in salads and Chinese cuisine, ground into flour, or made into soybean oil, milk, or curd called tofu. Often used as meat substitute.
Split Peas	May be split or whole (requiring different cooking times), yellow or green.		Good in soup.
White Beans	Include great Northerns, marrow beans, navy beans, white kidney, and white pea beans. Small or big flattish shape.		

THE BASIC PANTRY

Cooking vegetarian food requires no special equipment or fancy techniques. The goal of establishing a vegetarian pantry is simple: have on hand the best basic ingredients to combine with the fresh foods of each season. Basic recipes that will be used throughout the year follow information about major food groups.

Dairy Products

Cheese, milk, buttermilk, yogurt, butter, and sour cream provide calcium, minerals, vitamins, and essential amino acids important to every diet. If your diet includes some dairy products, you need not be too concerned with missing amino acids. One of the problems with dairy products is their high percentage of fats. Used in moderation, however, they add versatility and richness to the vegetarian diet.

Yogurt, which has a bacteria beneficial to digestion, is believed to have originated in Bulgaria, where it is still consumed in large quantities. The bacillus in yogurt changes the lactose, or milk sugar, to lactic acid, which makes yogurt digestible even for those unable to tolerate other dairy products. It is an excellent substitute for sour cream or cream when richness is not required.

BÉCHAMEL SAUCE

This classic white sauce contributes nutrients to a variety of dishes throughout the year including Spring Vegetable Cobbler (see page 29), Spinach Roulade (see page 49), Shiitake Potpie (see page 76), and Eggplant Moussaka (see page 105).

> 2 tablespoons butter
> 3 tablespoons flour
> 1¾ cups Vegetable Broth (see page 15)
> ½ teaspoon kosher salt
> ¼ teaspoon white pepper
> ¼ teaspoon nutmeg

Melt butter in a 1-quart saucepan over low heat. Whisk in flour, stirring to combine. Cook 2 to 3 minutes. Gradually add Vegetable Broth, whisking constantly until thickened. Season with salt, pepper, and nutmeg. Cook over low heat for 5 minutes. Use immediately or store in a sealed container in the refrigerator for up to 3 days.

Makes 2 cups.

Eggs

Chicken eggs are essential in baking and some cooking. The fat in eggs is found only in the yolks. When used in moderation, eggs add nutrients, flavor, richness, and leavening and thickening properties to cooked foods. Eggs are best purchased fresh and may be stored in the refrigerator for several weeks. Eggs are highly perishable at room temperature.

Fats and Oils

Fats carry the flavor and produce the aroma of foods. A balanced diet contains up to 30 percent fat, ideally only 10 percent saturated and 20 percent unsaturated fat. The A, D, E, and K vitamins are soluble in fat, which means that when a food is cooked in butter and the butter is drained away, these vitamins are lost.

Fats in the body contribute to a radiant complexion and glossy hair, provide insulation from the cold, and protect kidneys and mammary glands from vibrations and temperature changes. Fat stores energy in muscle tissue. Fat cells have unlimited storage capacity, which is why they continue to expand as supplied.

Saturated fat is hard at room temperature. This includes animal fats such as butter, suet, and lard, as well as hydrogenated (solid) margarine, and coconut and palm oils. Spoilage or oxidation can create health problems. Butter is preferred over margarine for flavor, but when following a strict vegan diet or reducing the amount of saturated fat in the diet, soft margarine or oils are allowed.

Unsaturated fat is liquid at room temperature. Oils such as safflower, sunflower, corn, sesame seed, soybean, and cottonseed are high in polyunsaturated fat. Safflower oil has the lowest amount of saturated fats of all vegetable oils. In preparing these recipes, choose an oil with a flavor that complements the food being cooked: corn oil when cooking corn or peanut oil when sautéing nuts.

Oils are highly perishable and should be purchased in amounts that will be used within eight weeks of opening. Oils are best stored in cool, dark areas, although refrigeration is not required except in the hottest climates. Some oils, when overheated, become hydrogenated or saturated. It is important, therefore, to avoid heating any oil to the smoking point.

Several grades of olive oil are available. The first pressing of the olives, without using extreme heat to cause pressure, is called virgin or extravirgin olive oil. The olives are pressed again using heat, and the product is called pure olive oil.

BASIC VINAIGRETTE

Miso, a fermented paste made of soybeans, is found in Asian markets.

> ¼ cup red or white wine vinegar
> 14 tablespoons oil
> 3 tablespoons miso
> 1 teaspoon kosher salt
> ½ teaspoon freshly ground pepper

In a small bowl or a 1-cup jar, shake or whisk vinegar, oil, miso, salt, and pepper. Use immediately or store tightly covered in the refrigerator for up to a week.

Makes 1¼ cups.

13

MOSAIC FRUIT COMPOTE

This jewellike dessert is made with always available dried fruit. Make it as part of the Emergency Dinner menu, which begins on page 20. Select a California port, or substitute apple juice, to macerate the fruit, then use the marinade as the base for the sauce. Try serving the slightly warm compote topped with a scoop of vanilla ice cream.

   1 *cup port or apple juice*
   ½ *cup water*
   2 *tablespoons honey*
   ½ *teaspoon dried mint*
   1 *piece (3 in.) vanilla bean*
   ¼ *pound dried pitted prunes*
   ¼ *pound dried calimyrna figs*
   ¼ *pound dried mission figs*
   ¼ *pound dried apricots*
   6 *fresh mint leaves, for garnish*

1. In a 2-quart saucepan stir together port, the water, honey, dried mint, and vanilla bean. Wash and dry prunes, figs, and apricots. Place fruit into port-honey-vanilla mixture and stir to cover. Macerate for 2 hours.

2. Bring port-fruit mixture to a boil. Immediately reduce heat to simmer and cook until fruit is tender (15 minutes). Remove fruit (use a slotted spoon) to a shallow serving bowl or individual bowls. Bring juices back to a boil, then cook over moderate heat until reduced by half. Strain sauce over fruit. Garnish with mint leaves.

Serves 8.

RED PEPPER SAUCE

Roasting bell peppers (and chiles) loosens their skins, making them easier to peel. You can roast over a flame, on an electric burner, or under a broiler. Red bell peppers, rich in Vitamin A, form a bright and attractive sauce for steamed vegetables or Summer Vegetable Chartreuse (see page 50).

   2 *large red bell peppers*
   1 *teaspoon kosher salt*
   ⅛ *teaspoon white pepper*
   1 *teaspoon red wine vinegar*
   ½ *cup whipping cream*
      (optional)

Corn Salsa is a super salad eaten as soon as it's made, or it can be canned and stored on the pantry shelf and used as a condiment to enliven the Ensenada Enchiladas (see page 32).

Fruits and Vegetables

Fruits and vegetables are the color in the fabric of a balanced diet. Most fruits and vegetables are low in fat while rich in fiber, complex carbohydrates, vitamins, minerals, and some protein.

Choose produce without mold or bruises. Often the aroma of the fruit or vegetable is evident when the produce is at its best. Try to select fruit that is neither soft and mushy nor hard. In general, store produce, including nuts and seeds, in the refrigerator or a cool room for best quality. To maximize nutritive value and peak flavor, use produce soon after purchase.

1. *To roast bell peppers:* Place peppers on a rack over a direct flame. Turn to roast all sides. When skin is blistered, remove pepper from flame, immediately place into a plastic bag, and seal. Let steam for about 20 minutes.

2. Remove bell peppers from plastic bag. Remove charred skin and seed under running water. Pat dry.

3. In a blender or food processor, purée peppers. Strain into a 1-quart saucepan. Add salt, pepper, vinegar, and cream (if used). Simmer until reduced by half (about 40 minutes).

Makes 1 cup.

CORN SALSA

Corn is mixed with lime and tomato to make a piquant condiment for Ensenada Enchiladas (see page 32). The volatile oils in jalapeño chile, found in the seeds and ribs, can cause the skin to feel burned. As a precaution, wear rubber gloves when removing seeds and ribs.

- 1 *ear fresh corn* or *1 cup frozen corn kernels*
- 1 *plum tomato*
- 2 *green onions*
- ½ *to 1 jalapeño chile, minced*
- 2 *tablespoons cilantro, minced*
- 2 *tablespoons lime juice*
- ½ *teaspoon kosher salt*
- ⅛ *teaspoon pepper*

1. If using fresh corn, slice kernels from ear and blanch for 1 minute. Remove from water and pat dry.

2. Slice tomato in half, remove seeds, and cut into a ¼-inch dice. Slice green onions into ⅛-inch rings.

3. In a 2-cup mixing bowl, combine corn, tomato, green onions, jalapeño chile, cilantro, lime juice, salt, and pepper. More jalapeño may be added for a spicier condiment. Chill until serving time.

Makes 1½ cups.

FRESH TOMATO SAUCE

Fresh tomatoes, diced and sautéed with onion, can be seasoned with a diversity of fresh herbs to vary the flavor of this sauce. During the height of summer when tomatoes are at their peak, prepare large batches and can using the Basics for Home Canning found on page 75.

- 2 *pounds ripe tomatoes* or *1 can (28 oz) whole plum tomatoes*
- 4 *tablespoons fresh chopped parsley* or *2 teaspoons dried parsley*
- 2 *tablespoons fresh chopped basil* or *1 teaspoon dried basil*
- 1 *tablespoon fresh chopped oregano* or *1 teaspoon dried oregano*
- 2 *tablespoons olive oil*
- 1 *medium onion, diced*
- 3 *cloves garlic, minced*
- ½ *teaspoon honey*
- 1 *teaspoon kosher salt*
- ½ *teaspoon pepper*

1. Remove stems from tomatoes and discard. Chop tomatoes into medium dice. If using canned tomatoes, drain them, discard juice, and then dice. Mince parsley, basil, and oregano.

2. Place oil in a 2½-quart saucepan over medium heat. Add onion and cook about 5 minutes. Stir in garlic and cook another 5 minutes. Add tomatoes, parsley, basil, oregano, honey, salt, and pepper and cook another 20 minutes. Remove from heat. Use immediately or store tightly covered in the refrigerator for 1 week or in an airtight container in the freezer for 1 month.

Makes 2 cups.

VEGETABLE BROTH

The principle of stock making is to create a canvas for other foods. Begin with cold water to extract the most flavor from the ingredients.

- 2 *leeks*
- 2 *yellow onions*
- 9 *small cloves garlic*
- 2 *small carrots*
- 1 *parsnip*
- 3 *small potatoes*
- 2 *stalks celery*
- ½ *pound mushrooms*
- 2 *tablespoons oil*
- 1 *teaspoon dried thyme*
- 1 *bay leaf*
- 1 *teaspoon dried oregano*
- 4 *sprigs parsley*
- 10 *cups cold water*
- 2 *teaspoons kosher salt*
- ½ *teaspoon pepper*
- 2 *tablespoons miso*

1. *To clean leeks:* Cut off root ends of leeks; remove and discard coarse outer leaves. Discard green tops. Split lengthwise, from leafy end, cutting to within 1 inch of root end. Soak in cold water for several minutes. Separate leaves under running water to rinse away any clinging grit.

2. Chop leeks across width into ½-inch pieces. Peel onions and chop into ½-inch pieces. Coarsely chop garlic cloves. Peel carrots and parsnip and cut into ½-inch rounds. Quarter potatoes. Cut celery into ½-inch slices. Halve mushrooms.

3. Place oil in a 6-quart stockpot over medium heat. Add leeks, onions, and garlic. Stir to coat with oil and cook about 5 minutes. Add carrots, parsnip, potatoes, celery, mushrooms, thyme, bay leaf, oregano, parsley, the water, salt, pepper, and miso. Bring to a boil, skim impurities from surface, and reduce heat to low. Cook for 30 minutes. Strain into a 3-quart bowl. Discard vegetables. Broth can be stored in the refrigerator in a covered container for up to 5 days or frozen in an airtight container for up to 1 month.

Makes 10 cups.

Grains

In approximately 7000 B.C., the cultivation of grains began to turn nomadic peoples into farmers, thus creating the start of community life. Cereals, as grains are also known, derive their name from the Roman goddess of the harvest, Ceres. Grains are made up of a germ or seed covered with a starchy endosperm, then with bran and an inedible hull. After the hull is removed, the whole grain is not only edible but loaded with nutrients. The refining process, when used, can reduce the amount of value contained in any grain.

Whole grains, called berries or groats, may be used in stews, salads, and pilafs. When grains are cut into two or three pieces, they are called steel cut or grits and are excellent for soups, salads, and side dishes. When grains are coarsely ground, with varying degrees of fineness, they are referred to as meal and are used for hot breakfast cereals, baking, and side dishes. As flour, the grains are more finely milled, either between stones or with metal rollers. Stone-ground grain is considered superior to grain processed with metal, which becomes hot during grinding, causing some of the nutrients to be lost. In addition, grains may be flaked, as rolled oats, rolled wheat, or rolled rye. Grains may be puffed—heated under pressure—or cracked, steamed, then dried.

Store all grains in a cool, dark place for up to one month. The germ of each grain contains some fat, which can turn rancid if not stored properly. Storage beyond one month should be in the refrigerator or freezer, tightly wrapped to prevent drying and loss of nutrients.

New grains are coming into the market to supplement wheat, rye, barley, corn, oats, and rice. Many are grains that have existed for centuries but have not been cultivated due to lack of demand or difficulty in growing. Amaranth, a staple of the Aztec diet, is similar to buckwheat—high in protein and rich in vitamins, fiber, and minerals. Quinoa, a newly revived grain currently grown in Colorado, dominated the Incan diet. Similar to millet, it can be used as a pilaf, a cereal, or a salad. Triticale, a highly nutritious cross between wheat and rye, has only been cultivated successfully in this century. It can be used in the same way as wheat or rye berries. Basmati rice, and its brown variety, often called *wehani*, come from India, where the nutty taste is extremely popular. It is currently raised in Texas, as well, where it is called Texmati.

Freshly ground grains provide an unsurpassed flavor for bread baking. Control over the degree of milling as well as added nutrients are benefits of cooking with whole grains.

PERFECT BROWN RICE

The simple steps to a perfectly cooked grain can be used for many different types and varieties. For a more intense flavor, grains may be toasted by placing in a dry skillet over medium heat, stirring constantly, until lightly browned, 8 to 10 minutes. Water or other liquid may then be added directly to the same pan to continue cooking.

> 1 cup brown rice
> 2½ cups water
> ½ teaspoon kosher salt

1. Wash rice under running water to remove starch, dust, stones, or broken grains. Place brown rice, the water, and salt in a 2-quart saucepan over medium heat.

2. Bring to a boil, reduce temperature to medium-low, and cover pan. Cook until grains are tender and separated (35 to 40 minutes). All the liquid will be absorbed. Let pan rest, covered, for 10 minutes before serving.

Makes 2½ cups, 6 servings.

A Variety of Grains

The vegetarian pantry should contain a variety of grains to add different tastes and textures, as well as important nutrients, to the diet. Grains with similar cooking times may be combined as in Wild-Rice Pilaf (see page 64). Following the steps for Perfect Brown Rice, prepare grains to use in various recipes.

BARLEY

Groats: Cook 1 cup raw in 4 cups liquid for 45 minutes to equal 3½ cups cooked. Grits: Cook 1 cup raw in 2 cups liquid for 15 minutes to equal 3 cups cooked.

BUCKWHEAT

Toasted buckwheat is known as kasha. Groats: Cook 1 cup raw in 2 cups liquid for 15 minutes to equal 2½ to 3 cups cooked. Grits: Cook 1 cup raw in 2½ cups liquid for 12 minutes to equal 2½ to 3 cups cooked.

BULGUR

Cook 1 cup raw in 2 cups liquid for 25 minutes to equal 2½ to 3 cups cooked.

CORNMEAL

Cook 1 cup raw in 3 to 4 cups liquid—depending on consistency—for about 25 minutes to equal 4 cups cooked.

MILLET

Cook 1 cup raw in 2 cups liquid for 25 minutes to equal 2½ cups cooked.

OATS

Rolled oats: Cook 1 cup raw in 2 cups liquid for 20 minutes to equal 1¾ cups cooked. Groats: Cook 1 cup raw in 2 cups liquid for 45 minutes to equal 2 cups cooked. Grits: Cook 1 cup raw in 3 cups liquid for 25 minutes to equal 2½ cups cooked.

PASTA

Cook 1 pound (5 cups raw) in 6 quarts boiling water and drain before serving to equal 8 to 10 cups cooked; 1 cup small pasta equals 1¾ cups cooked.

QUINOA

Cook 1 cup raw in 2 cups liquid for 25 minutes to equal 2½ cups cooked.

RICE

White rice: Cook 1 cup raw in 2 cups liquid for 20 minutes to equal 3 cups cooked. Short-grain white: Cook 1 cup raw in 1¾ cups liquid for 15 to 20 minutes to equal 3 cups cooked. Basmati rice: Cook 1 cup raw in 2 cups liquid for 15 to 20 minutes to equal 2½ cups cooked. Glutinous rice: Cook 1 cup raw in 1 cup liquid for 12 minutes to equal 1½ cups cooked. Arborio rice: Cook 1 cup raw while gradually adding 4 to 5 cups liquid in an uncovered pan for 20 to 25 minutes to equal 4 cups cooked. Wild rice: Cook 1 cup raw in 2 cups liquid for 45 to 60 minutes to equal 4 cups cooked.

RYE

Berries: Cook 1 cup raw in 2 cups liquid for 30 to 40 minutes to equal 2⅔ cups cooked. Cracked: Cook 1 cup raw in 2 cups liquid for 30 to 40 minutes to equal 2⅔ cups cooked.

SEMOLINA

Cook 1 cup raw in 3½ cups liquid for 25 minutes to equal 2⅔ cups cooked.

TRITICALE

Cook 1 cup raw in 2 cups liquid for 30 to 40 minutes to equal 2⅔ cups cooked.

WHEAT

Berries: Cook 1 cup raw in 2 cups liquid for 30 to 40 minutes to equal 2⅔ cups cooked. Cracked: Cook 1 cup raw in 2 cups liquid for 30 to 40 minutes to equal 2⅔ cups cooked.

WHOLE-GRAIN BAKING MIX

Store this baking mix in a cool, dark place or the refrigerator for up to eight weeks.

> 2 cups pecans, toasted (see page 108) and finely diced
> 4 cups unbleached flour
> 1½ cups whole wheat flour
> 2 cups cornmeal
> ½ cup buckwheat flour
> ½ cup wheat germ
> 1½ cups dried buttermilk powder
> ½ cup soy flour
> 4 tablespoons baking powder
> 2 tablespoons baking soda
> 2 tablespoons kosher salt
> 1¼ cups oil

1. In a 4-quart mixing bowl, combine pecans, unbleached flour, whole wheat flour, cornmeal, buckwheat flour, wheat germ, buttermilk powder, soy flour, baking powder, baking soda, and salt.

2. Stir in oil and mix well. Store in airtight tins or plastic bags.

Makes about 12 cups baking mix, enough for 6 recipes waffles, pancakes, muffins, or scones.

Serve Whole-Grain Waffles (see page 40) with sliced strawberries for a healthy start to an active day. The Whole-Grain Baking Mix recipe makes enough for about six mornings of waffles and is also used in pancakes, breads, muffins, and scones. Check the index, beginning on page 126, for a complete list of whole-grain recipes.

A successful marriage of vegetables, beans, and grains has offered Italy centuries of perfect vegetarian protein in this soup. Minestrone di Verdura (see page 71) can be made with fresh ingredients in autumn or with pantry items any time of the year.

Legumes

Beans have been a dietary mainstay for thousands of years. Kidney, navy, and pinto beans were harvested in Latin America 5,000 years ago. Soybeans were cultivated in China and fava beans in the Near East and Africa about the same time. Garbanzo beans, also known as chick-peas, played a role in early southwest Asian cuisine, then spread to the Mediterranean Basin, India, and the New World. Lentils and split peas, found by archaeologists at sites in the Middle East, date from 9,000 years ago.

The high food value found in beans has helped to make them popular in most of the world. Combined with grains, nuts, and seeds, beans provide more nutritional value than beef, cheese, fish, or poultry.

Dried beans, called shell beans when just picked, are dried in their pods, shelled, then dried again. Dried beans keep for a number of years stored in a cool, dry place, but are best used within the first year. When beans are soaked and cooked, they double or triple in volume. Most beans are high in protein, soybeans being the highest.

Soybeans are one of the most popular beans in the Pacific Basin. The beans are made into soy sauce, tofu, and a soybean paste called miso. Each of these products can be used alone or in combination to create the style of cooking indigenous to individual countries. Soy sauce, used extensively in Asian cuisines, is prepared with soybeans that have been fermented. It is extremely salty in flavor and content. People on salt-free diets should look for low-salt soy sauce in specialty food stores.

Tofu is made from soybeans that are soaked, then puréed, and cooked to create soy milk. The soy milk is then mixed with a substance similar to the rennet used in making cheese. As curds form, the soy milk is placed in a mold to drain and solidify.

Miso paste is found refrigerated in Asian markets and health-food stores. It is added, for nutritional value, to soups, stews, and salad dressings. When sealed airtight, it lasts almost indefinitely in the refrigerator. The flavor of miso resembles peanut butter, and the intensity is related to the color: light miso (yellow) is milder than dark miso (red).

BEST BEANS

Beans readily absorb the flavors of seasoned cooking liquid, so cook partially in water and finish cooking with the other ingredients used in the recipes. When beans boil, they give off a gray foam that is a combination of starch, protein, and minerals. Skim it away because it leaves a gritty taste on the beans. Salting beans before soaking and cooking tends to toughen them; instead, season beans as they are added to the recipes.

1 cup dried beans
8 cups water

1. Rinse beans and remove any stones, debris, and broken or split beans. Soak beans for 8 to 12 hours using 4 cups of the water in a large pan or bowl; or cover beans with 4 cups of the water in a 3-quart saucepan, boil for 10 minutes, cover, and let sit for 1 hour. Drain liquid.

2. Place soaked beans in a 3-quart pan and cover with remaining water. Bring to a boil over medium heat. Reduce heat to simmer and cook beans until tender but not mushy (1 to 1½ hours). Drain beans before using. Cooked beans will keep in the refrigerator for 5 to 7 days.

Makes 2½ cups cooked beans.

A Variety of Beans

Peas and lentils do not have to soak and need only to be boiled for 1 to 2 minutes then simmered 45 to 60 minutes before serving. This includes split peas, green lentils, black-eyed peas, pink lentils, garbanzos, yellow lentils, field peas, and pigeon peas. Other beans can be cooked following the steps for Best Beans. Specific cooking times are listed here. Yields will vary only slightly from the ratio of 1 raw equals 2½ cooked.

ADZUKI

Cook 1 cup raw beans in 3 cups water. Boil for 10 minutes, then simmer 1½ to 2 hours.

BLACK

Cook 1 cup raw beans in 3 cups water. Boil for 10 minutes, then simmer 1 to 1½ hours.

CRANBERRY

Cook 1 cup raw beans in 3 cups water. Boil for 10 minutes, then simmer 1½ to 2 hours.

FAVA

Cook 1 cup raw beans in 3 cups water. Boil for 10 minutes, then simmer for 2 to 2½ hours.

GREAT NORTHERN

Cook 1 cup raw beans in 3 cups water. Boil for 10 minutes, then simmer 1½ to 2 hours.

KIDNEY

Cook 1 cup raw beans in 3 cups water. Boil for 10 minutes, then simmer 1½ to 2 hours.

LIMA

Cook 1 cup raw beans in 3 cups water. Boil for 10 minutes, then simmer 1 to 1½ hours.

Nuts and Seeds

Nuts consist of an inner kernel of seed or fruit covered by a thin, soft skin, which is surrounded by a hard or leathery outer shell. Many foods commonly considered nuts are in fact seeds (almonds), legumes (peanuts), or tubers (water chestnuts). All are high in minerals (especially magnesium), vitamin B, carbohydrates, and polyunsaturated fat. Sesame seeds, for example, are extremely high in iron. Nuts and seeds also provide fiber.

Nuts and seeds have a good balance of the essential amino acids required for a healthy diet. They are extremely versatile: They can be toasted, ground into a paste or meal, and used in baking, in a sauce, or as a garnish. Nuts and seeds have the added benefit of low sodium content. For more information see the Basics on Nuts to You on page 108.

Salt

Sodium is found naturally in foods such as cheese, milk, meat, seafood, and vegetables. It sustains cell activity and helps carry water through the body. The body can use a maximum of 1½ teaspoons of salt per day. When used in moderation there are no dangers. However, those who are susceptible to high blood pressure should consult a physician for dietary advice. To reduce your sodium intake, experiment with peppers, herbs, and spices to add zest to food.

Salt, which is mined from the sea, comes in many forms and grinds. The recipes in this book use kosher salt, which is slightly coarser and is made without anticaking additives. Because the grains are larger, less kosher salt is required to achieve the taste of refined table salt. Medium-grind sea salt, available in health-food stores, is a good substitute for kosher salt. If refined table salt is preferred, use about two thirds of the amount called for in the recipes. Rock salt, required for making ice cream, is not interchangeable.

Using salted or unsalted butter is a matter of choice, although most cooks would rather regulate the amount of salt in their cooking and choose unsalted butter.

Sugar

Some kind of sweetener is used in moderation in most cuisines. Whether honey, molasses, brown sugar, confectioners' sugar, maple syrup, or granulated sugar, a sweetener imparts certain qualities to a dish. Tenderness in pastries and nicely browned color in loaves of bread are just two of the contributions of sweetener in doughs. Sugar, whether refined or not, provides no known nutrients, but it does supply calories. Tooth decay is the main problem caused by sugar in all its forms.

Don't be stymied by last-minute guests, lack of time to stop at the market, or bad weather. Keep a few ingredients at hand for a quick supper anytime.

EMERGENCY DINNER

Hot and Sour Soup

Brown Lentil Salad

Pantry Pasta

*Mosaic Fruit Compote
(see page 14)*

*Beverage Suggestion:
Milk*

Even the most organized and conscientious cook has days when the refrigerator shelves are bare. That is when this pantry menu comes to the rescue. This simple meal can be prepared from items on the pantry shelf. All recipes serve 8.

NUTRIENT BREAKDOWN	
Calories	496
Protein	13.5 gm
Fiber	6 gm
Cholesterol	34 mg
Vitamin C	32 mg
Calcium	259 mg
Sodium	906 mg

HOT AND SOUR SOUP

Some think this Chinese soup has medicinal qualities.

- ¼ cup dried black mushrooms
- ¼ cup dried lily buds
- 1 small can (4 oz) bamboo shoots
- ½ pound tofu
- 1 egg
- 5 cups Vegetable Broth (see page 15) or 4 packages instant broth plus 5 cups water
- 1 clove garlic, minced
- 1 teaspoon minced fresh ginger
- 1 cup (4 oz can) water chestnuts
- 3 tablespoons rice wine vinegar
- ¼ teaspoon white pepper
- ¼ teaspoon kosher salt
- 1 teaspoon sesame oil
- 1 teaspoon Asian hot oil
- 2 tablespoons soy sauce

1. Soak mushrooms in ½ cup water for 30 minutes. In a separate bowl soak lily buds in ½ cup water for 20 minutes. After soaking trim hard knobs and slice mushrooms into strips about ¼ inch wide. Trim hard ends from lily buds. Slice bamboo shoots and tofu into strips approximately 1½ inches by ½ inch. In a small bowl beat egg.

2. In a 3-quart saucepan, heat Vegetable Broth to boiling. Add mushrooms, lily buds, bamboo shoots, tofu, garlic, ginger, and water chestnuts. Reduce heat. Simmer for 15 minutes. Stir in egg, vinegar, pepper, salt, sesame oil, hot oil, and soy sauce. Simmer for 5 minutes before serving.

BROWN LENTIL SALAD

Carefully wash and sort lentils to remove debris before cooking.

- 1 package (12 oz) dried lentils
- 1 onion, diced
- 3 cloves garlic, diced
- 4 cups water
- 1 tablespoon dried parsley
- 1 teaspoon dried oregano
- 1 teaspoon dried basil
- ¼ cup red wine vinegar
- ½ cup oil
- 1 teaspoon kosher salt

1. In a 2-quart saucepan, combine lentils, onion, garlic, the water, parsley, oregano, and basil. Bring to a boil. Reduce heat to simmer and cook for 25 to 30 minutes. Pour into serving bowl to cool.

2. In a small bowl whisk vinegar, oil, and salt. Pour mixture over lentils and mix well. Chill 1 hour.

PANTRY PASTA

As with most pasta dishes, imagination and availability are guides to substitutes.

- ½ cup dried mushrooms
- 1 can (28 oz) whole plum tomatoes
- 1 tablespoon olive oil
- 1 onion, diced
- 2 cloves garlic, minced
- 1 teaspoon kosher salt
- 1 teaspoon dried basil
- 1 teaspoon dried oregano
- 1 teaspoon dried parsley
- ¼ teaspoon ground chiles
- 1 can (5¾ oz) black olives, quartered
- 1 can (15¼ oz) kidney beans
- 1 can (14 oz) artichokes, quartered
- 1 pound dried fusilli pasta

1. Soak mushrooms in ½ cup water for 30 minutes. Drain tomatoes and reserve juice. Chop each tomato into 6 pieces.

2. Heat oil in a 3-quart saucepan. Sauté onion until translucent (5 to 7 minutes). Add garlic and cook 5 minutes more. Drain mushrooms and cut into thin slices. Add mushrooms, tomatoes, salt, basil, oregano, parsley, chiles, and reserved tomato juice. Simmer for 10 minutes. Add olives, kidney beans, and artichokes. Simmer for 15 minutes.

3. Bring 6 quarts of water to a boil. Add pasta and cook for 12 to 15 minutes. Drain in a colander. Place pasta in a shallow serving bowl. Add sauce and toss to combine.

*Spring brings delicate-tasting
fruits and vegetables to
market and table. Plan your
herb garden now for bright
accents to future meals.*

Presenting Spring's Pantry

As winter loses its chilly hold and gives way to warming rains, most of us yearn to be out-of-doors. The gentle breezes, the light scents in the air, and the sight of new growth are energizing. March, April, and May are the months to plant a garden, whether a simple window box of herbs or an acre of vegetables. Growing some of your own food can provide a convenient as well as inexpensive store and increase the options in your kitchen. Make a centerpiece for your spring table of freshly cut blossoms or sprouting green foliage, which symbolize the vitality of the season.

SPRING PRODUCE

Whether or not you choose to garden, you should be aware of the arrival of the first foods of the season. Among them will be the many varieties of baby vegetables currently in vogue: tender young lettuces, asparagus, rhubarb, and early peas. The fresh, crisp flavor of these and other available produce, when simply combined with fresh herbs, best reflects the lightness of the season. As spring progresses, the mild evening weather beckons guests and hosts alike out onto the patio for pleasant conversations.

A spring-theme garden party could feature a meal of vegetables fresh from your yard. Then get your guests into the spirit of the season. Provide each with soil and seeds and invite them to plant their own box of edible herbs and flowers. A special feature on herb gardening and a photograph of a simple herb garden box appear on page 26.

QUICK COOKING

Spring vegetables and greens need to cook only a short time. Fresh legumes, such as fava beans, are shelled and sautéed for only a few minutes, in contrast to dried legumes of other seasons, which are soaked and cooked for long periods. Lengthy cooking would obscure the subtle flavors and textures of fresh vegetables and destroy their healthy supply of vitamins. These somewhat delicate flavors can be complemented with root vegetables from the winter larder such as carrots, beets, potatoes, or calcium-rich broccoli, cabbage, and cauliflower.

LENGTHEN THE SEASON

With a modest amount of time and energy, many of the fresh tastes of spring can be captured and preserved for delightful use later in the year. The Basics of Freezing Spring Produce are discussed on page 37. Herb Butters (see page 26) can be a frozen asset combining herbs, spices, and unsalted butter for a quick complement to steamed and grilled vegetables or for a speedy sauce in conjunction with the pan juices from a sautéed entrée. Meticulously wrapped and properly frozen spring produce can be saved for an encore later in the short spring growing season. Freezer jams and preserves add a sweet touch to the breakfast or luncheon table. Brief cooking times keep flavors intense and true.

Fresh fruit sorbets capture the color and essence of fragile fruits for enjoyment another day. Although prepared sorbets are best eaten within a few days of their making, fruit purées can be frozen and stored for several months and later drawn upon for light, refreshing desserts.

Capturing a special elegance, the brief spring season bridges a gap between hearty winter foods and lively summer fare. Each dish stands alone, more subtle and singular than those in other seasons.

SPRING SOUPS

The first greens of the season lend themselves to quick, light soups to start an evening meal or provide a modest lunch. Spring soups highlight seasonal freshness and are handy to have on hand in case a bit of winter wanders back onto your weather scene. Season these soups gently to preserve the subtle tastes.

ZUCCHINI-SPINACH SOUP

Zucchini and spinach create a palate-pleasing combination. Serve this soup either warm or cold with Charlie's Chive Toasts (see page 61).

  3 zucchini
  1 bunch spinach
  1 tablespoon oil
  2 onions, diced
  3 potatoes, cubed
  6 cups Vegetable Broth
     (see page 15)
  1 tablespoon kosher salt
  ¼ teaspoon pepper

1. Slice zucchini into ¼-inch thick circles. Thoroughly wash spinach, place in salad spinner and spin dry or on towels and pat dry.

2. Heat oil in a 3-quart saucepan. Add onions and cook for 6 to 8 minutes. Add zucchini, potatoes, and Vegetable Broth, bring to a boil, reduce heat, and simmer for 35 minutes. Add spinach, salt, and pepper, and cook 5 minutes more. Place half of the soup in blender or food processor and purée. Repeat with the other half. Reheat if needed and serve.

Makes 7 cups, 6 servings.

SPRING GREEN SOUP

Puff pastry makes this simple soup an elegant first course. Prepared puff pastry can be found in the frozen-food section of most supermarkets. If you prefer, you may omit both the puff pastry and the chilling step. In this case, cook the asparagus and sugar snap peas for 3 minutes when they are added in step 2 before serving the soup.

> 3 leeks
> 4 green onions
> ½ pound shiitake or domestic mushrooms
> 1 pound thin asparagus (about 24 spears)
> ¼ pound sugar snap peas or ¾ pound fresh peas
> 2 tablespoons butter
> 6 cups Vegetable Broth (see page 15)
> ½ teaspoon kosher salt
> ⅛ teaspoon white pepper
> ½ pound prepared puff pastry, defrosted
> 1 egg
> 1 tablespoon water

1. Clean leeks (see page 15). Slice crosswise into ¼-inch-thick pieces. Trim green onions, and slice diagonally into 1-inch pieces. Wash mushrooms, trim stems, and slice into strips about ¼ inch wide. Wash asparagus, discard any dry, tough ends, and slice on diagonal into 1-inch pieces. Remove stems from snap peas.

2. Heat butter in a 3-quart saucepan. Add leeks and cook over medium heat, stirring occasionally, until tender (about 8 minutes). Add mushrooms and cook for 5 minutes. Stir in onions and cook 1 minute. Add Vegetable Broth, salt, and pepper. Bring to a boil, reduce heat, and simmer 10 minutes. Add peas and asparagus. Turn off heat.

3. Pour into 2-quart soufflé dish. Cool slightly, then refrigerate until well chilled.

4. Cut puff pastry into a circle 2 inches larger than soufflé dish. Place pastry over top of dish, and press onto sides, smearing edges of puff pastry slightly to adhere to dish. Refrigerate until 45 minutes before serving time.

5. Preheat oven to 400° F. Mix egg and the water in a small bowl and brush on puff pastry. Bake until puff pastry is golden brown and crisp (about 40 minutes). Serve immediately; cut puff pastry open at the table. Ladle a piece of pastry and a serving of soup into individual bowls.

Makes 7½ cups, 6 servings.

Break the puffy pastry cover at the table and enjoy the dramatic presentation and subtle aroma of Spring Green Soup.

HERB GARDENING

Spice up almost any meal with a touch of fresh herbs. Mince them over pizza; julienne them onto salads; slow-cook them into soups and stews.

Most growing herbs prefer lots of sunlight—five to eight hours a day—and lots of water. Seeds can be started indoors in small pots and then transplanted outside or kept indoors on a sunny windowsill.

Plants can also be started directly outdoors by scattering seeds over raked soil and covering them to about twice their depth. Label beds carefully. Keep soil moist as seeds grow. After two to four weeks, carefully thin the tiny seedlings, and transplant the extra seedlings elsewhere or use them in cooking.

Herbs should be soaked rather than sprayed so that water reaches the roots. Fertilize only twice a year. Too much fertilizer creates lush foliage at the expense of flavor.

A Basic Herb Garden

Basil Rich flavor blends well with tomatoes; grow in full sun or partial shade; keep moist.

Chervil Dried has little flavor, fresh is delicate and aromatic; grow in partial shade; keep slightly moist.

Chives Use flowers as garnish; grow in full sun and moist soil.

Marjoram Can be substituted anytime a recipe calls for oregano; grow in full sun and moist soil.

Mint Easy to grow, likes partial shade and moisture; can easily overrun a garden so is best potted.

Nasturtium Beautiful in garden or salad, leaves edible but peppery, flowers edible; prefers full sun and overrich soil.

Oregano Hearty and tasty; grow in full sun and moist soil.

Parsley Easy to grow in partial shade and moist soil.

Rosemary Beautiful aromatic needles with edible flowers; use dried or fresh; grow in full sun and dry soil.

Tarragon French tarragon is preferred; grow in partial shade.

Thyme Extremely aromatic; grow in full sun.

HERB BUTTER

Mix available herbs for creative combinations. Mold in butter forms or ice-cube trays. Use on vegetables or as a spread for bread.

½ cup unsalted butter, softened
2 shallots, minced
3 tablespoons minced fresh herb
1 tablespoon white wine vinegar
½ teaspoon kosher salt
⅛ teaspoon white pepper

Place butter in a blender, food processor, or 2-cup mixing bowl. Add shallots, herb, vinegar, salt, and pepper. Mix well. Roll into a cylinder or place in mold. Wrap in foil for storage in the refrigerator for 1 week or the freezer for 2 months.

Makes ½ cup.

SPRING SALADS

The wide selection of lettuces, herbs, and vegetables available in spring makes for a great variety of salad choices. Showcase the greens of the season, and add herbs and baby vegetables from your garden or the produce stand. A different salad dressing can expand your repertoire as well. Experiment with the Basic Vinaigrette (see page 13) by substituting flavored vinegars and aromatic oils or tossing in chopped fresh herbs and grated cheeses.

ASIAN BLACK BEAN SALAD

Asparagus epitomizes spring produce: short-lived, bright, and subtle. It is best prepared to utilize the most of its long, thin stalk or, as in this recipe, cut into small pieces on the diagonal.

    1   cup cooked black beans
    ¼   small red onion, diced
    ¼   cup cilantro, minced
    1   tablespoon rice wine vinegar
    1   teaspoon soy sauce
    1   teaspoon Asian hot oil
    ⅛   teaspoon Asian sesame oil
    1   pound asparagus
    4   lettuce leaves

1. Place cooked beans in a 1-quart mixing bowl. Stir red onion, cilantro, vinegar, soy sauce, hot oil, and sesame oil into beans. Marinate for 20 to 30 minutes.

2. Bring 2 quarts of water to a boil. Trim dried, tough ends from asparagus stalks. Slice asparagus on the diagonal. Blanch in boiling water for 3 minutes. Remove from water and toss with marinated beans. Wash and spin dry lettuce leaves. To serve, place each leaf on a chilled salad plate. Place one fourth of the salad on each lettuce leaf.

Serves 4.

TOSSED GREEN SALAD

The most delicate salad greens—baby lettuce or trimmings from new plantings—are best served with light and delicate seasonings. Mâche, one of the first greens of spring, has spoon-shaped leaves, which have a mild flavor. Oils, vinegars, fruit, flowers, vegetables, and seasonings enhance the fragile greens while adding a contrasting note.

    2   tablespoons white wine
        vinegar
    5   tablespoons light fruity
        olive oil
    ¼   cup minced parsley
    2   teaspoons Dijon mustard
    ¼   teaspoon kosher salt
    ⅛   teaspoon pepper
    8   cups mixed salad greens:
        mâche; arugula (rocket);
        red-leaf, curly green, baby
        iceberg lettuce

1. In a small bowl, whisk vinegar, oil, parsley, mustard, salt, and pepper.

2. Wash, spin dry, and tear greens into bite-sized pieces. Place greens in a large serving bowl. Pour dressing over greens and toss well to combine. Serve immediately on chilled salad plates.

Serves 6.

ORANGE AND RADISH SALAD

This salad's sparkling fresh flavors of radish and orange enhance the pungent spices found in Ensenada Enchiladas (see page 32) for a light dinner, south-of-the-border style.

    10 radishes
    3   oranges
    2   green onions
        Juice of 1 lime
    ¼   cup cilantro (optional)
    1   tablespoon oil
    1   teaspoon white wine vinegar
    ¼   teaspoon kosher salt
    6   romaine lettuce leaves

1. Trim ends of radishes and cut into ⅛-inch-thick slices. Peel oranges and cut into ¼- to ½-inch-thick slices. Trim green onions and cut into ⅛-inch-thick slices.

2. Place radishes, oranges, and green onions in a 1-quart bowl. Toss with lime juice, cilantro (if used), oil, vinegar, and salt. Marinate for 30 minutes. Place ⅓ cup of salad on each lettuce leaf. Serve on chilled plates.

Serves 6.

ACAPULCO JICAMA SALAD

This salad is delicious as a first course and is a heartier accompaniment to Ensenada Enchiladas (see page 32) than the Orange and Radish Salad. Jicama is a large tuberous root with a brown outer skin covering a crunchy white pulp. It can be eaten raw, used as a substitute for water chestnuts, or steamed.

    ¼   cup cilantro
        Juice of 1 lime
    2   tablespoons white wine
        vinegar
    2   tablespoons oil
    ½   teaspoon kosher salt
    ¼   teaspoon pepper
    3   oranges
    1   avocado
    1   small jicama
    18 red-leaf lettuce leaves

1. Mince cilantro. Whisk together cilantro, lime juice, vinegar, oil, salt, and pepper.

2. Peel oranges, and slice into ¼-inch-thick circles. Peel and pit avocado; slice into 1-inch cubes. Peel jicama and slice into ½-inch cubes.

3. Marinate orange slices, avocado, and jicama in lime-cilantro vinaigrette for 30 minutes.

4. Wash, spin dry, and tear lettuce into bite-sized pieces. Arrange lettuce on chilled salad plates. Remove orange, avocado, and jicama from marinade and place on lettuce.

Serves 6.

27

SPRING FRESH PRODUCE

FRUITS	Purchase	Storage	Special Notes
Mangoes	May–Aug. Look for smooth skin, usually green with yellowish or red areas (red and yellow increase as fruit ripens), firm skin, hard central core, round to oval shape. Avoid wilting or discoloration.	Keep at room temperature until soft, then refrigerate; use promptly.	Contain some vitamin C.
Papayas	May–June. Look for large, oblong shape, yellow tinted with green, smooth skin. Avoid overly large fruit (less flavorful than medium sized).	Ripen at room temperature, then refrigerate; use promptly. Should yield slightly to pressure between the palms when ripe.	Contain papain enzyme, which breaks down protein; effective as digestive. Can range from 1 to 20 lbs.
Pineapples	Mar.–July. Look for bright color, fragrance, slight separation of eyes or pips (berrylike fruitlets spirally patterned on fruit core). The larger the fruit, the greater proportion of edible flesh. During ripening, the green turns orange and yellow. Fully colored are golden yellow, orange yellow, or reddish brown, depending on variety, and slightly soft. Avoid sunken or slightly pointed pips, dull yellowish green color, dried appearance of immature fruit, and mold.	If not fully ripe, keep at room temperature, away from heat or sun, until ready to eat. Then refrigerate at 45° F, relative humidity of 85 to 90 percent.	Good source of vitamins A and C. Also believed to be a digestive.

VEGETABLES

	Purchase	Storage	Special Notes
Artichokes	Apr.–May. Best in late spring, although available the year around. Cultivated in Calif. Look for compact, heavy, plump globes that yield slightly to pressure and large, tightly clinging, fleshy green leaf scales. Avoid browning (indicates old age, injury, or frost), light weight, small leaves with little or no globes.	Will keep briefly at 32° F, 95 percent relative humidity (to prevent wilting or drying).	The Jerusalem artichoke resembles the regular artichoke in flavor but is a member of the sunflower family.
Asparagus	Mid-Feb.–June. Look for closed, compact tips, smooth round spears, fresh appearance, rich green color, tender stalks (almost as far down as green extends). Avoid asparagus soaking in water, open and separated tips (indicates overripeness), moldy or decayed tips, ribbed spears (all indicate aging, toughness, poor flavor). Also avoid sandy asparagus, which is difficult to clean.	Refrigerate and use promptly.	Member of lily family. Good source of vitamin A, phosphorus, and niacin.
Corn	May–Aug. Varieties: white, yellow. Look for fresh, green, succulent husks. Avoid underdeveloped kernels lacking yellow color (in yellow corn), large kernels (of old ears), dark yellow kernels with depressed areas on outer surface, discolored stems, decayed silk.	Refrigerate and use promptly.	Contain trace amounts of phosphorus and potassium. Yellow also a good source of vitamin A.
Green Onions	May–Aug. A young onion harvested before bulb has enlarged. Also known as scallions. Look for crisp, green tops; medium-sized necks; well-blanched color for 2 or 3 in. from root. Avoid wilted, discolored, or decayed tips (indicate flabby, tough, or fibrous condition). Bruised tops do not affect quality of bulbs.	Refrigerate and use promptly.	Often added to salads.
Nasturtium Leaves and Flowers	Homegrown flowers and leaves provide the best quality.	Should be eaten immediately after picking; younger flowers and leaves preferred.	Young seeds pods can be pickled and used as a substitute for capers.
Okra	May–Oct. Look for young, bright green pods that are medium sized (2 to 4 in. long) and that snap or puncture easily (indicates tenderness). Avoid stiff tips (indicates tough, fibrous pods), hard pods, pale green color.	Refrigerate up to 3 days.	Sometimes called gumbo. Young pods popular in Creole cooking, excellent in soups and stews. A natural thickening agent. Do not cook in iron, copper, or brass.
Peas **Green Peas**	Mar.–July. Look for uniformly green, well-filled, young pods. Avoid very mature or yellowish pods.	Refrigerate and use promptly. Will keep briefly in pods at 32° F, 85 percent relative humidity.	Good source of vitamin A.
Sugar Snap Peas	Look for green color and well-rounded shape. Avoid yellowed or speckled pods.	Use same day as purchased.	
Radishes	May–July. Varieties: globular, long red, long white and long black, red and white. Look for smooth, firm, and crisp radishes that are medium sized, ¾ to 1⅛ in. in dia. Tops should be green, and can be cooked and eaten. Avoid cuts, black spots; pithy, spongy, or wilted texture.	Remove tops and refrigerate.	Often eaten raw, either alone or in salads. Daikon radishes are used in Asian dishes.
Red Onions	Look for shapeliness, dryness (enough to crackle), thin necks, bright and hard bulbs.	Keep in dry area with 70 to 75 percent relative humidity; at higher humidities may decay and grow roots. Never store with potatoes; will absorb moisture and decay.	Good in salads or as garnishes.

SPRING MAIN DISHES

Try quick-cooking techniques such as sautéing and steaming for the delicately flavored vegetables, fruits, and legumes mild spring weather produces. Use tantalizing herbs to highlight the unfolding bounty without masking the subtle flavors. Those same fresh herbs, grown in small pots in the garden or on a windowsill (see page 26), can double as aromatic centerpieces for springtime entertaining.

SPRING VEGETABLE COBBLER

This cobbler can be adapted to include any seasonal produce or legumes. The Cheddar Biscuits may be made as dinner rolls by baking them on an ungreased baking sheet at 400° F for 15 to 18 minutes.

- 2 *small zucchini*
- 2 *small yellow crookneck squash*
- 1 *red bell pepper*
- 4 *baby carrots*
- 8 *large mushrooms*
- ½ *pound broccoli*
- 2 *medium-sized potatoes*
- 2 *cups Béchamel Sauce (see page 13)*
- 2 *tablespoons butter*
- 1 *large onion, coarsely chopped*
- 4 *cloves garlic, minced*
- ½ *cup dried lentils*
- 1 *teaspoon kosher salt*
- 2 *tablespoons fresh tarragon*
- ¼ *teaspoon white pepper*

Cheddar Biscuits

- 2 *cups flour, plus flour for dusting*
- 1 *teaspoon kosher salt*
- 2 *teaspoons baking powder*
- 1 *tablespoon fresh tarragon*
- 3 *ounces Cheddar cheese*
- ¾ *cup milk*
- 3 *tablespoons butter, melted*

1. Preheat oven to 375° F.

2. Slice zucchini, squash, and red pepper into 1½-inch pieces. Cut carrots and mushrooms in half. Cut broccoli into individual florets about 3 inches long.

3. Peel and quarter potatoes. Place in a 1-quart saucepan and cover with water. Bring to a boil. Reduce heat and simmer until easily pierced with a knife (20 to 25 minutes). Place potatoes and Béchamel Sauce in a blender, food processor, or food mill, and purée.

4. Heat butter in a large skillet. Sauté onion and garlic for 5 minutes. Add zucchini, squash, pepper, carrots, mushrooms, broccoli, lentils, béchamel-potato mixture, salt, tarragon, and pepper. Toss to combine.

5. Pour mixture into a 3-quart casserole. Place Cheddar Biscuits over mixture. Bake until top is golden brown and vegetables are hot (about 1 hour). For each serving, top a generous scoop of vegetables with one or two biscuits.

Serves 8.

Cheddar Biscuits

1. Sift together flour, salt, baking powder, and tarragon into a 3-quart mixing bowl.

2. Grate cheese and toss with dry ingredients. Stir together milk and 2 tablespoons of the melted butter. Gently stir milk-butter into dry ingredients, mixing only until combined.

3. Place dough on a lightly dusted work surface and pat to ½ inch thick. Cut into 2-inch rounds. Place biscuits on casserole and brush with remaining melted butter.

Makes 10 to 12 biscuits.

RISOTTO PRIMAVERA

A staple of northern Italy, in addition to pasta, is small, oval arborio rice. This rice has the ability to absorb many times its weight in liquid while remaining tender and creamy. It should be stirred throughout the cooking process and served as soon as it is prepared.

- 4 *dried mushrooms*
- 4 *cups Vegetable Broth (see page 15)*
- 2 *green onions*
- 1 *tablespoon butter*
- 1 *tablespoon olive oil*
- 1 *onion, diced*
- 1½ *cups arborio rice*
- 2 *teaspoons kosher salt*
- 2 *small carrots, peeled and finely diced*
- 4 *mushrooms, quartered*
- 1 *pound peas, shelled*
- ½ *cup grated Parmesan cheese (optional)*
- 2 *tablespoons parsley*
- 2 *tablespoons basil*

1. Soak dried mushrooms in 1 cup of Vegetable Broth for 30 minutes. Slice green onions on the diagonal. In a 2-quart saucepan, heat butter and oil. Add diced onion and cook until translucent (5 to 8 minutes). Add rice and stir to coat with butter-oil mixture. Reduce heat to low, and add salt and 2 cups of the broth. When liquid is almost absorbed, add remaining 1 cup broth. Cook until broth is completely absorbed, stirring occasionally (total cooking time for rice is about 8 minutes).

2. Strain broth containing dried mushrooms, and add broth to broth-rice mixture in saucepan. Dice soaked mushrooms and add to mixture. Stir to incorporate and continue cooking. After 8 minutes add carrots and fresh mushrooms. Cook for 8 minutes. Add peas and green onions. Cook 6 minutes more.

3. Stir in cheese (if used), parsley, and basil. Serve immediately.

Serves 6.

HOW TO ROLL SUSHI

1. *Place rice in a large shallow bowl or baking sheet with sides. Slowly pour marinade over rice while stirring. Fan rice to cool it rapidly. Cover with a damp towel for up to 4 hours while preparing fillings. Do not chill rice.*

2. *Holding nori with metal tongs, place sheets about 2 inches above high-heat source, and pass them back and forth over flame for a few seconds. Nori will turn from black to dark green.*

3. *Put bamboo rolling mat on work table with sticks of bamboo parallel to edge of table. Place nori in center of mat. (If you do not have a bamboo rolling mat, cut a piece of aluminum foil about 8 inches square, and place nori in center of foil.) Gently spread sushi rice over nori, leaving ½ inch uncovered along all sides.*

4. *Place small amount of wasabi along length of rice and parallel to bamboo on mat. Wasabi is a fiery condiment and should be used sparingly.*

5. *Place strips of filling along length of sushi rice on top of wasabi and parallel to sticks of bamboo.*

6. *Lifting bamboo rolling mat from edge nearest to you, start to roll nori and rice over filling ingredients to enclose them. Use roller to press rice onto filling so that rice encloses filling and seals against itself to form a cylinder. Store rolls until serving time, loosely covered. To serve, slice into 1-inch-thick circles.*

VEGETARIAN SUSHI

The anxieties of eating unusual foods will be forgotten when the complementary flavors of this Japanese national dish are savored. *Nori,* although relatively flavorless, is a protein- and calcium-rich seaweed that holds the sushi rolls together. One type of nori is made especially for sushi. *Wasabi,* a green Japanese horseradish, gives a bit of bite to the rice and fillings. These more unusual ingredients can be purchased in Asian markets or in the produce section of large supermarkets. Vary the combinations of vegetables to your liking. It is traditional to make a dipping sauce of soy sauce and wasabi, to suit your taste, and to accompany sushi with pickled ginger root.

> *Perfect Brown Rice, using short-grain rice (see page 16)*
> 7½ *tablespoons sugar*
> 10 *tablespoons mirin or sweet sake (optional)*
> ½ *cup rice wine vinegar*
> 2 *teaspoons kosher salt*
> ¾ *cup water*
> ½ *cup soy sauce*
> ½ *English cucumber*
> 4 *large shiitake mushrooms*
> 1 *small avocado*
> ½ *lemon, juiced*
> ½ *red bell pepper*
> 10 *thin green beans*
> 6 *thin asparagus spears*
> 1 *medium carrot*
> 2 *eggs*
> *Pinch kosher salt*
> 1 *teaspoon oil for frying*
> 1 *tablespoon wasabi*
> 6 *nori for sushi*

1. Prepare Perfect Brown Rice (see page 16) using short-grain brown rice. While rice cooks, prepare marinade. In a small bowl, mix 3 tablespoons of the sugar, 2 tablespoons of the *mirin* (if used), vinegar, and 2 teaspoons salt.

2. When rice is cooked, place it in a shallow bowl, and slowly pour half the marinade over it, stirring rice to cool it as well as coat it with marinade. Fan rice to cool it rapidly. Add other half of marinade to taste. Cover with a damp towel for up to 4 hours while preparing fillings. Do not chill rice. This is now called sushi rice.

3. To prepare marinade for vegetables, stir together ½ cup of the water, 4 tablespoons of the sugar, the remaining mirin, and soy sauce.

4. Slice cucumber into strips approximately ¼ inch thick by 6 inches long. Cut shiitake mushrooms into strips about ¼ inch thick. Peel and pit avocado; slice into ¼-inch-thick strips. Drizzle avocado with lemon juice. Remove and discard seeds from red pepper, and slice into ¼-inch strips. Place vegetables in individual bowls. Drizzle half of the marinade evenly over these vegetables.

5. Bring 4 quarts of water to a boil. Cut stem ends from beans. Blanch for 3 minutes in boiling water. Remove and place in ice water to stop cooking and set color. Trim tough ends from asparagus. Blanch in boiling water for 2 to 3 minutes depending on thickness. Remove from boiling water and place in ice water. Peel carrots and cut into strips about ¼ inch thick by 6 inches long. Blanch in boiling water for 2 to 3 minutes. Remove from boiling water and place in ice water. Remove vegetables from ice water after they are cool. Pat dry, and place in individual bowls. Drizzle remaining marinade evenly over these vegetables.

6. In a small bowl, beat eggs, remaining sugar, and the pinch of salt. Heat half the oil in a 10-inch frying pan and pour in half the egg mixture. Cook for 2 minutes without stirring. Remove from pan in one piece and repeat with remaining oil and egg mixture. Slice into pieces about ½ inch wide and 6 inches long.

7. In a small bowl, mix wasabi with remaining ¼ cup water and reserve. Holding nori sheets about 2 inches over a medium-high heat source, toast until nori turns from black to dark green (about 2 to 3 seconds). Place nori on a foil square or a bamboo rolling mat. Gently spread sushi rice over center of the nori, leaving ½-inch borders. Smear a small amount of wasabi-water mixture along length of rice. Place strips of filling, alone or in combination, along the length of the sushi rice. Roll nori over ingredients to enclose them. For better sticking, use foil square or bamboo roller to press rice onto itself so that rice touches rice. Wrap tightly to form a cylinder. Press to seal. To serve, slice into 1-inch thick circles.

Makes about 36 pieces, 6 servings.

Vegetarian Sushi, garnished with a pickled ginger "rose" and a wasabi-paste "leaf," makes a superb appetizer or a luncheon entrée with Asian Black Bean Salad (see page 27).

ENSENADA ENCHILADAS

This south-of-the-border entrée can be prepared ahead to heat in the oven at serving time. A fresh green salad and lime-flavored mineral water round out the meal.

    12 flour tortillas
     8 ounces Monterey jack cheese
     6 cups Three-Bean Chile
        (see page 38)
        Corn Salsa (see page 15)
        Guacamole (see page 74)

Enchilada Sauce

     1 bell pepper
     1 large jalapeño chile
     2 cans (28 oz each) plum
        tomatoes
     2 tablespoons oil
     2 onions, minced
     6 cloves garlic, minced
    1½ teaspoons cumin
    2½ teaspoons kosher salt

1. Preheat oven to 350° F. Wrap tortillas in foil and place in preheated oven for 8 to 10 minutes. Shred cheese. Warm the Three-Bean Chile in a 1-quart saucepan. Place 2 cups Enchilada Sauce in a 10- by 15-inch baking dish.

2. Remove tortillas from oven and unwrap. Place ½ cup chile on each tortilla. Spread to form a strip of filling down center. Sprinkle 2 tablespoons cheese over chile. Drizzle with 1 tablespoon Enchilada Sauce. Roll up to enclose filling, leaving ends open. Place rolled enchilada in baking dish. Repeat with remaining tortillas.

3. Pour remaining sauce evenly over enchiladas. Sprinkle with remaining cheese. Place in preheated oven until cheese is melted and filling is heated (about 25 to 30 minutes). Serve on individual plates with Corn Salsa on the side. Top each enchilada with a dollop of Guacamole.

Serves 6.

Enchilada Sauce

1. Remove and discard seeds from bell pepper and jalapeño; dice pepper and jalapeño finely. Purée the tomatoes in a blender.

2. In a 3-quart saucepan heat the oil. Sauté the onion and garlic for 5 minutes. Add the peppers, tomato, cumin, and salt. Bring to a boil, reduce heat, and simmer for 30 minutes. Cool slightly.

Makes 5 cups.

LENTIL RAGOUT PRINTANIER

When spring rains make you long for a stew in a hurry, this combination of lentils and seasonal produce cannot be surpassed. The green lentils imported from France hold their shape a little better than their American counterparts although both are equally delicious.

     1 tablespoon oil
     2 onions, diced
     4 cloves garlic, minced
     2 cups French green lentils
     4 cups Vegetable Broth (see
        page 15) or water
    ½ cup parsley
     1 teaspoon oregano
     1 teaspoon thyme
     1 teaspoon kosher salt
    ½ teaspoon pepper
    12 baby turnips, about 1½
        inches in diameter
    12 small carrots
     6 green onions
    1½ pounds peas, shelled

1. In a 3-quart saucepan over medium heat, heat oil and cook onion and garlic together for 7 to 8 minutes.

2. Wash lentils. Sort and discard broken pieces. Add lentils, broth, parsley, oregano, thyme, salt, and pepper to saucepan. Simmer for 20 minutes.

3. Wash turnips and cut in half. Peel carrots and cut into 2-inch lengths. Clean green onions and cut into 1-inch pieces.

4. Add turnips and carrots to saucepan. Cook for 10 minutes. Add peas and green onions, and cook for 5 minutes more. Serve warm from 2-quart serving dish.

Serves 6.

SPRING VEGETABLE FANS

The secret to perfect crêpes is a thin batter and a well-seasoned crêpe pan. To season a crêpe pan, fill it with oil and heat to smoking. Turn off heat and, with oil still in pan, let pan rest for 4 to 12 hours. Discard oil. Wipe pan clean with paper towels, and prepare crêpes as directed below.

     5 small leeks
     4 green onions
    ¼ pound morels or domestic
        mushrooms
     1 bunch spinach
     2 tablespoons butter
     2 cloves garlic, minced
    ¼ cup plain yogurt
     1 teaspoon kosher salt
    ⅛ teaspoon white pepper
        Herb Butter (see page 26)

Buckwheat-Dill Crêpes

    ¾ cup water
    ½ cup milk
     2 eggs
     2 tablespoons oil plus oil
        for sautéing
    ¼ cup buckwheat flour
    ¾ cup unbleached flour
     2 tablespoons dill weed
    ¼ teaspoon kosher salt

1. Clean leeks (see page 15); pat dry. Trim root ends from green onions and slice on the diagonal. Rinse morels or mushrooms, and cut into quarters. Wash spinach in several changes of water. Remove and discard tough stems. Lift from water and drain, but do not pat dry. Place in a 10-inch skillet, and cook in the water retained from washing for 4 to 5 minutes over low heat. Remove from pan and chop.

2. Heat butter in an 8-inch skillet. Add garlic and leeks. Cook about 10 minutes over medium heat. Add green onions, morels, and spinach. Cook for 10 minutes. Stir in yogurt, salt, and pepper.

3. Preheat oven to 350° F. Spread 1 rounded tablespoon of filling on each Buckwheat-Dill Crêpe, leaving a ½-inch outside border. Fold in quarters and place in an ovenproof dish, slightly overlapping. Dot each filled crêpe with 1 teaspoon Herb Butter. Cover with aluminum foil and place in preheated oven until heated through (about 20 minutes). Remove foil and bake 5 minutes longer.

Serves 6.

Buckwheat-Dill Crêpes

1. In a blender, food processor, or 1-quart mixing bowl, combine the water, milk, eggs, and oil.

2. Add buckwheat flour, unbleached flour, dill, and salt. Whisk or blend until smooth. Let rest 30 minutes. Batter should be the consistency of heavy cream.

3. Heat a crêpe or 7-inch sauté pan over a medium flame. Brush with a light film of oil. When a drop of water sizzles on surface of pan, it is hot enough to cook crêpes. Holding pan with a pot holder, drizzle 2 tablespoons crêpe batter into pan; keep turning pan until bottom is coated with batter.

4. Return to burner for about 2 minutes. As crêpes cook, surface will appear dry and underside will be lightly browned. Loosen edges with a thin spatula or knife. Turn over and cook second side for 30 seconds. Do not brown second side. Place crêpes, loosely covered, on a plate until ready to assemble. Continue with remaining batter. Crêpes can be prepared ahead and stored in the refrigerator, covered in plastic wrap, for up to 3 days.

Makes 18 to 20 six-inch crêpes.

Buckwheat is a hearty grain originally cultivated in Siberia and northern Asia. The Buckwheat-Dill Crêpes enclose morel and spinach filling in Spring Vegetable Fans, which pair well with the French-inspired Lentil Ragout Printanier. The Herb Butter (see page 26) topping the crêpes shown here is made with dill and green onions.

Host a Sunday brunch to honor Mom or to simply celebrate the beauty of a sunny weekend afternoon. The menu is planned for fresh produce of late spring.

MOTHER'S DAY BRUNCH

Grapefruit Juice Fizzes

Morning Mint Tea

*Spring Pea and
Mushroom Salad*

Torta Milanese

Scrumptious Coffee Cake

Fresh Fruit

*Preparing a meal for
the lady of the house
is a Mother's Day
tradition in many
homes. This elegant
meal is not difficult,
but does take
advance planning.
Start a few days
ahead so that
everyone can relax
and enjoy the day.
Serve with your
favorite fresh fruit of
the season. All recipes
serve eight.*

NUTRIENT BREAKDOWN	
Calories	1,442
Protein	45 gm
Fiber	4 gm
Cholesterol	242 mg
Vitamin C	145 mg
Calcium	508 mg
Sodium	1,273 mg

GRAPEFRUIT JUICE FIZZES

This is equally delectable with orange
or tangerine juice.

>   4   *cups unsweetened grapefruit
>   juice*
>   4   *cups salt-free seltzer
>   Ice cubes*
>   8   *fresh mint leaves, for garnish*
>   8   *thin slices of orange, for
>   garnish*

Place juice and seltzer into a 2½-
quart pitcher. Add ice. Pour in glasses
and garnish with mint leaves and
orange slices.

Makes 8 cups.

MORNING MINT TEA

The same peppermint that is used for
seasoning may be stirred into boiling
water and served as tea. Other herbs
and flower buds—such as chamo-
mile, scented geraniums, lemon ver-
bena, rose hips, and hibiscus—can be
used to make *tisanes*, the French
term for restorative herbal teas.

>   6   *cups boiling water*
>   ⅓   *cup peppermint leaves, dried
>   and crushed
>   Honey (optional)
>   Milk (optional)
>   Lemon wedges (optional)*

1. Boil the 6 cups of freshly drawn
water in a 2-quart pot or teakettle.
Heat a ceramic or glass teapot by
filling with warm tap water and
letting it sit for 3 to 4 minutes.

2. Empty teapot. Place peppermint in
bottom of teapot. Carefully pour in
boiling water. Stir once to combine.
Let steep for 3 to 5 minutes. Traditionally, a pot of hot water is carried
to the table with the tea in case tea
needs to be diluted. Pour tea through
strainer and into individual cups.
Serve with honey, milk, or lemon
wedges, if desired.

Makes 6 cups.

SPRING PEA AND MUSHROOM SALAD

This salad is best made at least three
hours ahead of time so that the
flavors will meld. You can substitute
sugar snap peas or snow peas if fresh
green peas are unavailable. The Lemon Vinaigrette enhances the taste of
the mushrooms and prevents them
from darkening.

>   1   *pound unshelled green peas*
>   1   *pound small mushrooms*
>   4   *green onions*
>   8   *lettuce leaves*

Lemon Vinaigrette

>   ⅔   *cup lemon juice*
>   ⅓   *cup oil*
>   1   *teaspoon kosher salt
>   Freshly ground pepper*

1. Shell peas. Bring 2 quarts water to
a boil. Place peas in boiling water for
2 minutes. This blanching enhances
flavor of peas. Remove from water
and drain. Place in a 2-quart bowl of
ice water to stop cooking and cool.
When peas are cool (about 10 minutes), drain water. This will help to
retain bright green color of peas.
Place peas in a 3-quart mixing bowl.

2. If mushrooms are not too dirty,
just wipe surfaces with a damp towel.
If dirt adheres to them, briefly place
under running water while gently
brushing to remove soil. Trim stems.
Place mushrooms in mixing bowl
with peas.

3. Wash and slice green onions into
⅛-inch circles. Place in bowl with
mushrooms and peas. Toss with Lemon Vinaigrette and marinate for 3
hours in refrigerator. Serve on lettuce
leaves.

Lemon Vinaigrette Whisk together
lemon juice, oil, salt, and pepper.

Makes 1 cup.

TORTA MILANESE

By including scrambled eggs, a regional specialty of Milan, Italy, becomes a brunch favorite. Start the recipe a day before serving. The dough must be prepared at least 4 hours and up to 24 hours ahead of assembly, because it is easier to handle if it is rolled out while chilled. The vegetables may be sautéed and reserved in the refrigerator to wait assembly the morning of the brunch. Or the dish may be completely assembled and baked the day before, and just reheated the day of serving.

Dough

- 1 package active dry yeast
- 1½ teaspoons honey
- ⅓ cup warm water (not to exceed 100° F)
- 1 teaspoon kosher salt
- ½ cup butter, at room temperature
- 2 eggs
- 2¼ cups flour plus flour for dusting

Filling

- 15 fresh baby artichokes
- 2 teaspoons kosher salt
- 1 red bell pepper
- 1 green bell pepper
- 1 yellow bell pepper
- 1 onion
- 2 tablespoons olive oil
- 1 teaspoon oregano
- 2 bunches spinach
- ½ teaspoon freshly grated nutmeg
- 9 eggs
- 1 large bunch chives
- 3 tablespoons butter
- ½ pound mushrooms
- 2 small zucchini
- 2 cloves garlic
- 2 ounces fontina cheese, grated
- 6 ounces provolone cheese, grated
- 2 tablespoons water

1. *To prepare dough:* In a small mixing bowl, dissolve yeast and honey in the water. Place yeast mixture in a large mixing bowl; stir in salt, butter, eggs, and flour. Knead dough vigorously on a lightly floured work surface for approximately 5 minutes. Lightly oil a large mixing bowl, place dough in bowl, and cover with plastic wrap. Chill in refrigerator for 4 to 12 hours.

2. *To prepare filling:* Slice about 1 inch from top of artichokes. Peel back tough outer leaves and quarter artichokes. Bring 3 quarts of water to a boil, add artichokes, and simmer for 12 to 14 minutes depending on size of artichokes. They are done when a knife inserted into center pierces easily. Season with ¼ teaspoon of salt.

3. Remove and discard seeds from red, green, and yellow bell peppers and slice into long, thin strips. Slice onion into strips. In a 12-inch skillet, heat olive oil and add pepper and onion strips. Add oregano and ½ teaspoon salt and cook for 15 to 20 minutes over medium heat. Remove to a medium-sized bowl and chill.

4. Wash spinach. Remove large, thick stems. Heat a 12-inch skillet over low heat and add spinach. Stir to prevent sticking, and cook for about 10 minutes. Season with nutmeg and ½ teaspoon of the salt. Remove to a small bowl and chill.

5. In a medium-sized bowl, beat 8 of the eggs. Mince chives. Heat 1 tablespoon of the butter in a 10-inch skillet, and add beaten eggs. Cook over low heat, while stirring, for about 3 minutes. Season with ¼ teaspoon salt. Remove from heat while still slightly wet. Place in a small bowl and chill.

6. Wipe soil from caps of mushrooms and quarter. Slice zucchini into ½-inch-thick pieces. Peel and mince garlic. Heat 1 tablespoon butter in a 12-inch skillet and add garlic. Sauté briefly, and add mushrooms and zucchini pieces. Cook over medium heat for 12 to 15 minutes, and season with ½ teaspoon salt. Remove to a medium bowl and chill.

7. Mix together fontina and provolone cheeses. Beat remaining egg in a small bowl with 2 tablespoons water, and then chill.

8. *To assemble:* Preheat oven to 375° F. Using the last tablespoon of butter, coat bottom and sides of a 9-inch springform pan. Roll two thirds of the chilled dough into a 16-inch circle. Fold dough gently into quarters and lift into prepared pan. Open dough and press into pan bottom and against sides. Place edge of dough slightly over rim of pan. Brush interior of dough with egg-water mixture. Place artichokes in bottom of pan. Layer in this order: one fourth of cheese mixture, all the spinach, another one fourth of the cheese mixture, the peppers, another one fourth of cheese, the scrambled eggs, the mushroom-zucchini mixture, and finally the last of the cheese. Roll remaining dough into a 10-inch circle and brush with egg-water mixture. Place egg-coated side of dough next to filling and press edges of dough together to seal. Brush top of dough with remaining egg-water mixture. Use some of the dough trimmings to decorate top, if desired. Let Torta Milanese rise for 20 minutes in a draft-free area. Bake for 1 hour and 10 minutes. Cool for 20 minutes before serving.

SCRUMPTIOUS COFFEE CAKE

Discard the dark green leaves of the rhubarb because they are toxic.

Filling

4 cups rhubarb (about 8 stalks)
½ cup sugar
¼ cup flour plus flour for preparing pan
2 tablespoons butter plus butter for preparing pan
2 teaspoons cinnamon

Batter

¾ cup butter
1 cup sugar
2 eggs
1 teaspoon vanilla extract
1½ cups all-purpose flour
½ cup whole wheat flour
1 teaspoon baking powder
¼ teaspoon baking soda
¼ teaspoon kosher salt
Rind of 1 lemon, chopped
1 cup plain yogurt

Topping

¼ cup butter
½ cup brown sugar
1 teaspoon cinnamon
½ cup flour

1. Preheat oven to 400° F. Butter and flour a 9-inch springform pan.

2. *To make filling:* Wash and dry rhubarb stalks. Slice into 1-inch pieces and place in a 2-quart mixing bowl. Toss with sugar, flour, butter, and cinnamon. Set aside.

3. *To make batter:* In a large mixing bowl, beat butter and sugar together until light and fluffy. Beat in eggs and vanilla. Sift flours, baking powder, baking soda, and salt. Stir lemon rind into yogurt. Fold half of sifted flour mixture into butter-sugar-egg mixture. Fold in yogurt-lemon rind. Fold in remaining flour. Mix well.

4. *To make topping:* In a small bowl, mix butter, brown sugar, and cinnamon. Mix in flour until crumbly.

5. Place half the batter in prepared pan. Cover batter with filling. Top with remaining batter. Sprinkle on topping. Bake for 1 hour and 10 minutes.

FREEZING SPRING PRODUCE

Lengthen the spring produce season by freezing foods to use later. Choose the best produce available because the freezer can only maintain the quality of produce at the time of purchase. Produce can be frozen whole, chopped, or ready to cook (such as a pie). Produce can also be cooked in advance so that it is ready to reheat from the freezer. Freezing can be an aid or a bane depending on a few simple precautions.

☐ Prevent air from reaching frozen items and causing freezer burn and ice crystals, which can ruin all the beautiful foods that you freeze. Wrap all foods airtight, using heavy-duty aluminum foil, plastic bags from which the air has been pressed, or rigid containers filled to within ½ inch of the top so that there is room for expansion but not for oxidation.

☐ Food keeps best in a 0° F freezer. Produce cannot be kept indefinitely. Label, with a date, all items to be frozen, using an indelible marker. Keep a list (tape it to the freezer door) of everything stored in the freezer. Be sure to rotate the inventory of the freezer so that foods are not pushed to the back and forgotten.

☐ The flavor and texture of certain foods change after freezing. Raw salad greens, tomatoes, and cucumbers lose their crispness, for example. Raw onions and garlic intensify in flavor. Most frozen fruits lose their original texture and are best used as sauces or in cooking. Some fruits retain their shape better if they are served only partially defrosted.

☐ Thaw produce while still wrapped, preferably in the refrigerator, or place frozen produce directly from the freezer into boiling water, hot sauces, or preheated oven. There is a risk of spoilage when fruits and vegetables are thawed at room temperature.

☐ Fruit jams made using a freezer method use less sugar and no packaged pectin, can be made quickly, and maintain their bright natural colors. Although the final consistency is thinner than jams made from long-cooked preserves, freezer jams have a fresher flavor.

☐ Always sterilize jam jars and lids before using. Pour freshly prepared jam into the jars, cover with a lid, and seal immediately. Cool to room temperature. Date each jar and place it in the freezer for up to 3 months, using the earliest-dated jars first.

SPRING BERRY JAM

Use blackberries, olallieberries, raspberries, blueberries, or even peaches.

1½ pounds berries
1¾ cups sugar
1 tangerine

1. Stem berries. In a 2-quart saucepan, mash berries. Add sugar.

2. Cut rind from tangerine, taking care to remove only the colored part and none of the bitter white membrane. Dice rind and add to berries and sugar. Juice tangerine and strain out seeds. Discard seeds and membrane, and add juice to the fruit mixture.

3. Heat to a boil over low heat while stirring to dissolve sugar. Cook for 20 minutes and pour into sterilized jars, leaving ½ inch headroom for expansion. Seal with tight-fitting lids and cool to room temperature, 12 to 24 hours. Store in freezer for up to 3 months. Refrigerate after opening.

Makes 5 half-pints.

This harmonious trio, Three-Bean Chile, here served with Cheddar cheese, will be one of the mainstays of your kitchen. These beans provide complete protein when paired with either Jalapeño Corn Bread (see page 86) or Whole-Grain Bread (see page 123).

SPRING SIDE DISHES

These side-dish recipes are generally easier-to-assemble combinations of the same ingredients found in the main dishes. Using the Basics of Freezing Spring Produce on page 37, you can extend the season for several months, and enjoy this lighter fare through the summer months. Many of these side dishes take only a few minutes to prepare and can be served in a number of ways. Combine an assortment of side dishes for a beautiful buffet, put a salad and a side dish together as a light luncheon, or add a soup to one of these dishes for a super midnight supper.

THREE-BEAN CHILE

This combination of small white beans, kidney beans, and black beans creates a mosaic of color. For the simple cooking steps, refer to Best Beans (see page 19). Serve with condiments such as grated Cheddar cheese or as a filling for Ensenada Enchiladas (see page 32) or Huevos Rancheros (see page 113).

> 1   red bell pepper
> 1   green bell pepper
> 1   or 2 jalapeño chiles, to taste
> 6   fresh long green chiles, peeled and seeded or 1 can (4 oz) green chiles
> 1½ tablespoons oil
> 2   onions, diced
> 4   cloves garlic, minced
> 1   small bunch parsley, finely chopped
> 2½ cups small white beans, cooked
> 2½ cups kidney beans, cooked
> 2½ cups black beans, cooked
> 8   medium tomatoes, peeled and seeded or 1 can (28 oz) crushed plum tomatoes
> 4   teaspoons kosher salt
> 1   teaspoon cumin
> 1   teaspoon oregano
> 2   tablespoons chile powder
> 2   cups water
>   Cilantro, for garnish

1. Slice bell peppers in half, remove and discard seeds, and cut into ½-inch squares. Mince jalapeños (plastic gloves may be useful to prevent seeds from burning skin). Roast green chiles as described for Grilled Chiles Rellenos on page 50. Then cut in half lengthwise, carefully remove and discard seeds, and chop into ½-inch squares.

2. Heat oil in a 4-quart saucepan. Sauté onion over medium heat for 5 minutes and add garlic. Cook another 1 to 2 minutes. Stir in peppers, chiles, and parsley. Add cooked beans, tomatoes, salt, cumin, oregano, chile powder, and the water. Bring to a boil and reduce heat to a simmer for 40 minutes. Serve in shallow bowl with cilantro sprigs for garnish.

Makes 10 cups, 8 servings.

POTATO-BASIL FRITTATA

This simple pepper and potato omelet is based on the famous Spanish dish, *tortilla españa.*

> *Oil for baking dish*
> 2 *large boiling potatoes (about 1 lb)*
> 1 *small onion*
> 1 *red bell pepper*
> 1 *green bell pepper*
> 1 *bunch basil (15 to 20 large leaves)*
> 1 *tablespoon olive oil*
> 5 *eggs*
> 1½ *teaspoons kosher salt*
> ½ *teaspoon pepper*
> 2 *tablespoons Parmesan cheese (optional)*

1. Preheat oven to 350° F. Oil a 9-inch-round, 2-inch-deep baking dish. Wash and quarter potatoes, and place in a 1-quart saucepan. Cover with water and bring to a boil. Reduce heat and simmer for 12 minutes. Remove from pan, cool, and slice into ¼-inch-thick rounds.

2. Peel onion, and slice into ¼-inch-thick strips. Seed bell peppers and slice into ¼-inch-thick strips. Slice basil into thin strips.

3. Heat olive oil in a 10-inch sauté pan, and cook onion and peppers for 8 to 10 minutes over medium heat. Add potatoes and basil, and cook 1 minute more.

4. Beat eggs with salt and pepper in a 3-quart bowl. Add onion-pepper-potato mixture. Mix well and pour into prepared pan. Sprinkle with cheese (if used), and bake until top is dry and lightly golden (45 to 50 minutes).

Serves 6.

POMMES DE TERRE EN PAPILLOTE

Any vegetable can be steamed *en papillote,* the French term for *in paper.* Season with a little salt and pepper, dot with Herb Butter (see page 26), and seal for a great do-ahead side dish.

> 12 *small boiling potatoes (about 2½ inches in diameter)*
> 1 *teaspoon kosher salt*
> *Freshly ground pepper*
> ¼ *cup Herb Butter (see page 26)*

1. Preheat oven to 375° F. Cut 6 pieces of aluminum foil into 10-inch squares. Wash and dry potatoes, and slice into ¼-inch-thick pieces.

2. Place 2 potatoes on each piece of foil. Fan out pieces so that they overlap slightly. Sprinkle each potato package with about ⅛ teaspoon salt. Grind pepper over potatoes. Dot each potato with 1 teaspoon Herb Butter. Carefully seal each foil packet, crimping edges securely.

3. Place packages on a baking sheet and bake for 40 minutes.

Serves 6.

GRILLED VEGETABLES

Grilling accents the straightforward taste of fresh vegetables. Try this combination of spring produce, or use this technique for leftovers.

> 12 *small leeks*
> 12 *baby carrots*
> 12 *baby turnips*
> 4 *small yellow crookneck squash*
> *Herb Butter (see page 26)*

1. Bring 2 quarts of water to a boil. Clean leeks (see page 15), then blanch for 7 minutes. Remove and place in cold water until cool. Drain and dry. Peel carrots and blanch in boiling water for 3 minutes. Place in cold water until cool. Drain and dry. Cut turnips larger than 2 inches in diameter in half. Cut squash into ¼-inch-thick slices.

2. Heat grill and place vegetables on grate. Turn continuously until lightly grilled and warm throughout (about 3 to 4 minutes). Place on a serving plate, and dot with Herb Butter.

Serves 6.

STUFFED EGGPLANT BOATS

Eggplant absorbs many added flavors but none better than garlic and Parmesan cheese. These little boats can be prepared in the morning and just reheated for the evening meal.

> *Oil for pan*
> 3 *small eggplants*
> 2 *tablespoons butter*
> 4 *cloves garlic, minced*
> 3 *shallots, minced*
> 8 *mushrooms, minced*
> 8 *leaves kale or ½ bunch spinach*
> ½ *cup bread crumbs*
> ½ *cup chopped almonds*
> ¼ *cup Parmesan cheese*
> 1½ *teaspoons kosher salt*
> 2 *tablespoons parsley*
> 1 *teaspoon oregano*

1. Preheat oven to 350° F. Brush baking sheet with oil. Slice eggplant in half lengthwise. Place eggplant cut side down on baking sheet. Bake until tender when pierced with a knife (30 to 35 minutes).

2. Heat butter in a large skillet. Add garlic, shallots, and mushrooms. Sauté for 5 minutes. Julienne the kale and add with bread crumbs, almonds, Parmesan, salt, parsley, and oregano. Stir to combine.

3. Remove eggplant from oven. Leave oven on. Carefully scoop tender interior meat from eggplant shells. Chop and mix eggplant meat with vegetable mixture. Mound filling in eggplant shells, and bake for 30 minutes. Let rest for 10 minutes before serving.

Serves 6.

SPRING BREADS

Spring baking can take many forms. Serve breakfast waffles with seasonal fruits, breadsticks to complement soups and salads, and quick-baking flat breads to accompany stews and ragouts.

FOCACCIA PRIMAVERA

Focaccia in Italy is a simple flat bread. Here it is combined with the vegetables of the season. This is delicious served with Risotto Primavera (see page 29).

> 1 package active dry yeast
> 1 cup warm water
> ½ cup milk
> 2 tablespoons honey
> 2 tablespoons olive oil plus oil for brushing
> 1 cup whole wheat flour
> 2 teaspoons kosher salt
> 3 cups unbleached flour plus flour for dusting
> Oil for bowl
> 8 ounces Monterey jack cheese
> 4 ounces ricotta cheese
> 4 ounces goat cheese
> 4 cloves garlic
> 2 bunches spinach
> 8 to 10 stalks asparagus
> 6 to 8 green onions
> 1 can (10 oz) artichoke hearts
> ¼ cup capers

1. In a large mixing bowl, dissolve yeast in ¼ cup of the water. Stir in remaining water, milk, honey, oil, whole wheat flour, salt, and 2 cups of the unbleached flour. Stir dough vigorously in mixing bowl, incorporating remaining unbleached flour as needed. Dough should be soft and pliable and not sticky. Turn onto a lightly floured work surface, and knead for approximately 5 minutes. Lightly oil a large mixing bowl, place dough in bowl, and cover with plastic wrap. Let rise for 1 hour.

2. Shred jack cheese and place in a 1-quart mixing bowl. Stir together Monterey jack, ricotta, and goat cheeses. Mince garlic and stir into cheeses.

3. Wash spinach. Place spinach in a 12-inch skillet and let steam in liquid retained from washing. Chop coarsely. Slice asparagus and green onions on the diagonal into 1-inch pieces. Rinse and quarter artichoke hearts.

4. Preheat oven to 475° F. Punch down dough and cut into 3 equal pieces. Roll dough into 8-inch circles about ½ inch thick. Brush circles with olive oil. Crumble cheese over dough. Dot dough with spinach, asparagus, green onions, artichokes, and capers.

5. Bake until crust is crisp (about 15 to 20 minutes).

Makes 3 thin 6-inch breads.

WHOLE-GRAIN WAFFLES

A nonstick or well-seasoned waffle iron will not need additional oil to prevent sticking. If the waffle iron is new, it should be heated and brushed with oil to prepare it for the batter. Serve waffles with home-canned Raspberry Sauce (see page 75) or with sliced fresh fruit and a glass of milk for a special morning meal.

> 2 cups Whole-Grain Baking Mix (see page 17)
> 1 cup milk or water
> 1 egg
> 1 tablespoon oil plus oil for waffle iron

1. In a medium-sized mixing bowl, stir together Baking Mix, milk, egg, and oil. Let rest for 5 minutes while waffle iron is heating. Brush hot waffle iron with oil if necessary.

2. Place about one quarter of the batter in heated waffle iron and close lid. Cook waffles until steam no longer escapes from them (about 4 to 5 minutes). Remove waffles and serve at once.

Makes 4 waffles.

SPRING DESSERTS

Spring desserts focus attention on light seasonal fruits and gentle flavors. Sweet, tart apricots, strawberries, and mangoes can constitute a dessert by themselves, but when embellished in these recipes, they shine.

YOGURT-HONEY FLAN

Flan, the traditional dessert of Spain and Mexico, is an egg custard. In lieu of cream, this flan is made with yogurt to reduce the amount of fat in the recipe. It produces a delicious, tangy custard.

> ½ cup sugar
> ¼ cup water
> 3 cups plain yogurt
> 7 tablespoons honey
> 3 teaspoons vanilla extract
> 3 eggs
> 1 basket strawberries
> 1 mango

1. Preheat oven to 350° F. In a 1-quart saucepan, heat sugar and the water, and stir until clear. Cook over low heat until golden brown. Carefully pour into six ½-cup molds, and swirl to coat bottom of molds. Place molds in a 12-inch pan. Fill pan with 2 inches of water.

2. In a 2-quart mixing bowl, whisk together yogurt, honey, vanilla, and eggs. Strain and pour into molds. Bake until a knife inserted in center comes out clean (about 60 to 65 minutes). Cool for 30 minutes, then chill for 4 to 12 hours. To unmold, run a knife around flan, place a small dessert plate over top of mold, and invert.

3. Stem strawberries and slice each berry into two or three pieces. Peel, pit, and cube mango. Toss berries and mango, and spoon around flan.

Serves 6.

APRICOT MOUSSE

Apricots are available in late spring and early summer. One cup of dried apricots may be substituted when fresh are unavailable.

> 8 to 10 medium apricots
> ⅓ cup honey
> ⅓ cup white wine
> 1 lemon
> 1 package unflavored gelatin
> ½ teaspoon almond extract
> ½ teaspoon ground ginger
> 3 egg whites
> ⅛ teaspoon cream of tartar
> 2 tablespoons sugar
> ⅓ cup toasted sliced almonds, for garnish

1. Peel and pit apricots. Slice apricot and purée in blender, food mill, or food processor.

2. Place apricot purée, honey, and white wine in a 1-quart saucepan. Heat slowly at a low temperature, stirring constantly.

3. Remove rind from lemon, being careful to use only the yellow peel and none of the bitter white membrane beneath (a vegetable peeler or fruit zester will do the job). Mince yellow rind. Juice lemon, discard seeds and membrane, and dissolve gelatin in juice.

4. Stir gelatin mixture into apricot-wine mixture. Add almond extract, ginger, and lemon rind.

5. Beat egg whites with cream of tartar until foamy. Gradually add sugar and beat until soft peaks form. Stir one third of whites into apricot-wine-gelatin mixture. Then carefully fold in last two thirds of egg whites. Place in a 1½-quart soufflé dish or 6 tulip glasses, and chill for 4 to 12 hours. Garnish with toasted almonds at serving time.

Serves 6.

Apricots, high in potassium, iron, and vitamin A, have been cultivated since 2200 B.C. in China. Almonds, a close relative of the fruit, make a perfect garnish for this Apricot Mousse.

A profusion of colorful produce signifies the arrival of summer's bounty. Plan to preserve some of summer's succulence to savor in other seasons.

Relishing Summer's Repast

Summer bursts onto the scene with warm, sunny days that bring spring's gardening labors to delicious fruition. That well-tended garden now rewards with daily harvests. It is in the summer months of June, July, and August that we find the richest and most colorful spectrum of fruits and vegetables of the entire year. The garden unfolds with bold abundance, and color blooms on nearly every branch and vine. The volume and variety of produce available during the midst of summer provides nearly endless choices and combinations. Summer dining offers many options as well. Plan picnics and barbeques for added seasonal fun.

WARM-WEATHER DINING

Warm weather and more daylight hours allow us to maximize the time spent out-of-doors in leisure as well as productive activities. Swimming, waterskiing, gardening, fishing, hiking, and sports of every variety add to the lively tempo at which we live during this season. Sunny afternoons draw us outside for a walk or a few hours in the garden. The high energy needed for these pursuits is best fueled by light meals filled with small courses. The bounty of the season suggests meals based on salads. A salad buffet can be a pleasant way to serve a meal. Combine two or three diverse salads and homemade bread to supply the necessary nutrients. Incorporate fresh fruits, sliced or whole, into the summer diet as a delicious addition to the breakfast table or as a simple dessert. Have an abundant choice of vegetables, sliced or diced, readily available in the refrigerator for snacking. The crisp, clean flavors of the produce should prevail, so utilize brief cooking methods, such as steaming and marinating, rather than long simmers. Depend on fresh herbs for seasonings as they are most plentiful and aromatic now.

ETHNIC VARIETY

Summer is an excellent opportunity to sample dishes of different cultures. The foods of those places that enjoy an extended summer—such as France, Mexico, Italy, Greece, and the nations of North Africa and of the Pacific Basin—are a marvelous resource for inspiration. Many dishes have a common heritage based on available ingredients and cross-cultural migration. Historically, foods were heartily spiced to mask unappealing flavors caused by heat and lack of proper storage facilities. Now these same spices, herbs, and vegetables merely enhance the dishes we associate with those countries. For example, the spicy chiles of Mexico, Thailand, and Morocco complement and identify their cuisines. Additionally, the seasonings mix well with rice, couscous, cornmeal, and other grains, providing a wealth of flavors and nutrients, and a balanced diet.

SUMMER SOUPS

Summer is the perfect time to experiment with different temperatures, texture, and flavors of soup. Warm soups, prepared early in the day, can easily be chilled to serve at a later meal. All that is needed is a little heartier seasoning, as cold temperatures dull the flavor slightly. Chop fruits and vegetables into chunky pieces for rustic soups, or using the same recipe, partially or wholly purée ingredients for more elegant fare. Chilled soups travel well in a thermos for a picnic lunch at the beach or in a shady orchard.

CREAMY TOMATO-BASIL SOUP

The true taste of vine-ripened tomatoes is extolled in this soup. Water can be used in place of Vegetable Broth if the tomatoes are full-flavored. Add one-fourth cup of diced sun-dried tomatoes to enhance blander varieties.

> 1 tablespoon butter
> 2 tablespoons olive oil
> 2 onions, diced
> 2 cloves garlic, minced
> 6 large ripe tomatoes, finely diced
> 4 tablespoons tomato paste
> 2 bunches fresh basil, finely chopped
> 2 tablespoons fresh oregano, minced
> 1 teaspoon honey
> 1 tablespoon kosher salt
> ½ teaspoon freshly ground black pepper
> 5 cups Vegetable Broth (see page 15) or water
> ½ cup cream or milk

1. In a 2-quart saucepan over medium heat, melt butter and add oil. Add onions and cook for 5 minutes, stirring occasionally. Add garlic and cook for 3 minutes. Add tomatoes, tomato paste, basil, oregano, honey, salt, pepper, and Vegetable Broth. Bring ingredients to a boil, reduce heat, and simmer for 35 minutes.

2. Remove from heat and purée in a blender. Return to saucepan and add cream. Heat but do not boil. Serve hot or cold.

Makes 7½ cups, 6 to 8 servings.

SANTA ROSA PLUM SOUP

The dark skin of Santa Rosa plums hides succulent yellow fruit that makes a creamy, peach-colored soup. It is great served as either a palate-freshening starter or a light finale. Cherries, apricots, peaches, raspberries, or another variety of plum may be substituted for the Santa Rosas.

> 2 cups water
> ¼ cup sugar
> 1 cup dry white wine, fruit juice, or water
> 1 stick cinnamon
> 1 whole clove
> 1 piece (2 in.) vanilla bean
> 1 lemon
> 2½ pounds Santa Rosa plums, peeled
> 1 cup blueberries
> Mint sprigs, for garnish

1. Place the water, sugar, wine, cinnamon, clove, and vanilla bean in a 3-quart saucepan, and heat to a boil. Peel lemon and dice rind finely. Juice lemon. Add rind and juice to wine-spice mixture. Reduce heat and simmer for 10 to 15 minutes.

2. Slice peeled plums into about 8 sections, and add to wine-spice-lemon mixture. Cook until fruit is tender and translucent (14 to 18 minutes). In a blender or food processor, purée mixture. Pour into a 3-quart soup tureen and chill. At serving time stir in blueberries and garnish with mint sprigs. Serve chilled.

Makes 8 cups, 6 to 8 servings.

ANDALUSIAN GAZPACHO

From the hot Spanish plains comes a refreshingly crisp, chilled soup that is perfect on a hot summer day. It is sometimes called a salad in a broth because the ingredients are blended but not cooked. The midsummer pungency of ripe red tomatoes, peppers, and cucumbers stands out in this tangy, tasty soup.

  1 medium cucumber
  1 green bell pepper
  5 green onions
  2 cloves garlic, minced
  3 medium tomatoes
  2 stalks celery
  1 avocado (optional)
  1 small bunch parsley
 12 to 15 leaves fresh basil
  1 sprig fresh oregano
2½ cups small white beans, cooked
  2 tablespoons olive oil
  6 tablespoons red wine vinegar
  2 teaspoons kosher salt
  1 teaspoon cumin
  1 can (46 oz) tomato juice or 5½ cups Vegetable Broth (see page 15)

1. Peel cucumber and discard peel. Remove seeds and cut into ½-inch cubes. Remove and discard stem and seeds from bell pepper. Cube bell pepper. Trim root ends from green onions. Slice green onions crosswise about ¼ inch thick. Dice tomatoes into ¼-inch cubes. Slice celery and avocado (if used) into ¼-inch cubes.

2. Reserve 10 small, perfect sprigs of parsley for garnish. Mince remaining parsley, about enough to equal ⅓ cup. Mince basil to equal about ⅓ cup. Mince oregano to equal about 1 tablespoon.

3. Place cucumber, bell pepper, green onions, garlic, tomatoes, celery, avocado, parsley, basil, oregano, white beans, oil, vinegar, salt, cumin, and tomato juice in a 3½- to 4-quart soup tureen. Stir to mix thoroughly and chill 4 to 12 hours. Serve in shallow soup bowls, each garnished with a sprig of parsley.

Makes 12 cups, 10 servings.

LEEK AND POTATO SOUP

The "poor man's asparagus," as the leek was known in ancient times, blends well in this cold soup.

  6 leeks
  1 tablespoon butter
  1 clove garlic, minced
1½ potatoes, cubed
  5 cups water
2½ teaspoons kosher salt
  ¼ teaspoon white pepper
  2 cups milk
  1 bunch chives, minced, for garnish

1. Clean (see page 15) and dice leeks. Heat butter in a 3-quart saucepan, and sauté leeks and garlic for 6 to 8 minutes over low heat. Add potatoes, water, salt, and pepper. Bring to a boil.

2. Reduce heat to low, and simmer until potatoes are tender and easily pierced with a knife (35 to 40 minutes). Add milk. Remove from heat.

3. In a blender or food processor, purée mixture. Place in 3-quart soup tureen and chill. Serve in shallow bowls garnished with chives.

Makes 8 cups, 8 servings.

Vine-ripened tomatoes, peppers, and cucumbers reflect the fresh, clean tastes of summer in chilled Andalusian Gazpacho. Protein-packed small white beans contribute nutrients.

SUMMER FRESH PRODUCE

FRUITS	Purchase	Storage	Special Notes
Apricots	May-July. Varieties: Moorpark, Royal, Tilton. Look for plumpness and uniform golden orange color. Will yield to gentle pressure on skin when ripe. Avoid dull-looking, soft or mushy, pale yellow or greenish yellow fruit.	Will keep very briefly at cool temperature, out of direct sunlight.	Excellent source of vitamin A, potassium, and iron.
Berries	May-Nov.		
Blackberries	Black or deep-purple seedy fruit composed of numerous small cells on a fleshy receptacle. Look for brightness, uniform color, plump and tender cells, no attached stem caps. Avoid stained containers (indicates possible spoilage), either unripe or soft berries.	Perishable. Will keep briefly in dark, ventilated place at 32° F, 90 percent relative humidity, preferably not in refrigerator, which encourages mold.	Ideal for cereals, tarts, pies, and jams. Good source of vitamins A and C, calcium, iron, and phosphorus.
Blueberries	Look for dark blue color with silvery bloom (a natural protective coating); should be plump, firm, uniformly sized, dry, free from stems and leaves. Larger sizes better flavored than smaller. Avoid stained containers, soft berries.	Sturdier than other berries, will keep longer. *See Blackberries.*	Moderate source of vitamins A and C.
Boysen-berries	A large, aromatic bramble fruit with a raspberry flavor.	*See Blackberries.*	A trailing type of dewberry. *See Blackberries.*
Olallie-berries	Large, high-quality berries that are shiny black, firm, and sweet.	*See Blackberries.*	*See Blackberries.*
Raspberries	Any of various usually black or red berries that are aggregate fruits consisting of numerous small cells on a fleshy receptacle. Smaller and rounder than closely related blackberries.	*See Blackberries.*	Red are good source of vitamin A; black good source of calcium; both good sources of phosphorus and potassium.
Strawberries	Look for full red color, bright luster, firm flesh, attached cap and stem, dry, medium to small size. Avoid large uncolored or seedy areas (indicate poor flavor and texture), dull shrunken appearance, or softness (indicate decay), or mold.	*See Blackberries.*	Good source of vitamin C and potassium.
Cherries	May-Sept. Varieties: Bing, Black Republican, Black Tartarian, Chapman, Lambert, Schmidt. All range from deep maroon or mahogany red to black. Look for dark color (most important indication of good flavor and maturity); bright, glossy, plump appearance; and fresh-looking stems. Avoid soft berries, brown discoloration. Decay common but difficult to detect because of cherries' dark color.	Will keep at 32° F, 90 percent relative humidity. Handle carefully to avoid bruising.	Good source of vitamin A.
Cucumbers	May-Sept. Look for green color (may have some white), firmness over entire length, shapeliness (but not too large in dia.), many small lumps on surface. Avoid overgrown ones with large dia. and a dull, yellowish color (will have more seeds than meat), withered or shriveled ends (indicates toughness and bitterness).	Wash. Will keep a few days in refrigerator.	"Cool as a cucumber" derives from the cucumber's ability to be as much as 20° cooler than the outside air on a warm day. Contains more water than any other food except its relative the melon. Contains vitamins A and C. Often considered a vegetable.
Eggplant	Aug.-Sept. Look for firmness and heaviness, dark purple or purplish white skin. The Asian Ichiban is longer and smaller than the standard-sized one and may be cooked whole. Avoid blemishes, worm injury, wrinkles, or softening (indicate bitterness).	Keep in refrigerator at 45° to 50° F, 85 percent relative humidity. Use promptly.	Japan's third most important fruit. Often considered a vegetable. Also called aubergine, *berenjena,* "apples of love," guinea squash. A member of the nightshade family that includes poisonous weeds, the eggplant was shunned (along with the potato and tomato) in the 12th and 13th centuries.
Figs	June-Oct. Varieties. Adriatic: medium sized, white; Calimyrna: large, white; Kadota: small, white; Mission: large, dark purple. Look for ripe fruit that is soft to touch. Use immediately. Avoid sour odor (indicates overripeness) due to fermentation of juice.	Highly perishable; will keep briefly at 32° F, 90 percent relative humidity.	Fresh figs are tasty and attractive by themselves. Dried are better suited for mixing with nuts and seeds.
Grapes	Varieties. Perlette: June, green; Cardinal: June, bright red; Thompson Seedless: June, green; Ribier: August, jet black; Tokay: September, bright red; Emperor: October, deep red. Look for well-colored, plump grapes firmly attached to stem. White or green grapes are sweetest when color has yellowish cast and a tinge of amber. Red better when red predominates. Bunches sturdier if stems are pliable and predominately green. Avoid soft or wrinkled grapes (indicate freezing or drying), bleached areas around stem end (injury), soft berries (decay).	Highly perishable; will keep in refrigerator near 32° F, 90 percent relative humidity.	Grapes will neither ripen nor improve in color, sugar, or quality after harvesting. Contain small amounts of vitamin A and phosphorus.
Limes	June-Aug. (although available the year around). Florida Persians are seedless and bright green when ripe. Limes imported from Mexico and the West Indies are picked when green, turn yellow when fully ripe, and have heavy weight for size. Most grown in Florida. Look for glossy skin (dry skin indicates aging and loss of acid flavor). Avoid soft spots, mold, and skin punctures.	Wash to remove mold and dirt. Keep at 50° F, 85 percent relative humidity.	Flavorful when squeezed on salads. Excellent source of vitamin C, a natural disinfectant.

SUMMER FRESH PRODUCE (continued)

FRUITS	Purchase	Storage	Special Notes
Melons			
Cantaloupes	May–Oct. Look for no stem and a smooth symmetrical, shallow basin called a full slip; thick, coarse, corky netting or veining over some part of surface; yellowish rind and skin color (green indicates unripe or immature). Ripeness also indicated by pleasant odor and slight softening at blossom end. Small bruises are not normally damaging. Avoid pronounced yellow rind color (indicates overripeness), softening over entire rind; watery, insipid flesh; mold growth, particularly in stem scar; or soft and wet tissue (indicates decay). If any of stem base remains or if stem scar is jagged or torn, melon is probably not fully matured.	If melon is hard but properly colored, keep in warm room for several days, away from sunlight, preferably in high humidity, until aromatic and soft at stem and blossom ends.	Excellent source of vitamin A, good source of vitamin C.
Casabas	July–Nov. Look for golden yellow rind color and slight softening at blossom end (indicate ripeness). Casabas lack aroma. Avoid dark, sunken, water-soaked spots.	*See Cantaloupes.*	Moderate source of phosphorus and potassium. Any of several winter melons.
Crenshaws	July–Nov. Look for golden yellow rind, sometimes with small areas having a lighter shade of yellow; slight softening at blossom end; pleasant aroma. Avoid slightly sunken, water-soaked areas on rind (indicates decay, which spreads quickly).	Keep longer than cantaloupes and honeydews. *See Cantaloupes.*	
Honeydews	July–Nov. Look for yellowish white to creamy rind; soft, velvety texture; slight softening at blossom end; faint, pleasant aroma. Small, superficial, sunken spots do not damage fruit for immediate use. Avoid dead white or greenish white color, hardness (indicates immaturity), water-soaked bruised areas, cuts or punctures through the rind.	Will keep 5 to 8 days. *See Cantaloupes.*	Moderate source of phosphorous and potassium.
Watermelons	June–Sept. With cut melons look for firm, juicy, red flesh; dark brown or black seeds. Avoid pale, mealy, or watery flesh; white strands; or whitish seeds. With uncut melons look for smooth surface, slightly dull rind (neither shiny nor very dull), filled out and rounded ends, creamy underside.	Keep at room temperature until ripe; then use promptly.	Excellent source of vitamin A and potassium.
Nectarines	June–Oct. Look for plumpness, slight softening along seam, orange yellow skin between red areas (some have greenish ground color). Avoid hard, dull, or slightly shriveled fruits; softness or over-ripeness; cracked or punctured skin.	Bright-looking, firm to moderately hard fruits will probably ripen within 2 or 3 days at room temperature. Will keep at 32° F, 90 percent relative humidity.	Good source of vitamin A, moderate source of calcium and phosphorus.
Peaches	June–Oct. Look for plumpness, slightly softened surface, yellow or creamy color between red areas. Avoid very firm or soft fruit, distinctly green color, pale tan spots (indicate decay).	Will ripen rapidly at room temperature; will keep at 32° F, 90 percent relative humidity.	Contain vitamins A and C.
Peppers	May–Oct. Varieties. sweet: bell, pimiento; hot: cayenne, jalapeño. Sweet peppers are either yellow, green, or red, depending on maturity. Chiles (hot peppers) are sold dried or fresh. Look for shapeliness, thick walls, firmness, uniformly glossy color. Avoid pale color, soft seeds (indicates immaturity), sunken, blisterlike spots on surface (decay).	Keep briefly at 45° to 50° F, relative humidity 85 percent.	Raw sweet peppers are an excellent source of vitamin C, a moderate source of vitamin A. Hot varieties are good sources of vitamin A. Often considered a vegetable.
Plums	June–Sept. Varieties. European: blue or purple, generally smaller. Japanese: medium to large, known for juiciness. Look for plumpness, full color, slight yielding to light pressure. Avoid skin breaks, brownish discoloration, or hardness.	Keep at 32° F, 90 percent relative humidity.	Over 2,000 varieties. Rich in vitamin A, potassium, and fiber.
Tomatillos	Look for firm green or yellow fruits. Are green when ripe and later turn yellow.	Will keep in refrigerator for 2 weeks if not stored in plastic bag. Use canned only if fresh not available and drain strong liquid before use.	To use, remove papery husk and rinse well. Are never peeled. Popular in Mexican dishes.
Tomatoes	Use small sized for sauces and casseroles, medium sized or large for slicing, jumbo sized for stuffing or alone with dressing. Cherry tomatoes are 1 to 1½ in. in dia. Look for fully ripened, red color (for immediate use) or greenish color (for later use). Avoid yellowed, wrinkled, misshapen, angular, ribbed, or scarred tomatoes.	Will ripen quickly at room temperature, high humidity. After ripening, keep at 50° F or lower.	Good source of vitamins A and C and potassium. Often considered a vegetable.

VEGETABLES

Jicama	A knobby, earth-colored Mexican tuber with the crispness and whiteness of a turnip. Look for spindle shape, firmness.	Wash, keep in plastic container in refrigerator.	Use raw as hors d'oeuvres or in salads or slice thinly and stir-fry.
Summer Squash	Varieties: crookneck (yellow), Italian marrow, pattypan (greenish white), straight neck (large yellow), zucchini (slender green). Look for tenderness evidenced by glossy appearance and firm, not hard, surface. Avoid unshapely or stale or overmature squash, which have a dull appearance and a tough surface (usually indicating enlarged seeds and dry stringy flesh).	Refrigerate and use promptly.	Good source of potassium, vitamins A and C, and niacin. High water content.

SUMMER SALADS

A summer salad can fill the bill as either a delightfully refreshing course or a light but well-balanced meal. Utilizing the bounty of the garden in a creative fashion is the reward of the summer cook. Fresh corn, bright tomatoes, small green beans, a rainbow of bell peppers, and multihued fruits supply the paint box needed to create an edible masterpiece.

GREEN TOMATO AND AVOCADO SALAD

Near the end of the summer, a cold spell may prevent tomatoes from ripening fully. This can be seen as a blessing in disguise for it is an opportunity to use the tart, green tomatoes in salads and pies or dusted with bread crumbs and sautéed. Green tomatoes may be substituted for the tomatillo, a Mexican green tomato with a papery husk found in Latin American produce shops. For a simple luncheon, serve this salad with Grilled Chiles Rellenos (see page 50).

> 4 medium green tomatoes
> or 8 tomatillos
> 1 firm, ripe avocado
> 1 small onion, finely minced
> 1 lime, juiced
> 1 clove garlic, minced
> 1 small bunch cilantro, minced
> ½ jalapeño chile, minced
> 1½ cups cooked kidney beans
> ½ teaspoon kosher salt
> 6 to 12 lettuce leaves

1. Wash and core tomatoes. Discard cores. Cut tomatoes into a medium dice. Peel and pit avocado. Dice avocado into ½-inch cubes.

2. Place tomatoes, onion, and avocado into a 2-quart mixing bowl. Drizzle with lime juice. Stir in garlic, cilantro, jalapeño chile, kidney beans, and salt. Wash and pat dry lettuce leaves. To serve, place some mixture onto each leaf.

Serves 6.

CONFETTI CORN SALAD

Corn salad makes a delightful main course when served with soup or grilled vegetables. It travels well for picnics and is a beautiful addition to a buffet. This salad complements both Garden Pizza (see page 53) and Zucchini Tortillas (see page 52). Tomatillos are a member of the nightshade family, which includes eggplant, ground cherry, peppers (bell and chile), and potatoes. They are lemony, acid, green, tomato-shaped vegetables that arrive in the market in a papery husk. The husk is removed and discarded, and the tomatillos can then be cooked or diced and used raw in salads. End-of-summer green tomatoes are a suitable substitute in this recipe.

> 5 ears corn
> ¼ pound Monterey jack cheese
> or jalapeño jack cheese
> 1 red bell pepper, seeded
> and diced
> 1 green bell pepper, seeded
> and diced
> 1 small red onion, diced
> 2 tomatillos or green tomatoes,
> minced
> 1 small bunch cilantro, minced
> 1 jalapeño chile, minced
> 1½ cups cooked black beans
> or kidney beans
> 5 tablespoons red wine vinegar
> ¼ cup oil
> 1½ teaspoons kosher salt
> ½ teaspoon black pepper
> 8 to 12 leaves butter lettuce
> or radicchio, for garnish

1. Cut corn from cob to equal 3½ cups. Heat 2 quarts water to boiling. Cook corn for 2 minutes. Remove to colander. Rinse in cold water and pat dry. Place in a 3-quart mixing bowl.

2. Cut cheese into ¼-inch cubes.

3. Stir bell peppers, onion, tomatillos, cilantro, chile, cheese, and beans into corn to combine thoroughly. Add vinegar, oil, salt, and pepper. Mix well and marinate 1 to 12 hours before serving. Wash and pat dry lettuce leaves. To serve, place some mixture onto each leaf.

Serves 8 to 12.

MOZZARELLA SALAD

Italian mozzarella cheese is soft and tangy. It is worth the search in a specialty cheese store or delicatessen. Italian mozzarella comes in 8-ounce rounds or little balls the size of a walnut; either will be superb.

> 3 large ripe tomatoes
> ½ pound Italian mozzarella
> cheese
> 1 small bunch basil
> 2 tablespoons red wine vinegar
> 6 tablespoons olive oil
> ¼ teaspoon kosher salt
> Freshly ground black pepper

1. Slice tomatoes crosswise into ½-inch-thick rounds. Slice mozzarella into ¼-inch-thick rounds. This will be easier to do if cheese is chilled.

2. Reserve 6 to 8 small basil leaves for garnish and chop remaining leaves. In a 2-cup mixing bowl, whisk together vinegar, oil, and salt. Stir in chopped basil leaves.

3. Arrange tomatoes alternately with cheese on a serving dish. Drizzle with basil vinaigrette and grind black pepper over top. Garnish with reserved basil leaves.

Serves 6.

SUMMER BEAN SALAD

The addition of garbanzo beans makes this salad a hearty dish for a light supper.

> ½ English cucumber
> 1 large tomato
> ½ pound green beans
> 1½ cups cooked garbanzo beans
> Basic Vinaigrette (see
> page 13)
> 6 fresh dill sprigs,
> for garnish

1. Cube cucumber into ½-inch pieces. Dice tomato into ½-inch pieces. Bring 1 quart of water to a boil. Cut green beans into 3-inch pieces. Blanch beans by placing in boiling water for 3 minutes. Remove from water, and place in ice water to set color. Pat beans dry.

2. Mix cucumber, tomato, green beans, garbanzo beans, and Basic Vinaigrette together. Marinate in refrigerator for 3 to 4 hours. Serve garnished with dill sprigs.

Serves 6.

SPICY FRUIT SALAD

Fruit salads do not have to be sweet, as this spicy salad attests. This vibrant mixture of fruit and vegetables is a winning combination. It makes a perfect accompaniment to Tex-Mex Chile Salad (see page 50).

> 1 seedless English cucumber
>   or regular cucumber
> 3 medium tomatoes, cored
> ½ bunch (¾ c) cilantro, minced
> ½ pineapple, peeled
> ½ honeydew melon, peeled,
>   and seeded
> ½ papaya, peeled, seeded,
>   and cubed
> 1 red onion, diced
> 1 jalapeño chile, minced
> 1 tablespoon oil
> 2 tablespoons white wine
>   vinegar
> ¼ teaspoon kosher salt

1. If using a seedless cucumber, it is not necessary to peel or seed it. Peel other types of cucumber, remove seeds, and discard peel and seeds. Cut cucumber into ½-inch-thick slices. Cut each cored tomato into pieces about ½-inch square. Reserve 6 sprigs of cilantro for garnish, and mince the rest. Cut pineapple and honeydew melon into 1½-inch cubes.

2. Place pineapple, papaya, honeydew, red onion, cucumber, tomatoes, jalapeño chile, and minced cilantro into a 3-quart mixing bowl. Toss together with oil, vinegar, and salt. Chill for 4 to 8 hours. Remove from refrigerator for 30 minutes before serving. Garnish with reserved cilantro sprigs.

Serves 8 to 10.

SUMMER MAIN DISHES

No one wants to spend a hot afternoon working in a warm kitchen. Keep summer main-dish cooking time to a minimum, and utilize methods other than baking as often as possible. The components of these easily assembled courses can often be prepared ahead in the cooler morning. Supplement summer main courses with chilled soups and fresh salads.

SPINACH ROULADE

The word *roulade* indicates that this flat spinach soufflé is rolled. Tofu and ricotta combine with sautéed mushrooms for a tasty filling. This roulade is delicious served warm from the oven or chilled for a festive picnic. Parchment paper makes assembly and cleanup much easier.

> Butter and flour for pan
>   (optional)
> 2 bunches spinach
>   Béchamel Sauce (see page 13)
> ¼ teaspoon cayenne pepper
> 6 egg whites
> ⅛ teaspoon cream of tartar
> ⅛ teaspoon kosher salt
> ½ cup grated Parmesan cheese
> ½ pound mushrooms
> 1 tablespoon butter
> ¼ pound Monterey jack cheese
> 1 clove garlic, minced
> ¼ cup chives, minced
> ½ pound firm tofu
> 1 cup ricotta cheese
> 1½ teaspoons kosher salt

Tomato-Shallot Sauce

> 1 large tomato, minced
> 4 shallots, minced
> 2 tablespoons red wine vinegar
> 6 tablespoons olive oil
> 1 teaspoon oregano
> ½ teaspoon kosher salt
> ¼ teaspoon pepper

1. Preheat oven to 350° F. Line a 10-by 15-inch jelly-roll pan with parchment paper, or grease with butter and dust with flour (if desired).

2. Wash spinach leaves, and cook until wilted in a 14-inch skillet with water remaining on leaves. Pat dry and chop finely. Stir Béchamel Sauce and cayenne pepper into spinach. In a medium bowl, beat egg whites with cream of tartar and the ⅛ teaspoon salt until soft peaks form. Carefully fold egg-white mixture into spinach mixture. Spread spinach and egg-white mixture into prepared pan, and bake for 22 to 25 minutes.

3. While roulade is baking, place sheet of parchment or a towel on work surface. Sprinkle parchment with ¼ cup of the Parmesan cheese. When roulade has finished baking, cool in pan for 10 minutes. Loosen edges and invert onto cheese-covered parchment. Sprinkle with remaining Parmesan cheese. Roll parchment and roulade together jelly-roll fashion, and cool completely (about 1 hour).

4. Slice mushrooms about ¼ inch thick. Heat butter, and sauté mushrooms until lightly browned (12 to 15 minutes). Remove to a 3-quart mixing bowl to cool for 10 minutes.

5. Grate jack cheese and place in bowl with mushrooms. Add garlic, chives, tofu, ricotta, and the 1½ teaspoons salt. Mix well to combine.

6. Carefully unroll roulade and spread with filling, leaving 1 inch uncovered around the edge. Roll up again in parchment and refrigerate until serving time.

7. *To serve:* Remove and discard parchment. Cut roulade into 2-inch-thick slices. Place on individual plates. Top pieces with Tomato-Shallot Sauce.

Serves 8.

Tomato-Shallot Sauce In a small bowl, combine tomato, shallots, vinegar, oil, oregano, salt and pepper. Marinate for 1 hour before serving.

TEX-MEX CHILE SALAD

The states that border Mexico long ago transformed the seasonings of their neighbor to accommodate the American palate and regional ingredients. This Tex-Mex Chile Salad uses dry, red New Mexico chiles for depth of flavor and the tiny, green *serrano* chile for bite. Serve Spicy Fruit Salad (see page 49) as an accompaniment.

    3   cups black beans
    2   dry New Mexico chiles
    2   green bell peppers
    ½   tablespoon olive oil
    3   onions, diced
    4   cloves garlic, minced
    1   serrano chile, diced
    1   tablespoon cumin, toasted
    1   teaspoon oregano
    1½ tablespoons kosher salt
    4   cups water
    6   ounces Cheddar cheese
    6   plum tomatoes
    8   to 12 leaves Napa or Chinese
        cabbage
        Oil for deep-frying
    8   flour tortillas (14-in. dia)
        Guacamole (see page 74),
        for garnish
        Cilantro sprigs, for garnish

1. In a 3-quart saucepan, cover black beans with water and bring to a boil. Turn off heat, cover, and rest for 1 hour. After 1 hour, bring beans to a boil, reduce heat, and simmer until tender (1¼ hours). Drain and rinse.

2. In a 1-quart saucepan, cover New Mexico chiles with water and soak for 30 minutes. Strain 1 cup of soaking liquid from chiles and reserve. Discard remaining water and dice chiles.

3. Cut bell peppers into 1-inch cubes.

4. Place olive oil in a 5-quart Dutch oven over medium heat. Sauté onion and garlic for 6 minutes. Add New Mexico chiles, serrano chile, bell pepper, beans, cumin, oregano, reserved chile water, salt, and the 4 cups water. Stir to combine, reduce heat to low, and simmer uncovered for 1 hour.

5. Grate Cheddar cheese and reserve. Cut each tomato into 8 wedges. Wash cabbage and cut into ⅛-inch-thick strips.

6. Preheat oven to 200° F. In a wok or deep-fryer, heat oil to 375° F. Place one tortilla at a time into the hot oil. Press a 1-cup metal ladle with a long handle in the center of each tortilla for 30 to 45 seconds as it fries to create a bowl shape. Remove ladle and cook tortilla 30 seconds more. Remove tortilla from oil and drain on paper towels. Keep tortillas warm in preheated oven on baking sheets covered with paper towels.

7. *To assemble:* Place a tortilla on each dinner plate. On each tortilla layer about ¾ cup cabbage, 1½ cups black beans, ¼ cup Cheddar cheese, and 2 or 3 tomato wedges. Garnish with Guacamole and cilantro sprigs, and serve immediately.

Serves 8.

GRILLED CHILES RELLENOS

Roasting chiles (and peppers) loosens their skin, making them easier to peel. You can roast over a flame, on an electric burner, or under a broiler. If you would rather not perform this extra step, the long, green Anaheim chiles are often found in four- or seven-ounce cans labeled whole green chiles, which make a suitable substitute. *Relleno* is Spanish for *stuffed*.

    12 Anaheim chiles or 2 cans (4 oz
        each) whole green chiles
    ¾   pound jalapeño jack cheese
        or Monterey jack cheese
    12 sprigs cilantro
    12 lettuce leaves

1. *To roast chiles:* If using canned whole green chiles, start with step 2. Char fresh chiles on a rack over a direct flame. Turn to roast all sides. When skin is blistered, remove chiles from flame, immediately place into a plastic bag, and seal. Let steam for about 20 minutes. Remove from plastic bag, and slip off charred skin under running water.

2. Pat chiles dry. Slice cheese into 12 equal pieces. Make a small slit in the side of each chile, and slip in a slice of cheese and a sprig of cilantro. Chill until ready to grill.

3. Place stuffed chiles, slit side up, on a heated grill for 4 to 5 minutes. Remove when cheese is melted. The stuffed chiles may also be cooked in a 400° F oven for about 4 minutes. Serve on lettuce leaves.

Serves 6.

SUMMER VEGETABLE CHARTREUSE

In classic French cooking, *chartreuse* refers to a vegetable-lined mold filled with partridge, made for a special occasion. In this version of the visual masterpiece, a mixture of summer vegetables replaces the meat.

    2   tablespoons butter
    2   medium potatoes (about ¾ lb)
    1   tablespoon kosher salt
    1   small eggplant
    1   to 2 medium zucchini
    2   carrots
    2   tomatoes
    ½   pound small green beans
    1½ tablespoons olive oil
    2   cloves garlic, minced
    1   onion, minced
    ½   pound broccoli, diced
    6   to 8 medium mushrooms,
        quartered
    3   tablespoons fresh basil
    ¼   cup chopped parsley
    ¼   teaspoon freshly ground
        black pepper
        Red Pepper Sauce (see
        page 14)

1. Preheat oven to 350° F. Butter a 1½-quart soufflé dish or 6-cup charlotte mold. Peel and cube potatoes. Place in a 2-quart pan of boiling water and cook for 20 minutes. Remove, drain, and purée. Season with 1 teaspoon of the salt. Cube eggplant and sprinkle with ½ teaspoon of the salt. Place in a colander or on a towel-lined baking sheet for 30 minutes. Rinse and pat dry.

2. Measure height of mold. Cut zucchini to equal height of dish. Slice into ⅛-inch-thick strips. Peel carrots and cut to equal height of dish. Slice into ⅛-inch-thick strips. Line mold alternately with zucchini and carrot slices. Trim a ¼-inch by 3-inch diameter slice from the bottom of one of the tomatoes. Place in the center of the bottom of the mold. Slice green beans to fit space between tomato and edge of the mold so that they radiate like spokes on a wheel. Carefully smear inside of the vegetable-lined mold with two thirds of the potato purée to a thickness of about ⅜ inch.

3. Dice leftover zucchini, carrots, and tomatoes. Cut green beans in half.

4. Heat oil in a 5-quart saucepan over medium heat, and sauté garlic, onion, carrots, eggplant, and broccoli about 8 minutes. Add the beans and mushrooms. Cook for about 5 minutes more. Stir in tomato, zucchini, basil, parsley, pepper, and remaining salt. Cook for 3 to 4 minutes and remove from heat. Place sautéed vegetables in center of potato- and vegetable-lined mold. Spread remaining potato purée over top of vegetables. Cover top with aluminum foil. Bake for 30 minutes, remove aluminum foil, and bake for 20 minutes more.

5. Let chartreuse rest for 10 minutes before unmolding. Invert serving plate over chartreuse, and turn over plate and mold together. Lift off mold. Pour warmed Red Pepper Sauce around base before serving.

Serves 6 to 8.

The potato, with approximately 100 calories, contributes protein, vitamins, and minerals to Summer Vegetable Chartreuse served in a pool of Red Pepper Sauce. This makes an elegant main course accompanied by tossed green salad.

51

Whole wheat spaghetti, available in health-food stores, is combined with long, thin strands of carrot and green and yellow zucchini for a colorful pasta supper. Accompany Vegetable Spaghetti with Summer Bean Salad (see page 48) or Green Tomato and Avocado Salad (see page 48) for a well-balanced, visually exciting dinner.

VEGETABLE SPAGHETTI

The julienned carrots and zucchini mimic the shape of the spaghetti. Feel free to substitute your favorite pasta for the whole wheat version featured here. You may substitute crookneck squash for yellow zucchini.

> ½ *pound whole wheat spaghetti*
> 3 *carrots*
> 3 *green zucchini*
> 3 *yellow zucchini*
> 1 *tablespoon olive oil*
> 1 *tablespoon butter*
> 2 *cloves garlic, minced*
> 1½ *cup packed fresh basil, minced*
> ¾ *cup parsley, minced*
> ½ *cup fresh chives, minced*
> 2 *tablespoons fresh marjoram, minced*
> 1½ *teaspoon kosher salt*
> ½ *cup grated Parmesan cheese*

1. Bring 4 quarts of water to a boil. Stir in whole wheat spaghetti and cook for 12 minutes. Drain. Peel carrots. Cut carrots and green and yellow zucchini into long, thin julienne strips (about ⅛ inch thick) to resemble spaghetti.

2. In a Dutch oven or large skillet, heat oil and butter over low heat. Add garlic and carrots. Sauté for 5 to 7 minutes. Add whole wheat spaghetti, green and yellow zucchini, basil, parsley, chives, marjoram, and salt. Stir to combine and cook for 4 to 5 minutes. Remove from heat and place in a shallow serving bowl. Sprinkle with Parmesan cheese. Toss to combine. Serve immediately.

Serves 6 to 8.

ZUCCHINI TORTILLAS

This straightforward sauté of zucchini and onions can be turned into a terrific luncheon or light supper with the addition of Green Tomato and Avocado Salad (see page 48) or Black Bean Salsa (see page 74).

> 3 *zucchini*
> 1 *onion*
> 1 *teaspoon butter*
> 2 *cloves garlic, minced*
> ½ *teaspoon kosher salt*
> ½ *pound jalapeño jack cheese or Monterey jack cheese*
> 8 *flour tortillas (8-in. dia)*

1. Shred zucchini. Slice onion into thin strips. Heat butter in a medium skillet, and sauté onion and garlic until translucent (about 8 minutes). Add zucchini, and cook for about 5 minutes, stirring to mix thoroughly with onion and garlic. Season with salt. Cool slightly. Grate cheese.

2. Spread about 3 tablespoons of onion-garlic-zucchini filling over one half of each tortilla, sprinkle with about ⅓ cup grated cheese, and fold tortilla in half. Place 2 or 3 folded tortillas in a large skillet over a medium flame, and heat until cheese is melted.

Serves 4 to 8.

GARDEN PIZZA

Although baking is not a typical summer pastime, pizza is always a welcome treat. This is especially true when it is made with some of the beautiful produce of summer. The crispiest crust comes from rolling the dough thin and prebaking it before the topping is added. A baking stone or unglazed terra-cotta tiles also contribute to a crispier pizza. Whole pickled chiles are available in Latin American markets.

2 cups warm water
1 tablespoon honey
1 tablespoon active dry yeast
1 tablespoon olive oil
¾ cup whole wheat flour
5 teaspoons kosher salt
4¼ cups unbleached flour plus flour for work surface

Topping

3 small boiling potatoes
6 ounces teleme cheese
2 ounces feta cheese
2 tomatoes
8 black olives, pitted
1 yellow bell pepper
6 to 8 whole pickled chiles (optional)
15 to 20 leaves fresh basil Cornmeal for baking sheets
2 cups Fresh Tomato Sauce (see page 15)
4 cloves garlic, minced
1 small bunch parsley, minced
8 to 10 sprigs fresh thyme, minced

1. Place the water, honey, and yeast in a large mixing bowl. Stir to dissolve yeast. Add olive oil, whole wheat flour, and salt. Stir well to combine. Add unbleached flour gradually to make a firm dough. Stir vigorously. When dough becomes too stiff to stir, lightly dust work surface with flour and knead dough. Return dough to large bowl, cover loosely, and let rise for 1 hour.

2. Place potatoes in a small pan and cover with water. Bring to a boil, reduce heat, and simmer until potatoes are tender (20 minutes). Remove from pan and cool. Slice potatoes about ¼ inch thick.

3. Slice teleme cheese and crumble feta cheese. Slice tomatoes into thin slices about ¼ inch thick. Slice olives. Cut yellow pepper into thin strips. Cut pickled chiles (if used) crosswise into ¼-inch-thick slices. Reserve 6 of the basil leaves, and mince remaining basil.

4. Near end of rising time, preheat oven to 500° F. When dough has risen, punch down, and form into 2 balls. Roll each to about 12 inches in diameter by ½ inch thick. Place pizza crusts on baking sheet sprinkled with cornmeal, and let rise for 15 minutes.

5. Bake crusts in preheated oven for 10 minutes. Remove from oven. Spread 1 cup of Fresh Tomato Sauce over each pizza. Place tomato slices, yellow bell pepper, olives, potatoes, garlic, teleme cheese, feta cheese, and pickled chiles on pizzas. Return pizzas to oven and bake another 15 to 20 minutes. Remove from oven and sprinkle with basil, parsley, and thyme. Garnish with reserved basil leaves and serve immediately.

Makes 2 pizzas, 4 to 8 servings.

EGGPLANT AND GARLIC MOUSSE

Garlic is the main flavoring of this "meaty" mousse. If you are reluctant to use a garlic press because of the tedious cleaning, try this method: Place an unpeeled clove in the garlic press. The garlic purée comes through the press while the papery skin stays behind, preventing any purée from lodging in the tiny holes of the press.

1 tablespoon butter
2 small eggplants or 5 Japanese eggplants
1 tablespoon kosher salt
2 tablespoons olive oil
8 cloves garlic
1 onion, sliced
½ pound firm tofu
2 eggs
1 small bunch parsley
2 teaspoons thyme
1 teaspoon oregano
1 teaspoon pepper
Tomato Pearl-Onion Chutney (see page 59)

1. Butter a 1½-quart soufflé dish or a 5-cup charlotte mold. Slice eggplant into ½-inch-thick rounds. Cut each round into 6 to 8 pieces. Sprinkle with 2 teaspoons of the salt, and drain in a colander for 30 minutes.

2. Preheat oven to 350° F. Rinse and pat dry eggplant slices. Heat 1 tablespoon of the oil in a 14-inch skillet, and sauté one half of the eggplant for 10 minutes over medium heat. Remove and repeat with remaining eggplant and oil. Press garlic, add garlic and onion to eggplant, and cook for another 5 minutes.

3. Place reserved eggplant and eggplant-onion-garlic mixture in a blender or food processor, and add tofu and eggs. Purée. Remove to a mixing bowl, and stir in parsley, thyme, oregano, remaining 1 teaspoon salt, and pepper.

4. Place into buttered soufflé dish, and bake until knife inserted in center comes out clean (40 minutes). Cut mousse into 6 pieces. Serve with Tomato Pearl-Onion Chutney.

Serves 6.

Whatever your sunny-day pleasure—baseball, biking, or basking in the rays—top off the outing with a picnic featuring fruits of the season.

FRUIT-PICKING PICNIC

Pita-Bread Sandwiches

Greek Salad

Hummus

Egg and Caper Salad

Tofu Salad

Pesto Dipping Sauce

Grandmother's Date Bars

*Anne's Almond
Shortbreads
(see page 67)*

*Beverage Suggestion:
Apple Juice*

---

*If you keep a picnic
basket ready to
travel with plates,
utensils, cups, and
napkins, then
putting together an
outing is a simple
matter. Plan a visit
to an orchard and
pick your fruits from
the tree. All recipes
serve 8.*

NUTRIENT BREAKDOWN	
Calories	1,125
Protein	36 gm
Fiber	4 gm
Cholesterol	187 gm
Vitamin C	10 mg
Calcium	368 mg
Sodium	831 mg

PITA-BREAD SANDWICHES

Mediterranean pocket or pita bread makes an easily handled sandwich. To maintain freshness, it is best to wrap the sliced bread in an airtight container and store the components in an ice chest. Assemble the sandwiches at the picnic site.

    8   whole wheat pita breads
   16   romaine lettuce leaves
  2½   cups Greek Salad
  1¾   cup Hummus

To serve, slice pita bread in half, and place a lettuce leaf in each half. Place 2 tablespoons of Hummus in each pita-bread half. Top with ¼ cup of Greek Salad.

GREEK SALAD

This salad utilizes bell peppers, cucumbers, and tomatoes, which are all rich in vitamins A and C. Serve it as a sandwich filling or with lettuce as a salad.

    2   green bell peppers
    1   cucumber
    3   tomatoes
    2   stalks celery
   ¼   pound feta cheese
   ½   red onion, diced
   ½   teaspoon kosher salt
        Freshly ground pepper
    3   tablespoons vinegar
   ¼   cup oil
   ½   teaspoon oregano
    1   tablespoon fresh basil, minced

1. Wash and seed peppers and cut into 1-inch cubes. Peel cucumber and cut into 1-inch cubes. Wash tomatoes and cut into 1-inch cubes. Wash celery and slice on the diagonal into ½-inch-thick pieces. Cut feta cheese into ½-inch cubes.

2. In a 2-quart bowl, mix peppers, cucumber, tomatoes, celery, feta cheese, and red onion. Season with salt, pepper, vinegar, oil, oregano, and basil.

HUMMUS

Garbanzo beans, or chick-peas, have one of the highest protein contents of any of the legumes and are the basis of this condiment. They are puréed with tahini, a Middle Eastern condiment made from toasted sesame seeds, and served with pita bread as a high-protein sandwich spread. Peanut butter can be substituted for tahini.

    1   lemon, juiced
  1⅔   cups cooked garbanzo beans
        or 1 can (15¼ oz)
    2   cloves garlic, minced
    2   tablespoons tahini
   ⅛   teaspoon kosher salt

In a blender or food processor, combine lemon juice, garbanzo beans, garlic, tahini, and salt. Blend to a smooth paste.

Makes 1¾ cups.

EGG AND CAPER SALAD

Capers are the unopened buds of a flowering bush found primarily in the Mediterranean. The buds are traditionally harvested in the morning before they have opened, then are pickled in vinegar and herbs. The piquancy they add to the egg salad is similar to the taste of olives or *cornichons* (small French pickles).

    4   eggs, hard-cooked
    2   stalks celery
    2   tablespoons mayonnaise
    2   tablespoons plain yogurt
    1   tablespoon Dijon-style
        mustard
   ¼   teaspoon kosher salt
    1   tablespoon capers
    4   slices Whole-Grain Bread
        (see page 123)
   16   small sprigs fresh oregano

With a sharp knife, dice hard-cooked eggs and place into a 1-quart mixing bowl. Mince celery and add to eggs. Add mayonnaise, yogurt, mustard, salt, and capers. Stir to mix well. Place ½ cup on each slice of Whole-Grain Bread, garnish with sprigs of oregano, cut into quarters, and serve as open-faced sandwiches.

PACKING A PICNIC

It is important that you keep cold food cold and hot food hot and never try to store the two together. Do not store food at room temperature either before a picnic or while traveling. Place cold food in an ice chest with a tightly fitting lid. Do not pack too much into the chest, because some of the chilling capability will be lost. Keep food in the ice chest until serving time. Try to avoid picnic leftovers, as foods that have been unrefrigerated for any length of time are vulnerable to spoilage. Bacteria thrive between 42° and 140° F. When planning a picnic, choose foods that can be transported cold and cooked at the picnic site. Pack foods in the order they will be served, placing the last item served in a sturdy, rigid-sided container on the bottom. Prepare salads in plastic bags and toss in the dressings when you arrive. Casseroles are best wrapped in many layers of insulation (newspaper works well) and should be carried only short distances.

Choose a picnic basket with durable, comfortable handles. Picnic aficionados always keep ready eating and serving utensils, plastic glasses and plates, napkins, tablecloth, corkscrew, bottle opener, a sharp knife, and a small cutting board.

Perishable food is best kept in a cooler or ice chest. Many coolers have tight lids that lock in place, as well as trays to hold food away from melting ice. These coolers are available in several sizes.

Thermoses hold beverages and soups at the proper temperature for several hours. Freeze plastic jugs filled with juices. They will defrost on the way to the picnic but meanwhile help keep food well chilled.

TOFU SALAD

When serving these open-faced sandwiches for a picnic, wrap the sliced bread in foil or plastic wrap and place the tofu mixture in an airtight container in an ice chest. Assemble just before eating.

> ½ cucumber
> 1 pound firm tofu
> 1 carrot, shredded
> 2 shallots, minced
> 3 to 4 radishes, finely minced
> ⅓ cup mayonnaise
> 1 teaspoon kosher salt
> ¼ teaspoon black pepper
> 4 lettuce leaves
> 4 slices Whole-Grain Bread (see page 123)

1. Peel cucumber, slice in half lengthwise, remove and discard seeds, and cut into a fine dice. Dice tofu into ¼-inch cubes.

2. In a 2-quart bowl, combine cucumber, carrot, shallots, radishes, tofu, mayonnaise, salt, and pepper. Stir to combine and store in airtight containers.

3. At serving time, place a lettuce leaf on each slice of Whole-Grain Bread. Scoop ¾ cup of sandwich filling on top and spread evenly. Cut into quarters and serve open-faced.

PESTO DIPPING SAUCE

Pesto is a blend of fresh basil leaves, olive oil, and garlic. Best made in the summer when basil and garlic are at their peak, pesto can be stored in airtight jars in the freezer to be tossed with pasta and Parmesan, stirred into vegetable soups, or made into a dipping sauce for raw vegetables. Cherry tomatoes, green beans, broccoli, and zucchini are all delicious topped with pesto sauce.

> 1 bunch fresh basil
> 2 cloves garlic, peeled
> ½ cup olive oil
> 1 teaspoon kosher salt
> 1 cup plain yogurt or sour cream
> 2 tablespoons toasted pine nuts (see page 108)

1. Wash basil, and remove and discard large stems. Using a blender or food processor, purée basil leaves and garlic. Gradually add olive oil in a thin stream. Season with salt.

2. In a small mixing bowl, stir together yogurt and basil-garlic mixture. At serving time mix in toasted pine nuts. Serve with vegetables.

Makes 2 cups.

GRANDMOTHER'S DATE BARS

Dates contain vitamins A, B, C, and D, and minerals, as well as fiber. Because they are naturally sweet, little sugar or honey is required in the dough. These cookie bars, which travel well when packed in a rigid container, make a delicious counterpoint to a selection of fresh fruit.

> ½ pound dates
> ¾ cup water
> 1 tablespoon honey
> 1 cup toasted walnut pieces (see page 108)
> ¾ cup brown sugar
> 1 cup unsalted butter
> 2½ cups rolled oats
> 2 cups flour
> 1 teaspoon baking soda
> 1 teaspooon vanilla extract
> 2 tablespoons milk

1. Preheat oven to 350° F. Chop dates into ½-inch-thick cubes.

2. In a 1-quart saucepan, combine dates, the water, and honey. Bring to a boil, reduce the heat, and simmer for 7 minutes. Cool for 10 minutes. Stir in walnuts. Reserve.

3. In a large mixing bowl, crumble together brown sugar, butter, rolled oats, flour, and baking soda. In a small bowl, mix vanilla and milk, then stir into dry ingredients to form a crumbly mixture.

4. Pat two thirds of the crumbly mixture onto the bottom of an 8-inch-square baking pan. Spread date mixture onto crumbs. Sprinkle remaining crumbly mixture on top. Bake until lightly browned (35 to 40 minutes).

Makes 16 squares.

VEGGIE BURGER

Vegetarians need not be left out of summer barbecues with this superb "burger" made of wheat and beans to provide complementary protein. Wrap the patty to take to a party, and place on the grill at mealtime. Garnish with all the usual burger fixings, or serve in pita bread topped with Cilantro Raita (see page 101).

¼ cup bulgur
1 cup boiling water
1 small onion, minced
3 cloves garlic, minced
15 to 18 sprigs parsley, minced
2 eggs
3 cups cooked garbanzo beans
2 tablespoons plain yogurt
1 teaspoon kosher salt
½ teaspoon coarsely ground black pepper
½ teaspoon cumin
½ teaspoon cayenne pepper
½ cup bread crumbs
1 tablespoon oil

1. Place bulgur in a 1-quart bowl, and cover with the water. Let rest for 30 minutes. Drain.

2. Place bulgur, onion, garlic, parsley, eggs, garbanzo beans, yogurt, salt, pepper, cumin, and cayenne in a blender or food processor. Purée to a smooth paste.

3. Shape ½ cup into a patty, and pat on bread crumbs. Chill for 1 hour. To cook in a skillet, heat oil over medium heat, add burgers to skillet, and sauté for 7 minutes. Turn burgers over, and sauté on second side for 3 minutes. To grill, place patties over a heated barbecue, and cook for 3 minutes. Turn, and cook on second side for 3 minutes more.

Serves 8.

Combining bulgur with garbanzo beans in a patty, the Veggie Burger contains all the protein and amino acids required for proper nutrition. And, it's fun to eat!

You and your guests can celebrate on the Fourth of July with this easily assembled Gratin of Summer Squash. Serve either hot from the oven or at room temperature. Serve with Red, White, and Blue Cheesecake (see page 66) for dessert and you'll have a meal fit for Miss Liberty.

SUMMER SIDE DISHES

Those lazy, hazy, crazy days of summer are the perfect time to try a collection of light side dishes made of vegetables, grains, and legumes. For extra variety in your diet, experiment with a meal of several side dishes, without any true "main dish" at all. Many of these recipes can be served warm from the stove on the day they are prepared or chilled and served as a salad course the next day. This time-saver technique is a special bonus for entertaining when the weather is hot and the cook would rather be relaxing with guests.

CAPONATA

Italian caponata and French ratatouille are based on the same types of ingredients; just the seasonings vary. In this adaptation, the eggplant, zucchini, and bell peppers are grilled briefly before being added to the cooked tomato mixture. The tomato mixture can be prepared ahead to await the grilled eggplant, zucchini, and peppers. At serving time, grill vegetables, stir in, and simmer for a few minutes while the rest of your meal, perhaps the Veggie Burgers (see page 57), cooks. If you do not have time to barbecue the vegetables, you can broil them.

1 large eggplant
2 teaspoons kosher salt
3 zucchini
2 green bell peppers, seeded
4 tablespoons olive oil
2 red onions, diced
4 cloves garlic, minced
6 plum tomatoes, diced
3 stalks celery, diced
2 tablespoons fresh basil
2 tablespoons oregano
½ tablespoon pepper
2 tablespoons tomato paste
5 tablespoons red wine vinegar
2 tablespoons capers
½ cup green olives

1. Prepare the barbecue for grilling or heat the broiler. Slice eggplant into ½-inch rounds, and quarter. Place in a colander and sprinkle with 1 teaspoon of the salt. Reserve for 30 minutes. Cut zucchini and bell peppers into 1-inch chunks.

2. In a 4-quart saucepan over medium heat, place 2 tablespoons of the oil. Add onions and garlic, and sauté for 8 minutes. Add tomatoes and celery. Cook for 10 minutes more. Season with basil, oregano, remaining 1 teaspoon salt, pepper, tomato paste, vinegar, capers, and olives. Simmer for 20 minutes.

3. While the sauce is simmering, rinse salt from eggplant and pat dry. Brush eggplant, zucchini, and bell peppers with the remaining oil. Place eggplant, zucchini, and bell peppers on grill or under broiler for about 3 minutes. Turn and grill or broil the other side for 3 minutes. Remove from grill and place in tomato mixture. Simmer for 20 minutes. Serve warm or chilled.

Serves 8 to 12.

GARBANZO RAGOUT

Rosemary, a main flavoring in this recipe, is an earthy herb signifying remembrance in folklore. This quick sauté is even delicious when canned garbanzo beans are used. Chilled and tossed with Basic Vinaigrette (see page 13), the ragout becomes a delicious salad.

- 1 *bunch broccoli*
- 1 *small tomato*
- 2 *sprigs fresh rosemary* or *1 tablespoon dried rosemary*
- 1 *tablespoon oil*
- 1 *onion, diced*
- 2 *cloves garlic, minced*
- 3½ *cups cooked garbanzo beans*
- ½ *teaspoon kosher salt*
- ¼ *teaspoon coarsely ground black pepper*
- 1 *tablespoon red wine vinegar*

1. Cut broccoli into bite-sized pieces. Cube tomato. Strip leaves from sprigs of rosemary. Discard sprigs.

2. Place oil in a 2-quart saucepan over medium heat. Add onion and garlic, and sauté for 5 to 6 minutes. Add broccoli, tomato, and garbanzo beans. Stir to combine and season with rosemary, salt, pepper, and vinegar. Cook over low heat for 10 minutes to heat through. Serve warm or at room temperature.

Serves 4 to 6.

GRATIN OF SUMMER SQUASH

This quick gratin can be prepared ahead, held for baking, and served hot or prepared and baked ahead and served at room temperature.

- 2 *tablespoons olive oil, plus oil for baking dish*
- 1 *small red onion*
- 3 *zucchini*
- 2 *plum tomatoes*
- 3 *cloves garlic, minced*
- ½ *teaspoon kosher salt*
- ¼ *teaspoon freshly ground black pepper*
- 1 *tablespoon fresh thyme, minced* or *1 teaspoon dried*
- 3 *ounces Gruyère cheese, grated*

1. Preheat oven to 350° F. Lightly oil an 8-inch round baking dish. Slice onion into rounds. Slice zucchini and tomatoes about ½ inch thick.

2. In a large skillet over medium heat, place 1 tablespoon of the oil, and sauté onion and garlic until translucent (5 to 8 minutes).

3. Place zucchini slices vertically along the edge of the baking dish (cut edge against the side of the dish). Place the tomato slices against the zucchini, then some of the sautéed onion-garlic mixture against the tomato slices so that the vegetables stand up around perimeter of baking dish. Repeat with zucchini, tomato, and onion-garlic mixture to form alternating rings. Place remaining vegetables in center. Sprinkle with salt, pepper, thyme, and cheese.

4. Bake for 25 minutes. Serve warm or at room temperature.

Serves 6.

TOMATO PEARL-ONION CHUTNEY

The easiest way to peel a pearl onion is to dip it in boiling water for 3 minutes, cut off the end, and then squeeze the onion out of the skin. This chutney is a delicious condiment served with Eggplant and Garlic Mousse (see page 53).

- 10 *ounces pearl onions*
- 1 *tablespoon olive oil*
- 1 *large yellow onion, minced*
- 2 *cloves garlic, minced*
- 5 *tomatoes, diced*
- 1 *tablespoon minced ginger*
- 2 *tablespoons tomato paste*
- 1 *teaspoon dry mustard*
- 2 *tablespoons apple cider vinegar*
- 1 *teaspoon kosher salt*
- 1 *tablespoon honey*
- ¼ *teaspoon ground dried red chiles*
- ¼ *cup raisins*
- 2 *tablespoons parsley, minced*
- 1 *teaspoon fresh oregano, minced*

1. In a 2-quart saucepan, bring 1 quart of water to a boil, and drop in pearl onions. Blanch for 3 minutes and remove. Trim off root ends and slip onions out of papery skins.

2. Place oil in a 2-quart saucepan over medium heat. Add onion and garlic. Sauté for 5 minutes, and add tomatoes, ginger, tomato paste, dry mustard, vinegar, salt, honey, dried chiles, raisins, parsley, and oregano. Cook for 20 minutes. Add pearl onions and cook for 25 minutes more. Cool slightly before serving.

Makes 3¼ cups.

HARICOTS VERTS WITH SHALLOTS AND HAZELNUTS

Bright green beans are quickly blanched, then sautéed with shallots and hazelnuts for a light summer side dish. The shallots may be roasted on a grill rather than in the oven. The shallots may be roasted, hazelnuts toasted, and green beans blanched in the morning and sautéed later for the evening meal.

    16 shallots
    4 tablespoons olive oil
    ½ pound toasted hazelnuts (see page 108)
    1 pound small French green beans or small Blue Lake green beans
    1 teaspoon kosher salt
    ¼ teaspoon pepper
    2 tablespoons fresh tarragon

1. Preheat oven to 350° F. Peel shallots and place in a small ovenproof baking dish. Drizzle with 3 tablespoons of the oil, and place in preheated oven for 30 minutes. Remove from oven and reserve.

2. Remove toasted hazelnuts from oven and cool. Place cooled hazelnuts in a towel, and rub against each other to remove some of the skins. Reserve.

3. Bring 3 quarts of water to a boil. Remove stem ends from green beans, but leave beans whole. Place beans in boiling water for 3 minutes to blanch. Remove beans, rinse in cold water to stop cooking and set color. Pat dry.

4. Place remaining 1 tablespoon of oil in a large skillet over medium heat. Add beans, shallots, hazelnuts, salt, pepper, and tarragon. Sauté until heated through (3 to 5 minutes). Serve immediately.

Serves 6.

SUMMER BREADS

Rely on quick breads such as muffins, scones, and grilled breads for a delightful accompaniment to light summer foods. These breads should not be saved only for the warmer months. Muffins are easily packed for lunches all year long.

WHOLE-GRAIN MUFFINS

Any fruit or spice may be added to the muffins for variety. These may be assembled and refrigerated, then baked 4 to 12 hours later.

    Oil for muffin cups or paper muffin liners
    1 apple, peeled and cored
    2 cups Whole-Grain Baking Mix (see page 17)
    1 teaspoon baking powder
    ½ cup brown sugar
    1 tablespoon cinnamon
    ½ cup buttermilk or milk
    2 eggs

1. Preheat oven to 400° F. Lightly oil 12 muffin cups, or line muffin cups with paper liners.

2. Cube apple. In a 3-quart mixing bowl, combine Whole-Grain Baking Mix, baking powder, sugar, and cinnamon. Stir in apple cubes. In a separate bowl, stir together buttermilk and eggs. Using as few strokes as possible, blend buttermilk-egg mixture into dry ingredients.

3. Bake muffins until lightly browned and dry on top (20 to 22 minutes). Remove and serve immediately.

Makes 12 muffins.

WHOLE-GRAIN SCONES

Scones are an excellent quick biscuit made to accompany a summer soup and salad meal. Serve with Basil Jelly (see page 61) or any favorite jam.

    2 cups Whole-Grain Baking Mix (see page 17)
    1 teaspoon baking powder
    2 tablespoons sugar
    5 to 6 tablespoons buttermilk or milk
    2 eggs
    ¼ cup dried currants or raisins
    1 tablespoon water

1. Preheat oven to 400° F. In a 3-quart mixing bowl, sift together Whole-Grain Baking Mix, baking powder, and sugar. In a small bowl, stir together buttermilk and 1 egg. Gradually stir buttermilk-egg mixture into dry ingredients. Add currants. Stir as little as possible or dough will become tough.

2. Pat dough to about ¾ inch thick. Cut dough into 2-inch circles and place on an ungreased baking sheet. In a small bowl, whisk together remaining egg and the water and brush mixture onto dough circles. Bake scones until lightly browned (10 to 12 minutes).

Makes 10 to 12 scones.

CHARLIE'S CHIVE TOASTS

These crunchy toasts make a great snack food. They also marry well with soups for a lovely first course to an elegant dinner.

> 3 ounces French goat cheese
> 4 tablespoons butter
> ¼ cup minced chives
> 1 tablespoon rosemary
> 1 whole wheat baguette, cut in 24 to 28 slices

1. Preheat oven to 350° F.

2. In a small bowl, mix together cheese and butter. Add chives and rosemary. Mix well. Spread 1 teaspoon per baguette slice. Bake toasts until cheese is melted (10 minutes). Serve warm.

Serves 8.

ITALIAN BRUSCHETTA

The aromatic rosemary-and-garlic-scented olive oil will taste better if it steeps for one week before being used. The recipe provides enough oil for three to four loaves of French bread and keeps for up to two months in a cool, dark room.

> 1 cup olive oil
> 1 large sprig rosemary or 6 tablespoons dried, coarsely chopped
> 6 to 8 cloves garlic, coarsely chopped
> 1 loaf French bread

1. In a 2-cup jar, stir together olive oil, rosemary, and garlic. Close with lid. Store in a cool, dark place a minimum of 4 hours.

2. At serving time, heat grill or broiler. Slice bread about ¾ inches thick to make about 16 slices. Brush 1½ teaspoons of rosemary-garlic oil on each side of bread. Place bread on grill or under broiler for about 1 minute per side. Remove and serve immediately.

Serves 8 to 12.

PRESERVING FRUITS

As the seasonal charts show, some of the best produce comes into the markets for only a short time. One way to preserve produce for out-of-season use is to utilize the natural acidity of fruits in conjunction with sugar, honey, and high-heat cooking to create an environment hostile to bacteria.

☐ Choose perfect, flavorful fruit, wash carefully, and remove any bruises. Store in refrigerator if you are unable to proceed immediately. Preparing preserves as soon as produce is picked ensures a superior-tasting product.

☐ Prepare jams and jellies according to the directions, as the proportions in each recipe may act as a preservative rather than just a flavoring.

☐ A deep, nonaluminum kettle with a metal rack is required so that jars can rest on the rack and still be covered with boiling water by one to two inches. Fruits, jams, preserves, and tomatoes are safely prepared with this process.

☐ Clean pots, utensils, work surfaces, cloths, and hands are the first safety factor. Jars must be clean and hot when filled. Lids must be boiled, not just scalded, to activate the rubber seal on the lids.

☐ Use tempered glass jars without cracks or chips, flat metal lids with rubber sealing compound, and metal screw ring caps without rust or dents. Jars and screw ring caps are reusable, but flat metal lids should be replaced each time they are used.

☐ A jar lifter makes the task of removing hot jars from boiling water safe.

☐ Label foods with type and date of preservation, and keep an inventory of preserves. Always use the earliest dated jars first. Store in a cool, dark room for the longest shelf life (about one year).

BASIL JELLY

Any herb can be substituted for the basil. Fresh mint, rosemary, and thyme are especially flavorful. Herb jellies are delicious condiments served with meat, for those who indulge.

> 1¼ cups white wine
> 2 cups sugar
> ½ cup white vinegar
> 1¼ cups tightly packed fresh basil leaves, minced
> 3 ounces (1 pouch) liquid pectin

In a 1-quart saucepan over medium heat, cook wine, sugar, and vinegar, stirring until sugar is dissolved. Add basil and mix well. Bring to a boil and stir in liquid pectin. Immediately remove from heat and pour into 3 sterilized half-pint (1-cup) jars. Seal with sterilized lids and cool. Store in a cool, dark room until used. Refrigerate after opening.

Makes 3 cups.

Whether the backyard is many lush, green acres or a city fire escape, summertime demands a barbecue. Grilling is a great way to enjoy seasonal produce.

SUMMER BARBECUE

Bouquet of Crudités

Basil-Garlic Dip

Tofu and Vegetable Brochettes

Wild-Rice Pilaf

Tomato and Spinach Braided Bread

Deep-Dish Berry Pie

Yogurt Ice Cream

Beverage Suggestion: Iced Tea

A vast array of delicious foods lend themselves to grilling, making for great gatherings around backyard barbecues. All vegetables benefit from being tossed in a marinade before they go on the grill. All recipes serve 8.

NUTRIENT BREAKDOWN	
Calories	1,559
Protein	64 gm
Fiber	2 gm
Cholesterol	220 gm
Vitamin C	122 mg
Calcium	138 mg
Sodium	1,708 mg

BOUQUET OF CRUDITÉS

Crudités is simply the French word for raw vegetables. A well-chosen assortment of vegetables can be a palate-pleasing substitute for the more customary dinner salad. Cucumbers, radishes, yellow bell peppers, cauliflower, and broccoli are all especially good dipping vegetables.

BASIL-GARLIC DIP

Basil is synonymous with summer. Serve this dip with the Bouquet of Crudités assortment or as a dressing on fresh tomato, potato, or pasta salad. Potato chips or pieces of the braided bread are great with this dip as well. A cored red bell pepper makes an interesting, edible "bowl" for this white and green dip.

- 20 *leaves fresh basil*
- 1 *egg yolk*
- ½ *cup oil*
- 2 *cloves garlic, minced*
- 1 *lemon, juiced*
- ½ *teaspoon kosher salt*
- ½ *cup plain yogurt*

Cut basil leaves into thin strips. In a 1½-quart mixing bowl, blender, or food processor, beat egg yolk until it is pale yellow. Add oil by the teaspoonful, whisking constantly, until it is incorporated. Stir in basil strips, garlic, lemon juice, salt, and yogurt. Place in a small bowl and serve with raw vegetables.

Makes 1 cup.

TOFU AND VEGETABLE BROCHETTES

This main course may be broiled when barbecuing is not possible. Note that you will need 16 skewers. The bamboo skewers must be soaked in cold water for about one hour prior to use to avoid burning.

- 9 *tablespoons olive oil*
- 9 *tablespoons red wine vinegar*
- ¾ *teaspoon kosher salt*
- 1½ *cups parsley, minced*
- 6 *cloves garlic, minced*
- 1 *pound firm tofu*
- 2 *medium carrots*
- 1 *red bell pepper*
- 4 *zucchini*
- 16 *medium mushrooms*
- 1 *small red onion*
- 16 *cherry tomatoes*

1. In a large mixing bowl, whisk together olive oil, vinegar, and salt. Add parsley and garlic.

2. Cut tofu into 1½-inch cubes. Place in a small bowl and drizzle with 3 tablespoons of olive-vinegar marinade. Marinate for 1 hour.

3. Peel carrots. Cut each into 8 pieces about 1 inch long. Bring 2 quarts of water to a boil. Blanch carrots in boiling water until they are tender but not soft (about 3 minutes). A knife inserted will easily pierce the carrot. Immediately remove from boiling water and place in cold water to stop cooking and set color.

4. Cut bell pepper into 16 pieces about 1½ inches square. Cut each zucchini into 4 pieces about 1½ inches long. Wipe tops of mushrooms and trim dry ends of stems. Cut onion into 16 pieces about 1½ inches square. Stem cherry tomatoes.

5. Place carrots, bell pepper, zucchini, mushrooms, onion, and tomatoes into the remaining marinade, cover with plastic wrap, and reserve until ready to barbecue.

6. Spear vegetables and tofu with bamboo or metal skewers, and baste with remaining marinade. When coals are hot, place skewers over fire. Cook for 4 minutes, turn, and cook for 4 minutes on second side.

WILD-RICE PILAF

This pilaf offers an opportunity to try a mixture of different grains that lend balance, protein, and flavor to a meal. Triticale, a hybrid of wheat and rye, is an especially nutritious substitute. Barley could also be exchanged for the wheat berries.

2 tablespoons oil
1 onion, minced
2 carrots, finely diced
1 stalk celery, finely diced
1 cup wheat berries
1 cup brown rice
½ cup wild rice
4½ cups Vegetable Broth (see page 15) or water
½ tablespoon kosher salt

Heat oil in a 2-quart saucepan over medium heat. Stir in onions, carrots, and celery, and cook until softened but not browned. Add wheat berries, brown rice, wild rice, Vegetable Broth, and salt. Stir to combine. Cover and cook for 40 minutes over medium to low heat.

TOMATO AND SPINACH BRAIDED BREAD

Each of these doughs makes a single delicious loaf. Together they make two spectacular free-form braided loaves. The doughs can also be shaped as dinner rolls and placed alternately into a baking pan to create a multicolored pan roll.

Oil for coating bowls
1 egg
1 tablespoon water
Cornmeal for baking sheets

Tomato Dough

1 cup water (not to exceed 100°F)
1 package active dry yeast
½ tablespoon honey
3 ripe tomatoes
½ tablespoon kosher salt
½ cup whole wheat flour
2¾ to 3 cups unbleached or bread flour

Spinach Dough

1 bunch spinach
1 cup water (not to exceed 100°F)
1 package active dry yeast
½ tablespoon honey
½ tablespoon kosher salt
½ cup whole wheat flour
2 cups unbleached or bread flour

Tomato Dough

1. In a large mixing bowl or bowl of a heavy-duty mixer, mix the water, yeast, and honey. Let rest for 5 minutes to dissolve yeast.

2. Peel tomatoes by placing in boiling water for 1 to 2 minutes. Slice in half crosswise, hold over sink, and gently squeeze out seeds. Chop tomatoes into a fine dice.

3. Add tomatoes to yeast-water-honey mixture. Add salt, whole wheat flour, and enough of the unbleached flour to form a firm dough. When dough becomes too stiff to stir, lightly dust work surface with unbleached flour and knead remaining flour into dough. Knead dough vigorously for

10 minutes by hand or about 5 minutes in a heavy-duty mixer. Place dough in a lightly oiled bowl, cover with plastic wrap, and let rise for 1 hour. To complete, see steps 4 and 5.

Spinach Dough

1. Remove large, tough stems from spinach. Wash spinach leaves but do not dry. Place in a 14-inch skillet over low heat, and steam for about 5 minutes. Cool and mince.

2. In another large mixing bowl or bowl of a heavy-duty mixer, mix the water, yeast, and honey. Let rest for 5 minutes to dissolve yeast.

3. Stir spinach into yeast-water-honey mixture. Add salt, whole wheat flour, and enough of the unbleached flour to form a firm dough. When dough becomes too stiff to stir, lightly dust work surface with unbleached flour, and knead remaining flour into dough. Knead dough vigorously for 10 minutes by hand or about 5 minutes in a heavy-duty mixer. Place dough in a lightly oiled bowl, cover with plastic wrap, and let rise for about 1 hour.

4. After the rising time, punch down tomato dough and spinach dough. Divide each dough into 4 equal pieces. Working with 2 pieces of spinach dough and 2 pieces of tomato dough at a time, shape into a braid. Cover remaining dough with a cloth to prevent drying while first braid is being shaped. Pinch both ends and tuck under to seal. Sprinkle 2 baking sheets with cornmeal. Place loaves on sheets and let dough rise for 45 minutes.

5. Near end of rising time, preheat oven to 375° F. In a small bowl, whisk egg with the water. Carefully brush mixture onto loaves. Bake loaves for 55 minutes. Remove from pans. Test loaves by tapping bottom of each. If loaf sounds hollow, it is done. Place on cooling racks for 10 minutes and serve.

Makes 2 loaves.

DEEP-DISH BERRY PIE

Olallieberries, raspberries, boysenberries, or blueberries can be substituted with equal success, but the aromatic ripeness of blackberries tells us that summer has arrived. Although the thorns often make picking difficult, it is worth persisting for blackberries have a relatively high amount of vitamin B_1 and calcium combined with a sweet, tart flavor.

> *Butter for baking dish*
> 4   *cups blackberries*
> ½   *cup sugar, plus 1 teaspoon*
> ¼   *cup all-purpose flour, plus flour for dusting*
> 1   *lemon*
> 1½ *cups pastry flour*
> ½   *cup whole wheat flour*
> ¼   *teaspoon kosher salt*
> 1   *tablespoon baking powder*
> 6   *tablespoons cold unsalted butter*
> ⅔   *cups plain yogurt*
> 1   *tablespoon milk*

1. Preheat oven to 350° F. Lightly butter a shallow, 2-quart baking dish. Wash blackberries and drain in a colander. Place in a 2-quart mixing bowl, and add ¼ cup of the sugar and all-purpose flour. Using a vegetable peeler or sharp knife, remove only the colored part of the rind from the lemon. Mince rind into fine pieces. Juice lemon and add with rind to blackberry mixture. Gently mix and place in prepared baking dish.

2. In a 3-quart mixing bowl, stir together pastry flour, whole wheat flour, ¼ cup sugar, salt, and baking powder. Add unsalted butter by crumbling into flour mixture using fingertips, two knives or pastry blender until dough resembles coarse crumbs. Stir in yogurt, using a minimum of mixing, to make a light, tender dough. Dust work surface with flour, place dough on work surface, and carefully pat dough to fit top of baking dish. Gently fold dough into quarters and lift onto fruit mixture. Brush dough with milk, sprinkle with the 1 teaspoon sugar, and place into preheated oven. Bake for 55 to 60 minutes.

YOGURT ICE CREAM

Plain yogurt is added to French custard to make a tangy ice cream. Fresh fruit can be stirred into the ice cream just before serving. If the fruit is mixed with the ice cream too far ahead, the water in the fruit will cause the fruit to become too hard. If you plan to store the ice cream in the freezer, be sure to seal the container to keep out odors. It will be best served within two weeks.

> 1   *cup milk*
> 3   *egg yolks*
> ½   *cup sugar*
> 2   *cups plain yogurt*
> 1   *teaspoon vanilla extract*

1. In a 1-quart saucepan over low flame, heat milk, taking care not to scorch it. In a 1½-quart mixing bowl, beat egg yolks and sugar. When milk forms small bubbles around edge of pan, quickly remove it from heat and stir into egg-sugar mixture.

2. Mix thoroughly and return mixture to saucepan. Stir constantly over low heat until mixture has thickened.

3. Pour custard through a strainer placed over a clean 1-quart mixing bowl. Do not press any of the solids from strainer into custard. Cover bowl with plastic wrap pressed down onto surface of custard to prevent a skin from forming. Place in refrigerator to cool.

4. When custard mixture is cold, stir in yogurt and vanilla. Mix thoroughly and place in the chilled bowl of an ice-cream machine. Process ice cream according to manufacturer's instructions (approximately 20 to 25 minutes). Remove from ice-cream machine container, place in a small airtight storage container, and keep in the freezer until serving time.

Makes 4 cups.

Tips

HOW TO MAKE YOGURT ICE CREAM

All that is required to turn a delicate custard into a delicious ice cream is agitation and cold temperature. The three basic methods are explained here. See page 66 for special Step-by-Step instructions for preparing delicious Yogurt Ice Cream.

Ice Cream Machine A conventional ice-cream mixture is placed in a chilled cannister, a paddle is inserted, and a top secured. The cannister is placed in the center of a larger bucket, which is then surrounded with alternate layers of chipped ice and rock salt. A handle or motor is attached to the top and is turned for 20 to 30 minutes until ice cream is firm. A variation of this machine is to use ice cubes and table salt. Follow manufacturer's directions.

Freezer Model These machines come as a feature on some freezers. Portable machines are available and can be placed in the freezer or stored there for continual use. An electric motor churns the chilled ice cream mixture without requiring salt or ice.

Ice-Cube Trays Ice cream can be made in ice-cube trays, although the final product will not be as smooth. Agitation and freezing become alternating rather than simultaneous steps. Follow step 1 through step 4 on page 66, then freeze the mixture for 45 to 60 minutes in ice-cube trays, remove, and stir vigorously by hand, with the paddle of an electric mixer, or in a food processor. Freeze again. Repeat the stirring and freezing two more times. When a mixture is stirred as it freezes, the ice crystals become smaller and smoother. Stirring also incorporates some air into the mixture, which lightens it and makes it easier to scoop.

MAKING ICE CREAM

Yogurt Ice Cream (see page 65) makes a refreshing frozen dessert. There are several methods available for making ice cream discussed in How to Make Yogurt Ice Cream (also on page 65). Once you have chosen your recipe and your method, use these steps for a variety of delicious frozen desserts.

1. *Heat milk in a 1-quart saucepan until bubbles appear on edges of pan. In a 1½-quart bowl, stir egg yolks and sugar together until pale yellow and thickened. Using a wooden spoon, stir warm milk into beaten egg yolk. Return mixture to saucepan. Heat slowly over medium to low heat, stirring constantly. This must be watched carefully, for it thickens only slightly as small bubbles appear around edges of pan.*

2. *Be careful to stir in corners of pan, where mixture will start to thicken first. Be careful not to boil mixture because eggs will curdle and milk may begin to scorch. Test*

for thickening by placing a metal or wooden spoon into mixture. Remove spoon and draw a line through the center with your finger. If custard flows together, it will need to cook a bit longer. If the impression stays, custard will have thickened enough. An instant temperature thermometer will register about 170° F. Pour mixture through a strainer placed over a clean 1-quart mixing bowl. Place plastic wrap on the surface of the mixture, and chill for 3 to 4 hours.

3. *When ready to prepare the ice cream: Stir yogurt and vanilla into chilled custard mixture. Place into chilled container of ice-cream machine. Chill according to manufacturer's instructions. When removing ice cream, be careful to wipe top, sides, and bottom of inner cannister clean to prevent salt from mixing with contents.*

4. *Store finished ice cream in an airtight container for no more than two weeks. Place a piece of plastic wrap between ice cream and lid to help prevent ice crystals.*

SUMMER DESSERTS

Summer desserts can be as straightforward as slices of watermelon or a bowl of ripe berries. When special occasions arise, fruit pies, cobblers, and cookies can still take advantage of seasonal opulence while maximizing the succulent flavors.

RED, WHITE, AND BLUE CHEESECAKE

Cheesecake, though it is a bit of decadence, is a glorious dessert worthy of a splurge. The fruit topping can consist of only one fruit, but this combination is more alluring.

Almond Crust

½ cup shelled almonds
1 cup flour
2 tablespoons sugar
⅛ teaspoon kosher salt
6 tablespoons unsalted butter

Cheesecake Filling

2 lemons
2 pounds ricotta cheese or cottage cheese
¾ pound cream cheese
1 cup sugar
4 eggs
2 tablespoons flour
2 teaspoons almond extract
1 teaspoon vanilla extract
1 tablespoon dark rum (optional)
1 pint strawberries
2 cups blueberries
1 banana
¼ cup currant jelly
2 tablespoons kirsch or water

1. *To prepare crust:* Grind almonds together with ½ cup of the flour. Mix with the remaining ½ cup flour, sugar, and salt. Cut butter into small cubes, and rub into flour mixture with fingertips or pastry blender until it resembles coarse crumbs. Add enough water to form a dough, and chill for 30 minutes. Roll out to fit a 9-inch springform pan.

2. *To prepare filling:* Preheat oven to 350° F. Remove rind from lemons and dice finely. Juice lemons. In a 3-quart mixing bowl or the bowl of a food processor, beat ricotta cheese together with cream cheese. When smooth, gradually add sugar. Beat in eggs one at a time. Add flour, lemon rind, and lemon juice to cream cheese filling with almond extract, vanilla, and rum (if used). Place in crust, and bake for 1 hour and 20 minutes. Remove from oven and cool for 1 hour.

3. Chill filling for a minimum of 4 hours. It will keep in the refrigerator for 10 days. Before serving time, stem strawberries and blueberries. Slice banana into ¼-inch-thick slices. Decorate top of cheesecake with alternating strawberries, blueberries, and banana slices.

4. In a small saucepan, mix currant jelly with kirsch. Heat briefly to dissolve jelly. Brush currant-jelly glaze on fruit to keep fruit from drying out, retain the fresh color, and give it a jewellike appearance.

Serves 10 to 12.

ANNE'S ALMOND SHORTBREADS

These cookies are a simple accompaniment to a picnic lunch. You can freeze them for up to two weeks.

> ½ *pound unsalted butter*
> ½ *cup sugar*
> 2 *cups flour*
> ½ *cup cornstarch*
> *Pinch salt*
> ½ *pound toasted almonds*
> *(see page 108)*

1. Preheat oven to 350° F.

2. In a large mixing bowl or a food processor, combine butter, sugar, flour, cornstarch, and salt. Chop cooled almonds and add to mixture. Place in an 8-inch-square baking pan and bake until golden brown (35 to 40 minutes). Cut while warm. Serve at room temperature.

Makes 16 squares.

CHERRY-NECTARINE PIE

This combination of cherries and nectarines is just one configuration possible for a summer fruit pie. The oil pastry requires patience, as it is a crumbly dough; using parchment paper, waxed paper, or aluminum foil makes rolling easier. The glaze is optional, although oil pastry does not brown without it.

> 2 *cups plus 2 tablespoons flour*
> ½ *teaspoon kosher salt*
> ½ *cup safflower oil*
> 4 *tablespoons cold water*
> 6 *nectarines, peeled and pitted*
> 1¼ *pounds sweet cherries, pitted and halved*
> ½ *lemon, juiced*
> 5 *tablespoons sugar*
> 1 *tablespoon kirsch (optional)*
> ½ *teaspoon almond extract*
> 1 *tablespoon milk*

1. Sift the 2 cups flour with salt into a large mixing bowl. In a small bowl, mix oil and the cold water. Stir water-oil into the flour-salt using as few strokes as possible.

2. Divide dough into thirds. Form two thirds of the dough into a disk and place between two sheets of parchment paper. Rolling from center of dough to edge, roll dough into a 9-inch circle ¼ inch thick. Rotate dough and parchment so that you are rolling away from yourself.

3. Place dough and parchment on a flat baking sheet. Remove top sheet of parchment. Place a pie pan upside down over pastry on baking sheet. Invert pie pan, dough, parchment, and baking sheet together. Carefully remove baking sheet and parchment. Gently shape pastry into pan. Prick shell in several spots, and chill to rest dough for 30 minutes.

4. Preheat oven to 375° F. Slice each nectarine into about 8 sections. In a 2-quart mixing bowl, toss cherries with nectarines. Add lemon juice, 4 tablespoons of the sugar, the 2 tablespoons flour, kirsch (if used), and almond extract. Stir to combine and place fruit mixture into dough-lined pie pan.

5. Roll remaining one third of dough between sheets of parchment into a 9-inch circle, as directed above. Cut dough into strips 1½ inches wide. Lift strips with a long, thin metal-bladed pastry spatula or the edge of a baking sheet without sides. Place strips in a lattice pattern on fruit-filled pie. In a small bowl, whisk milk and remaining tablespoon of sugar, and brush onto strips.

6. Bake until light brown (55 to 60 minutes). Cool for 10 to 15 minutes before serving.

Serves 8.

PEACH MELBA

Peaches and strawberries are a divine combination. Serve this dish in sherbet glasses or over biscuits for an unusual shortcake. Accompany with Yogurt Ice Cream (see page 65) as an even grander finale.

> 1 *pint strawberries*
> 3 *tablespoons confectioners' sugar*
> 2 *tablespoons bitter-orange liqueur or orange flower water (optional)*
> ½ *teaspoon almond extract*
> 6 *peaches, peeled and pitted*
> 6 *sprigs mint, for garnish*

1. Wash strawberries and remove stems. Place in a blender or food processor, and purée. Add confectioners' sugar, liqueur (if used), and almond extract, and mix well.

2. Slice each peach into 6 to 8 slices, and place in a 2-quart mixing bowl. Pour strawberry purée over peaches and stir to combine. Cover and chill for 30 minutes. Remove from refrigerator 15 minutes before serving. Place in stemmed goblets, each garnished with a sprig of mint.

Serves 6.

The autumn harvest features a variety of earthly delights. Lengthen the season by canning sauces and relishes and drying herbs to use later in the year.

Sharing Autumn's Harvest

The hearty yields of September, October, and November contribute to vegetarian cooking throughout the year. Store root vegetables, which are harvested now, for months in a cool, dark place. Dry herbs from your garden for flavorings and garnishes until fresh herbs are available again in spring. Use fresh fruits and vegetables, in colors that rival the brilliance of autumn leaves, in recipes unique to the season. Continue the seasonal theme by combining baskets of leaves, gourds, and flowers as centerpieces on your autumn table. Nature's last hurrah before the dormancy of winter is a spectacle of delicious and eye-pleasing delights.

Cooler weather calls for rich-tasting vegetable soups. Serve the earthy Corn and Pepper Chowder with Black Bean Salsa (see page 74). Both dishes can be made in advance and together make a well-balanced quick meal on a busy autumn night.

FUEL FOR ACTIVE LIVES

The frivolous activities of summer fade as fast as the heat. Robust pursuits like cycling, vigorous walking, raking leaves, and harvesting the garden take over now. As the weather cools there is more energy to tackle new projects, new athletics, and new hobbies. However you spend the crisp autumn afternoons—band practice, cheering the local football heros at the stadium, or getting in a golf game—you'll return from the outdoors rosy cheeked and renewed from your endeavors.

Outdoor activities, as well as work and school chores, require more sustaining fare than was needed in the indolent summer months. The time from Indian summer to the first storm of the season calls for a return to the warming and nourishing soups, casseroles, and stews of the cooler months. Make a quick bread and start a pot of soup to simmer, then take a brisk, late afternoon walk to enjoy the autumn colors. When you return the one-pot meal will be ready for dining in front of that first fire of the season.

PLANNING AHEAD

Preparation should be the catchword for autumn. Gear up now for the serious tasks of going back to school and making plans for the upcoming holidays. Think ahead and take full advantage of all the available produce. Like squirrels storing nuts for the cold months ahead, plan for winter by putting up preserves and jams, freezing and canning ripened produce, and drying fruits and vegetables for future enjoyment. The bounty of autumn should not only provide splendor in its own season but a bright accent to many meals during the monochromatic months of winter. With a little organization and effort, the flavor of autumn can be just behind your cupboard doors for months to come.

Prepare pantry items for yourself or as special holiday gifts. Maximize originality by creating chutneys, making cranberry sauces, and bottling herb-scented oils and vinegars for future presents. Let the abundance of the season inspire you to create foods that are simple yet delicious. The recipients of your generosity will feel your personal attention, and you will avoid all the last-minute pressures of gift buying. Why not invite guests for an intimate evening of baking or gift making, or have canning or baking be the central theme of a preholdiay gathering for friends or relatives? As old-fashioned farm families used to do, assemble jars, mixing bowls, and produce for a preserving party. Or if the home-canned products are already prepared, spend an evening wrapping them whimsically. Create your own traditions by repeating these pleasurable activities each year.

AUTUMN SOUPS

As the weather turns cold, steamy soups return to favor. The aromatic scent of vegetables cooking in broth punctuates the air. Homemade soups can be prepared one day and stored, tightly wrapped, in individual servings in the freezer for quick heating in the microwave later in the week. Each soup can be accompanied with herb bread, pizza, or crackers for a hearty, balanced meal.

MINESTRONE DI VERDURA

Minestrone in Italian refers to all hearty soups, so *minestrone di verdura* indicates that it is a vegetable soup. *Fusilli* are long corkscrew-shaped egg noodles that add texture to the soup. Any noodle may be substituted. This satisfying soup can be served as a main course.

     2 *carrots*
     ½ *pound green beans*
     2 *zucchini*
     8 *whole plum tomatoes or 1 can (28 oz) whole tomatoes*
     1 *tablespoon olive oil*
     1 *onion, diced*
     2 *stalks celery, diced*
     4 *cloves garlic, diced*
     ½ *cup parsley, minced*
     3 *tablespoons fresh basil, minced*
     3 *tablespoons fresh oregano, minced*
     2 *bay leaves*
    12 *cups water*
     4 *teaspoons kosher salt*
     1 *teaspoon pepper*
     3 *cups cooked, small white beans (see page 19)*
     ½ *pound fusilli*
     2 *ounces grated Parmesan cheese, for garnish*

1. Peel carrots and cut into ½-inch sections. Trim stem ends from green beans and cut into ½-inch lengths. Cut zucchini into ½-inch cubes. Core tomatoes and cut into ½-inch cubes.

2. Heat oil in an 8-quart stockpot or Dutch oven over low flame. Cook onion, celery, and garlic for 6 minutes. Add carrots, tomatoes, parsley, basil, oregano, bay leaves, the water, salt, pepper, white beans, and pasta. Bring to a boil, reduce heat to medium, and simmer for 20 minutes. Add green beans and cook for 5 minutes. Add zucchini and cook for 3 minutes more. Ladle into individual shallow soup plates and sprinkle with Parmesan cheese.

Makes 14 cups, 8 to 12 servings.

CARROT-THYME SOUP

Saturated with vitamins A and C, this vibrant soup is a great start to a family supper.

     9 *carrots*
     2 *potatoes*
    12 *sprigs fresh thyme*
     8 *cups water*
     1 *tablespoon kosher salt*
     1 *teaspoon freshly ground pepper*
     ½ *cup plain yogurt, for garnish*

1. Peel carrots and potatoes. Cut into 1-inch pieces. Mince 4 sprigs of thyme, reserving remainder for garnish. In a 5-quart saucepan, combine the carrots, potatoes, and minced thyme. Add water, salt, and pepper. Bring to a boil, reduce heat to medium, and simmer until carrots and potatoes are tender (30 minutes).

2. Place in a blender or food processor and purée until smooth. Return to saucepan to reheat if necessary. Serve in individual soup bowls. Garnish with a tablespoon of yogurt and a sprig of thyme.

Makes 12 cups, 8 servings.

CORN AND PEPPER CHOWDER

Roasting the corn enhances the flavor of this soup, but the step is optional. Serve this soup country-style by leaving the vegetables in large chunks, or present it elegantly by puréeing the ingredients into a pale green canvas for red pepper bits and yellow corn kernels. For a spicier version increase the amount of dried chiles.

     5 *ears corn in the husk (2½ cups kernels)*
     1 *red bell pepper*
     2 *cans (7 oz each) whole green chiles*
     ½ *tablespoon oil*
     2 *onions, diced*
     5 *cloves garlic, minced*
     2 *cups Vegetable Broth (see page 15) or water*
     2 *cups milk*
     ½ *teaspoon kosher salt*
     ¾ *teaspoon ground dried red chiles*
     ⅛ *teaspoon freshly ground black pepper*
     ½ *cup whipping cream*

1. If using whole ears of corn, place ears in water to cover for 1 hour. On a medium-hot barbecue or under a broiler, grill 7 to 8 minutes, turning 3 or 4 times. Cool briefly, remove husks, and slice corn from ears.

2. Seed bell pepper and dice into ½-inch cubes. Coarsely chop whole green chiles.

3. Place oil in a 3-quart saucepan over medium heat. Sauté onions and garlic for 7 to 8 minutes. Add corn, bell pepper, whole green chiles, Vegetable Broth, milk, salt, dried red chiles, and black pepper. Bring to a boil, reduce heat to medium, and simmer for 20 minutes.

4. Stir in cream and warm briefly. Serve in shallow soup plates.

Makes 8½ cups, 6 servings.

AUTUMN FRESH PRODUCE

FRUITS	Purchase	Storage	Special Notes
Coconuts	Oct.-Jan. Look for heavy weight and sound of milk sloshing inside when shaken. Avoid moldy or wet eyes, fruits without milk.	Will keep for 1 or 2 mo. at 32° F, relative humidity 80 to 95 percent.	
Cranberries	Sept.-Feb. Look for plump, firm berries with reddish lustrous color. Vary from bright red to dark blackish red according to variety. Avoid spongy or leaky berries, which may have off flavor.	Wash and dry. Will keep up to 1 week in refrigerator.	Juice aids in cleansing bladder and urinary tract. Unsweetened cranberry concentrate is available.
Dates	Sept.-May. Look for plumpness, lustrous and golden brown color, smooth skin. Available pitted or unpitted.	Will keep for several months at 32° to 40° F, relative humidity 70 to 75 percent (to prevent absorbing moisture and odors).	Classified as soft, semidry, or dry depending on softness of ripe fruit. Also classified according to type of sugar in ripe fruit. Good source of minerals, but high in sugar; commonly carries undetectable mold.
Pears	Aug.-Dec. Varieties. Anjou or Comice: light green to yellowish green, tough skin, stocky neck, aromatic; Bartlett: pale to bright yellow, thin skinned; Bosc: greenish yellow to heavy russet, firm flesh, aromatic; Winter Nellis: light to medium green. Look for good color and firmness beginning to soften, ripen. Avoid wilting or shriveling, dull appearance, weakened flesh near stem, or spots (indicates corky tissue beneath).	Wash. Keep at room temperature or in plastic container with other pears (to ripen); then refrigerate, will keep 3 to 5 days.	When slightly underripe pears are best for baking and cooking. Moderate source of vitamins A, B₁, and C and minerals.
Pomegranates	Sept.-Nov. Look for size of apple; thin, tough, pink or bright red rind; and pulpy crimson flesh composed of many small seeds. Avoid dry or hard fruit.	Will keep briefly in refrigerator.	Seeds are good in fruit salads, used to make syrup (cooked with sugar and water) that is sold commercially as grenadine.

VEGETABLES

Broccoli	Look for green heads, leaves, and stems; tender and firm stalks; compact dark green or purplish green buds. Avoid yellow or purple flowers visible inside buds.	Wash immediately. Will keep only briefly at 32° F, 95 percent relative humidity.	Excellent source of vitamin A (½ cup cooked = ½ RDA); good source of calcium, fiber, vitamin C, and minerals. A cruciferous vegetable, may reduce risk of colon cancer.
Brussels Sprouts	Oct.-Mar. Close relative of cabbage. Look for bright green color, tightly fitting outer leaves, firm body. Avoid puffy or soft sprouts (usually poor in quality and flavor), wilted or yellowing leaves (indicate aging).	Keep at 32° F, 90 percent relative humidity. Use promptly.	Rich in vitamin C and B₁, but prolonged cooking can destroy vitamins.
Cauliflower	Sept.-Jan. Look for an outer shell of fresh green stem and leaves, white or creamy white head, clean and solid formation. Neither head size nor leaves growing through curds affect quality. Avoid obvious small flowers in head, yellow withered leaves.		Rich in calcium.
Horseradish	Grown mainly for root from which the condiment is made. Belongs to the cabbage, turnip, mustard family. Look for firm, longish, tan to beige root. Avoid dark, soft spots.	Will keep 1 mo. in refrigerator.	Pungent, highly volatile oil gives it a hot taste.
Leeks	Sept.-Nov. Look for broad green tops and medium-sized necks that are whitish green 2 to 3 in. from root. Leeks should yield slightly to pressure. Avoid woody insides.	Will keep 1 week in refrigerator.	Wash carefully, separating leaves, to remove sand that clings inside sharp creases.
Pumpkins	Late Oct. Look for golden orange color, hard rind, heaviness. Avoid soft spots.	Will keep 1 or 2 mo. in cool location.	Good source of vitamin A, moderate source of potassium. Keep cool until ready to use.
Rutabagas	Look for yellowish color (distinguishes from whiter-fleshed turnips), slightly elongated shape, thick neck. Avoid dark, soft spots.	Keep in refrigerator at 32° F, relative humidity 95 percent.	Good source of vitamin B₁.
Sweet Potatoes	Oct.-Apr. Look for thick, chunky, clean, medium-sized sweets that taper toward ends. Disregard color. Avoid blemishes and decay; deterioration spreads rapidly, affecting taste of entire potato, even in portions not immediately adjacent to the decayed area. Yams are sweeter and moister than the dry-fleshed sweet potatoes.	Keep at 55° F, relatively low humidity.	Excellent source of vitamin A, good source of vitamin C and minerals, high energy food.
Winter Squash	Varieties: acorn, banana, buttercup or turban, butternut, golden delicious, Hubbard (green and blue). Look for full maturity (indicated by tough rind), heaviness (indicates a thick wall and more flesh). Slight variations in skin color do not affect flavor. Avoid cuts, punctures, sunken or moldy spots on rind. A tender rind indicates immaturity, a sign of poor eating quality.	Keep at 50° F, relative humidity 70 percent. Do not keep in a warm room.	Excellent source of vitamin A.

AUTUMN APPETIZERS AND AUTUMN SALADS

Break the usual meal routine by serving an appetizer first course instead of a salad. Or, combine several appetizers as a party buffet. Autumn salads take advantage of brilliantly colored vegetables and the fresh harvest of beans and put them together in winning combinations. Many of the salads can be served as a single-course lunch or as a starter for a family-style soup and salad supper.

GAZPACHO PÂTÉ

For a light and savory hors d'oeuvre to complement a summer meal, make this do-ahead pâté. Full of fresh, crunchy vegetables in a tomato-wine base, it uses just enough gelatin for a spreadable consistency.

  2   envelopes unflavored gelatin
  ¼   cup white wine or water
  2½   cups tomato juice
  1   cucumber
  1   green bell pepper
  ½   medium onion
  1   avocado
  ¼   cup parsley, minced,
  1   tablespoon fresh basil, minced
       or ½ teaspoon dried basil
  1   tablespoon fresh oregano,
       minced or ½ teaspoon dried
       oregano
  1   teaspoon cumin seed, toasted
       (see page 108)
  1½   tablespoons olive oil
  1   tablespoon red wine vinegar
  1   tablespoon tomato paste
  1   teaspoon kosher salt
  ½   teaspoon hot-pepper sauce
       or to taste
  6 to 8 romaine lettuce leaves

1. In a 2-cup, stainless steel bowl, sprinkle gelatin over wine. Stir to combine and place bowl in a shallow pan of water. Add ½ cup of tomato juice to gelatin mixture. Place pan over low heat and stir mixture to dissolve gelatin. When mixture is clear, it is dissolved. Cool.

2. Dice cucumber, bell pepper, and onion into ¼-inch cubes. Peel, pit, and dice avocado.

3. In a blender or food processor, combine mixture of gelatin, wine, and tomato juice; one half of the cucumber; one half of the bell pepper; the onion; parsley; basil; oregano; cumin; oil; vinegar; tomato paste; salt; and hot-pepper sauce. Purée until smooth.

4. Stir the remaining tomato juice into the puréed gelatin-tomato-juice-vegetable mixture. Add the reserved cucumber, bell pepper, and avocado. Pour into a 1½-quart mold and chill 4 to 12 hours.

5. Serve as a spread for breads or crackers.

Serves 10 to 12.

Whether the Gazpacho Pâté is served as an elegant appetizer on toasted baguette slices or as a savory first course to complement the Shiitake Potpie (see page 76), it's sure to become a favorite recipe.

73

Fiber- and nutrient-rich jicama, bell pepper, and tomato combine for an easy, festive autumn salad. Serve Provençal Salad with Lasagne Verdi (see page 81 and the cover photograph) for a hearty autumn meal.

GUACAMOLE

The dark-skinned Hass avocado has the firmest meat of the many varieties, but any type makes a fine guacamole. Use as a dip for corn chips, a condiment for an omelet or Huevos Rancheros (see page 113), or as a dressing for a variety of vegetable salads. It is best to serve any avocado within 3 hours of cutting. The browning caused by oxidation is unsightly, though harmless.

  2 *large avocados*
  1 *large tomato, finely diced*
  1 *jalapeño chile, finely diced*
 12 *sprigs cilantro, finely minced*
  1 *onion, finely minced*
  2 *cloves garlic, finely minced*
  1 *lime, juiced*
 1½ *teaspoons kosher salt*

Peel and pit avocados. In a large mixing bowl, mash avocados with a fork until combined but not smooth. Stir in tomato, jalapeño chile, cilantro, onion, garlic, lime juice, and salt. Serve immediately or place plastic wrap on the surface of the guacamole (to prevent browning) and store in the refrigerator for up to 3 hours.

Makes about 2 cups.

BLACK BEAN SALSA

Black beans provide nutrients as well as color for this simple salsa salad.

  2 *large tomatoes, diced*
  1 *white onion, diced*
  2 *green tomatoes or*
      4 tomatillos, diced
  1 *serrano chile, or to taste, diced*
  2 *cloves garlic, minced*
 ½ *cup parsley, minced*
 ¼ *cup cilantro, minced*
  2 *limes, juiced*
  3 *cups cooked black beans*
  1 *teaspoon kosher salt*
  1 *teaspoon cumin seed, toasted*
      (see page 108)
 ¼ *teaspoon freshly ground*
      pepper

In a small bowl, stir together tomatoes, onion, green tomatoes, serrano chile, garlic, parsley, cilantro, lime juice, black beans, salt, cumin seed, and pepper. Chill for 30 minutes before serving.

Serves 6 to 8.

PROVENÇAL SALAD

Jicama is a brownish root with crisp, white meat. Choose a small jicama, which will be tender and not fibrous.

  1 *small jicama*
 20 *Calamata olives or 1 can*
      (6 oz) ripe olives
  1 *large yellow bell pepper*
  1 *large green bell pepper*
  3 *large tomatoes*
  1 *red onion, minced*
  1 *cup Basic Vinaigrette*
      (see page 13)
 12 *romaine lettuce leaves*

1. Peel jicama and dice into ½-inch cubes. Pit and halve olives. Dice bell peppers into ½-inch pieces. Cut tomatoes into ½-inch cubes.

2. In a 3-quart mixing bowl, combine jicama, olives, yellow and green bell peppers, tomatoes, and onion. Toss with Basic Vinaigrette. Marinate 1 to 4 hours.

3. To serve, place 1 to 1½ cups of salad on each lettuce leaf.

Serves 8 to 12.

HOME CANNING

Ripe, succulent seasonal produce, properly canned, is far superior to refrigerated and transported or hot-house foods. Remember: The better the produce, the superior the home-canned foods. It is imperative that, after choosing delicate and delicious produce, you care for it properly.

☐ Although canning should commence as soon as possible after harvesting, produce can be refrigerated for several hours or days after picking. Canning immediately will provide a better product.

☐ Safety must be the first consideration in home canning. Many elements can damage the quality or safety of home-canned produce. Enzymes, bacteria, and microorganisms cause deterioration of all foods. When in the contained environment of a canned good, they can multiply and cause food to become rancid, bad tasting, or even toxic. Some bacteria are so virulent that they are destroyed only after hours of boiling, and other bacteria are benign until stored in an airless environment like a canning jar where they become dangerous. Carefully following canning instructions is the only way to prevent these hazards.

☐ Clean pots, utensils, work surfaces, cloths, and hands are the first safety requirement. Jars must be clean and hot when filled. Lids must be boiled, not just scalded, to activate the rubber sealing ring.

☐ Use tempered glass jars without cracks or chips, flat metal lids with rubber sealing compound, and metal screw-ring caps without rust or dents. Jars and screw-ring caps are reusable. Flat metal lids should

be replaced each time. Use a jar lifter to remove hot jars from boiling water. This will make the job easier and safer.

☐ A pressure canner is necessary when canning low-acid foods such as vegetables, meats, and poultry. (It is not the same thing as a pressure cooker.)

☐ Jars can be filled with hot or cold foods. When filling jars, allow space for a little expansion, however, too much air space could cause food to discolor and spoil.

☐ As jars are processed in the canner, the contents expand slightly. While this occurs, some of the air is forced out of the jars. When jars cool, the remaining air contracts and causes the lids to be pulled tightly against the rims. If a rubber sealer on a lid is inadequate, or a crack prevents a tight seal, the food will not be airtight. To check the seal, press the center of the flat metal lid after it has cooled. If the center stays down, the jar has sealed.

☐ If one or two jars fail to seal properly, simply refrigerate those jars and eat the contents within a day or two. Store properly canned goods away from the sun and heat in a cool, dry place for up to one year. As jars are opened, remember to store them in the refrigerator.

RASPBERRY SAUCE

This vibrant red sauce, rich in vitamin C, can be used in lieu of raspberry juice in the Peach Frappé (see page 89)—just reduce the amount of sweetener in the frappé—or poured over Whole-Grain Waffles (see page 40) for a special morning treat.

- *4 pints (8 cups) fresh raspberries*
- *1 cup water*
- *½ cup honey*
- *⅓ cup sugar*
- *1 orange rind, finely minced*

Place the berries in a 3-quart saucepan over low heat and mash them. Add the water, honey, sugar, and orange rind. Continue to cook, stirring occasionally, for 20 minutes. Place a strainer over a 2-quart mixing bowl; pour the raspberry mixture through the strainer, pressing with a wooden spoon to extract as much juice as possible. Pour strained sauce into sterile glass jars to store.

Makes 2 cups.

PECAN-NECTARINE CHUTNEY

The flavors of the chutney develop over several days, so resist the urge to eat this immediately. Mix it with cream cheese for a delicious spread.

- *1 teaspoon oil*
- *2 medium onions, diced*
- *4 cloves garlic, minced*
- *1 tablespoon minced fresh ginger*
- *2¼ pounds nectarines, peeled and sliced ½ inch thick (6 cups)*
- *1 cup (6 oz) dried apricots*
- *1 cup currants*
- *1 lemon rind, minced*
- *1 cup apple cider vinegar*
- *¼ cup water*
- *½ cup honey*
- *½ cup brown sugar*
- *1 teaspoon dry mustard*
- *¾ teaspoon cinnamon*
- *½ teaspoon kosher salt*
- *½ teaspoon cayenne pepper*
- *¼ teaspoon ground allspice*
- *1 cup pecans*

Heat oil over medium heat in a 3-quart saucepan. Add onions, garlic, and ginger and sauté until pale but not browned (about 10 minutes). Add nectarines, apricots, currants, lemon rind, cider vinegar, water, honey, brown sugar, dry mustard, cinnamon, salt, cayenne, and allspice. Stir well to combine and bring to a boil. Reduce heat to low and simmer for 35 minutes. Stir in the pecans and cook for 5 minutes more. Pour into sterile canning jars and seal.

Makes 5 cups.

AUTUMN MAIN DISHES

Crisp autumn temperatures allow us to enjoy hearty meals once again. Restore the energy spent harvesting the garden, raking leaves, or returning to schoolwork with comforting, earthy ragouts, pizzas, and potpies.

BARLEY RAGOUT

Barley is believed to be the first cultivated grain. The barley motif was often used on ancient coins, and the grain was considered important enough to serve as a basis of measurement (3 barleycorns = 1 inch) in the United States until 1888. It is sold unhulled, which is more nutritious, or hulled, which is called pearl barley. See page 16 for cooking tips on grains.

> 4 ears corn (2 cups kernels)
> 2 zucchini
> 1 pound broccoli
> 4 leeks
> 2 tablespoons oil
> 6 shallots, minced
> 8 garlic cloves, minced
> ½ cup water
> 2 red bell peppers, diced
> 2 tablespoons chives, minced
> 20 sprigs fresh thyme, minced
>   or 3 tablespoons dried thyme
> 7 cups cooked barley
> 2 teaspoons kosher salt
> 1 teaspoon pepper

1. Cut corn from cobs. Dice zucchini and broccoli into 1-inch pieces. Clean leeks (see page 15), then cut into ½-inch-thick slices.

2. Place oil in a 5-quart Dutch oven over medium heat. Cook shallots, garlic, and leeks for 5 minutes. Add broccoli and the water and cook for 3 minutes. Stir in red peppers, chives, thyme, barley, corn, and zucchini. Season with salt and pepper. Serve immediately.

Serves 6 to 8.

SHIITAKE POTPIE

The pastry topping adds a special touch to stewed autumn vegetables.

> ¾ pound shiitake mushrooms
> 16 baby carrots
> ½ pound green beans
> ½ pound tofu
> 8 green onions
> 1 tablespoon butter
> 1 large onion, diced
> 3 cloves garlic, diced
> 2 cups Béchamel Sauce
>   (see page 13)
> 1 tablespoon fresh rosemary,
>   minced
> 1½ tablespoons parsley, minced
> 1 tablespoon fresh oregano,
>   minced
> 1 tablespoon fresh basil, minced
> 1 teaspoon kosher salt
> ½ teaspoon pepper
> 2 recipes oil pastry from Cherry-
>   Nectarine Pie (see page 67) or
>   1 pound purchased puff pastry
> 1 egg
> 1 tablespoon water

1. Slice mushrooms into ¼-inch-thick slices. Cut baby carrots into 1-inch lengths. Stem green beans and cut into 1-inch lengths. Cut tofu into 1-inch-thick cubes. Trim green onions and cut into 1-inch lengths.

2. Melt butter in a 5-quart Dutch oven over medium heat. Sauté onion and garlic for 6 to 7 minutes. Add mushrooms and cook for 5 minutes more. Add carrots, green beans, tofu, green onions, Béchamel Sauce, rosemary, parsley, oregano, basil, salt, and pepper. Cook for 5 minutes. Remove from heat and place in 8 individual 1-cup ovenproof dishes or a 2½-quart baking dish. Cool in refrigerator (about 2 hours).

3. While vegetable mixture is cooling, prepare oil pastry or defrost purchased puff pastry. Preheat oven to 400° F. Beat egg with the water to form a glaze. Roll out pastry 1 inch larger than the diameter of the baking dishes. Wet edges of dishes, and place pastry over tops. Press pastry against dishes to seal. Brush with egg glaze. Bake for 30 minutes.

Serves 8.

STUFFED GRAPEVINE LEAVES

Fresh grapevine leaves can be picked from the vines of a willing vintner. To prepare, simply blanch the leaves in boiling water, remove, and dry thoroughly before using. Store in the freezer, wrapped tightly in freezer paper. Hollowed tomatoes, or bell peppers, or cabbage leaves can substitute for the grapevine leaves.

> 1 tablespoon oil
> 2 small onions, minced
> 2 cloves garlic, minced
> 1 cup brown rice
> 1½ teaspoons kosher salt
> 5 cups water
> 3 lemons
> 2 ounces almonds, toasted
>   (see page 108)
> ½ cup dried currants
> 2 cups parsley, minced
> 40 fresh grapevine leaves or 1 jar
>   (12 oz) grapevine leaves

1. Place oil in a 3-quart saucepan over medium heat. Add onions and garlic, and cook for 5 minutes. Stir in rice, salt, and 2 cups of the water. Reduce heat to low, cover pan, and cook for 35 to 40 minutes.

2. Reserve 1 lemon for garnish, and juice remaining lemons. Coarsely chop almonds. Stir lemon juice, almonds, currants, and parsley into cooked rice mixture. Cool.

3. If using preserved grapevine leaves, rinse and drain leaves. Defrost frozen leaves. Place leaves on a work surface with shiny side down and point of leaf away from you. Place 1 tablespoon of filling at base of each leaf. Fold sides toward the center. Roll leaves around filling. Place in a single layer in a shallow 12- to 14-inch skillet or sauté pan.

4. Carefully pour in remaining water. Weight leaves with a heat-resistant plate to keep them from unfurling. Place a lid on the pan and simmer 20 minutes. Slice remaining lemon into 8 pieces. Serve stuffed grapevine leaves, garnished with lemon wedges, hot or at room temperature.

Makes 40 stuffed leaves, 8 servings.

INDIAN SUMMER SALAD WITH PICKLED ONIONS

The area in the south of France around the town of Nice is famous for the olives, olive oil, capers, peppers, and tomatoes grown there. This salad was originally created to showcase these magnificent Mediterranean products. You can personalize this recipe by choosing vegetables that are available in the market in early fall.

24 small new potatoes, unpeeled (2½ lb)
24 small yellow beets, unpeeled
½ pound green beans
2 recipes Basic Vinaigrette (see page 13)
1 red bell pepper
1 green bell pepper
1 head romaine lettuce
18 cherry tomatoes
3 eggs, hard-cooked
12 Niçoise olives
2 tablespoons capers

Pickled Onions

1 large red onion
⅓ cup red wine vinegar
½ cup water
2 teaspoons honey
¼ teaspoon kosher salt
4 to 5 peppercorns, crushed
1 teaspoon dried oregano
1 teaspoon dried basil

1. In a vegetable steamer over boiling water, keeping each group of vegetables separate, steam the well-scrubbed potatoes for 20 minutes, the well-scrubbed beets for 15 to 20 minutes, and the green beans for 6 minutes. A vegetable is done when a knife is inserted and meets no resistance.

2. Plunge beans immediately into ice-cold water to stop cooking and set color. Cool potatoes and beets.

3. Place potatoes, beets, and beans in 3 separate mixing bowls and toss each with 4 tablespoons Basic Vinaigrette. Reserve for 2 hours.

4. Slice red and green bell peppers into ½-inch-thick strips. Wash and separate lettuce leaves. Wash cherry tomatoes and remove stems. Quarter hard-cooked eggs.

5. At serving time arrange lettuce leaves on individual serving plates. Mound potatoes in center of each plate. Place green beans, beets, bell peppers, egg slices, tomatoes, and Pickled Onions around potatoes. Top with olives and capers. Drizzle with remaining vinaigrette.

Serves 6.

Pickled Onions

1. Thinly slice onion. In a 4-quart saucepan, bring onion, vinegar, the water, honey, salt, peppercorns, oregano, and basil to a boil. Reduce heat to low and simmer until onion is tender (8 minutes).

2. Chill onion in juices for 2 to 12 hours. Store in refrigerator for up to 1 week.

Makes about 2 cups.

Although perfect baby vegetables are best for this picture-pretty Indian Summer Salad With Pickled Onions, leftover steamed vegetables can turn last night's side dish into tonight's salad.

Peppers, lima beans, and corn bring the Autumn Compote to life with the tastes and colors of the season. Potato Pillows (see page 84) are delicious alone and are amino acid–balancing accompaniments to the compote, providing a nutritionally complete meal.

CAULIFLOWER HASH

Colorful autumn vegetables, quickly sautéed with basil and olive oil, taste delicious with Jalapeño Corn Bread (see page 86).

- 1 pound cauliflower
- 1 large red onion
- 4 tomatoes
- 3 zucchini
- 1 tablespoon olive oil
- 3 cloves garlic, minced
- ¼ cup water
- 2 teaspoons kosher salt
- ¼ cup fresh basil, minced
  Freshly ground pepper
- 3 cups cooked kidney beans

1. Dice cauliflower into 1½-inch pieces. Cut onion, tomatoes, and zucchini into a ½-inch dice.

2. Place olive oil in a 14-inch sauté pan over medium heat. Add onion and garlic, and cook for 6 to 7 minutes. Add cauliflower and water, cover, and cook for 4 minutes. Stir in tomatoes, zucchini, salt, basil, pepper, and kidney beans. Cook for 10 minutes, stirring constantly, to heat thoroughly. Serve immediately.

Serves 6 to 8.

AUTUMN COMPOTE

This harvest of autumn vegetables makes a colorful combination that may be quickly cooked for an after-work supper. Serve over a bright Potato Pillow (see page 84).

- 2 red bell peppers
- 4 ears corn (2 cups kernels)
- ½ pound small green beans
- 1 tablespoon olive oil
- 2 onions, diced
- 3 cloves garlic, minced
- 2 cups cooked lima beans or 1 can (17 oz) lima beans
- ½ cup water
- ¼ teaspoon cayenne pepper
- 1 teaspoon dried thyme
- ½ teaspoon dried oregano
- 2 teaspoons kosher salt
- ½ teaspoon pepper

1. Cut red peppers into ½-inch-square pieces. Cut corn from cobs. Trim stem ends from beans and cut into 2-inch lengths.

2. Place oil in a 3-quart pan over medium heat. Sauté onions and garlic for 7 to 8 minutes. Add red peppers, corn, and green beans, and cook 5 minutes. Add lima beans, the water, cayenne, thyme, oregano, salt, and pepper. Cook 10 minutes.

Serves 6.

CHICAGO–STYLE PIZZA

The Windy City is famous for a deep-dish rather than a traditional flat pizza. A dark, metal cake pan with sides at least 2 inches deep or a cast-iron skillet is great for baking this pizza. The variation here uses escarole, tomato, two cheeses, and roasted garlic. Baked garlic is a sweet, mellow vegetable that is also good squeezed from the papery husk and spread on a baguette with a little cream cheese for an appetizer.

   1 *head garlic*
  3½ *tablespoons olive oil*
   ½ *tablespoon active dry yeast*
   ½ *cup cornmeal*
   ¾ *cup warm water*
   1 *teaspoon kosher salt*
  1½ *cups flour plus flour*
       for dusting
   1 *bunch escarole or spinach*
   6 *ounces mozzarella cheese*
   2 *ounces dry Monterey jack*
       cheese
   1 *green bell pepper*
   1 *cup Fresh Tomato Sauce*
       (see page 15)

1. Preheat oven to 350° F. Slice about ½ inch from top of garlic head. Remove some of the papery covering from garlic but leave the head intact. Place the garlic in a small baking dish and pour 2 tablespoons oil over it. Bake until garlic is tender (50 to 60 minutes). Cool slightly. Squeeze garlic from papery shell and reserve for pizza topping.

2. In a large mixing bowl, stir yeast and cornmeal into the water. Stir in salt, 1 tablespoon oil, and flour to form a soft dough. Knead dough vigorously on a flour-dusted work surface for 5 to 10 minutes. Place dough in a bowl. Brush top with the remaining oil and cover to prevent dough from drying. Let rise until doubled (about 1 hour).

3. Wash escarole in cool water to remove any sand or grit. Chop coarsely and heat in a skillet until wilted. Remove and reserve. Grate mozzarella and jack cheeses. Slice bell pepper.

4. Increase oven temperature to 450° F. Punch down dough and let rest 10 minutes. Roll into a circle about ½ inch thick and 15 inches in diameter. Press into baking pan. Bake for 5 minutes.

5. Place garlic, escarole, bell pepper slices, Fresh Tomato Sauce, and mozzarella and jack cheeses on pizza. Bake until cheeses are melted and crust is lightly browned (20 minutes). To serve cut in 8 pie-shaped wedges.

Serves 4 to 8.

Good and good-for-you cheeses and cornmeal add sensational flavor to this all-time favorite, Chicago-Style Pizza.

MAKING FRESH PASTA BY HAND

Follow individual recipes for the exact ingredients and specific type of pasta used in the dishes. This example is Spinach Pasta from the Lasagne Verdi recipe on the opposite page. *To store:* Dust pasta with cornstarch or flour to prevent sticking. If not cooking it immediately, let it dry where air can circulate around the strands on a cooling rack, in a basket, or on specially designed pasta racks. When completely dry, pasta can be stored in sealed plastic bags on a pantry shelf for up to 3 months.

1. Make a ring of flour on clean work surface. Place beaten egg in center of well.

2. Use a fork or your fingertips to incorporate the flour into beaten egg to form a firm dough. On a flour-dusted work surface, knead dough until it is smooth and cohesive (5 to 8 minutes). Cover with damp cloth. Rest for 15 minutes.

3. Lightly flour work surface. Start with one third of the dough at a time. Starting from the center and moving to the edge, roll the pasta using as few strokes as possible. If dough becomes too elastic, cover it for a few minutes with a damp cloth to prevent it from drying out. Roll about ⅛ to ¹⁄₁₆ inch thick.

4. Lightly flour dough and roll into a cylinder or jelly-roll shape. Cut to desired thickness for flat shapes (spaghetti, fettuccine, or lasagne) or a variety of pasta shapes.

GREEN CHILE SOUFFLÉ

This quick soufflé is equally good as breakfast, brunch, or late-night supper. Either Black Bean Salsa (see page 74) or Green Tomato and Avocado Salad (see page 48) add the necessary protein complement to the menu. A 27-ounce can of whole green chiles can be used when fresh chiles are unavailable.

 1 teaspoon butter
20 fresh Anaheim or California long green chiles
 1 jalapeño chile
 4 eggs
 1 teaspoon kosher salt
 ¼ cup flour
 3 cups cooked brown rice
 6 ounces Monterey jack cheese, grated

1. Butter a shallow, 1½-quart, oval gratin dish. Preheat oven to 400° F.

2. Roast and peel Anaheim chiles as described for Grilled Chiles Rellenos on page 50. Pat dry. Remove stem from jalapeño chile.

3. Separate egg yolks from egg whites. Reserve egg whites. Place yolks, 5 Anaheim chiles, jalapeño chile, salt, and flour into a blender or food processor. Purée until smooth. Place egg whites in a 5-quart mixing bowl, and beat until they are stiffened and soft peaks form. Stir one third of the egg whites into chile-egg mixture. Fold in remaining egg whites.

4. Place 5 Anaheim chiles in bottom of prepared dish. Cover with one third of the rice, one third of the cheese, and one third of the chile-egg mixture. Layer 5 more Anaheim chiles, half of the remaining rice, half of the remaining cheese, and half of the remaining chile-egg mixture. Finish with the last 5 Anaheim chiles and the remaining rice, the cheese, and the chile-egg mixture.

5. Bake until top is golden brown (30 to 35 minutes). Serve immediately.

Serves 8.

RED PEPPER PASTA WITH CILANTRO SAUCE

Cilantro and bell peppers marry tastefully in this pasta for a perfect light lunch. You can prepare pasta several days ahead, dry it thoroughly, and wrap it airtight until you're ready to make this dish. Do not precook the pasta. Add a little more liquid and a slightly longer baking time for dried pasta than for fresh pasta.

> 2 red bell peppers
> 1 egg
> 4 cups flour plus flour
>   for dusting
> 2 ounces Asiago cheese, grated

Cilantro Sauce

> 4 cloves garlic, finely minced
> 1 cup walnuts, toasted (see page 108) and finely minced
> 4 cups parsley, minced
> 1 lime or lemon, juiced
> 2 cups cilantro, minced
> ⅓ cup olive oil
> 1½ teaspoons kosher salt
> 4 ounces Asiago cheese, grated

1. Place red peppers over a medium flame, turning constantly, until lightly charred on all sides. (On an electric stove place peppers on a rack about ½ inch above burner.) Place in a plastic bag, tightly seal, and let rest for 20 minutes. Place peppers under running water to slip off charred skins. Discard skins. Pat dry.

2. *If using a food processor:* Place peppers in food-processor bowl. Add egg and flour, and whirl in processor until dough forms a ball. *If using a food mill:* Purée red pepper into a 2-quart mixing bowl, add egg, and enough flour to form a firm dough. Knead dough on a lightly floured work surface until smooth.

3. Prepare pasta with a pasta machine following manufacturer's directions. Using the cutting roller on the pasta machine, cut pasta into ¼-inch-thick strands. If preparing pasta by hand, as directed on opposite page, slice pasta ¼ inch wide. Lightly flour pasta to prevent sticking.

4. In a 4-quart pan, bring 6 cups of water to a vigorous boil. Stir in pasta. Keep stirring to prevent it from sticking to pan. Cook for 30 seconds. Drain pasta and toss with Cilantro Sauce. Sprinkle with cheese and serve immediately.

Serves 8.

Cilantro Sauce In a 2-quart mixing bowl, stir to combine garlic, walnuts, parsley, lime juice, cilantro, oil, salt, and cheese.

Makes 2 cups.

LASAGNE VERDI

This colorful dish is featured in the cover photograph. You can substitute 1 pound of fresh or ¾ pound of dried store-bought noodles for the recipe.

> 1 medium eggplant
> 1 teaspoon kosher salt
> 2 medium zucchini
> 12 shiitake mushrooms or ½ pound domestic mushrooms
> 3 leeks
> 1 tablespoon butter
> 1 tablespoon olive oil
> 3 cups Fresh Tomato Sauce (see page 15)
> 4 ounces Parmesan cheese, grated
> 3 cups ricotta cheese
> 3 ounces Monterey jack cheese, grated

Spinach Pasta

> 1 bunch spinach
> 2 cups flour plus flour for dusting
> 1 egg

1. Preheat oven to 350° F. Slice eggplant in half. Slash ½-inch deep cuts into each half. Place slices on a towel and sprinkle with salt. Let rest for 30 minutes. Place in colander, rinse, and pat dry. Place eggplant on a baking sheet and bake for 40 to 50 minutes. After baking, let cool slightly, cut into ¼-inch-thick pieces, and reserve.

2. Slice zucchini lengthwise into ⅛-inch-thick pieces and reserve. Slice shiitake mushrooms about ¼ inch thick. Clean leeks (see page 15), then slice into ½-inch-thick slices. Heat butter and oil in a 12-inch skillet, add leeks and mushrooms, and cook together for 10 to 12 minutes over medium heat. Add Fresh Tomato Sauce and simmer together for 15 minutes.

3. Spread one quarter of the tomato-shiitake-mushroom-leek sauce on the bottom of baking dish. Place lasagne noodles on sauce, and sprinkle with one third of the Parmesan cheese and half of the ricotta and jack cheeses. Cover cheeses with eggplant slices. Repeat layers using one third of the remaining sauce, one half of the lasagne noodles, half of the remaining Parmesan cheese, all of the remaining jack and ricotta cheese, and the zucchini slices. Cover with one half of the remaining sauce and the remaining lasagne noodles. Cover with the remaining sauce and Parmesan cheese. Cook for 35 to 40 minutes. Cool for 5 minutes before serving.

Serves 6.

Spinach Pasta

1. Wash spinach and remove stems. In water retained from washing, cook over low heat for 10 minutes. Squeeze dry. Purée in a food processor or with a food mill. This should equal ½ cup purée. If using a food processor, add flour and egg, and whirl in processor until dough forms a ball. When using a food mill, purée spinach into a 2-quart mixing bowl, and add egg and enough flour to form a firm dough. Knead dough on a lightly floured work surface until smooth.

2. Prepare pasta using a pasta machine or as described on opposite page. Roll sheets 16 inches long. Cut pasta into sheets approximately 12 inches long to fit a 9- by 12-inch baking dish.

Much of the Autumn Family Supper may be prepared ahead, allowing the evening meal to be a relaxing, social event for the entire family.

AUTUMN FAMILY SUPPER

Allium Bisque

Walnut Bread

Curried Vegetable Stew

Cinnamon Brown Rice

Apple and Cheddar Cheese Crumble

Beverage Suggestion: Cranberry Juice

Make each evening at home special. Dining together while catching up on the day's events is a wonderful family custom. This menu is a perfect weeknight meal, as much of it can be prepared in advance, kept in the refrigerator, and heated at the last minute. All recipes serve 8.

NUTRIENT BREAKDOWN	
Calories	1,913
Protein	43 gm
Fiber	8 gm
Cholesterol	272 mg
Vitamin C	155 mg
Calcium	363 mg
Sodium	1,449 mg

ALLIUM BISQUE

Allium is the scientific name for chives, garlic, leeks, onions, and shallots. These bulblike roots are related to the lily. Flowers from these plants are also edible and provide an attractive, tasty garnish. To reduce eye irritation generated by the volatile oils of onions, hold them under running water while peeling.

> 4 onions
> 4 leeks
> 4 potatoes
> 2 tablespoons butter
> 2 tablespoons oil
> 10 cloves garlic, minced
> 4 shallots, minced
> 6 cups Vegetable Broth (see page 15)
> 2 teaspoons kosher salt
> 1 teaspoon dried basil
> 1 bay leaf
> 1 teaspoon dried oregano
> ½ teaspoon dried marjoram
> Chives, minced, for garnish

1. Slice onions into a large dice. Clean leeks (see page 15), then cut into ¼-inch-thick slices. Peel potatoes and cut into ½-inch cubes.

2. In a 3-quart saucepan, heat butter and oil. Add onions, garlic, shallots, and leeks. Cook slowly over low heat until lightly browned. Add potatoes, Vegetable Broth, salt, basil, bay leaf, oregano, and marjoram. Bring to a boil, reduce heat to simmer, and cook for 40 minutes. Serve immediately or refrigerate and warm before serving. Garnish with minced chives.

WALNUT BREAD

This recipe makes 2 country loaves or 2 dozen rolls. Well wrapped, a loaf will keep in the freezer for up to two months. Freeze after initial baking and reheat from the frozen state at 350° F for 40 minutes.

> 2 packages active dry yeast
> 2 tablespoons honey
> 1 cup water (not to exceed 100° F)
> 1 cup warm milk
> ½ cup walnut oil or olive oil
> 1 tablespoon kosher salt
> 2 cups whole wheat flour
> 1 medium onion, finely diced
> 3 cups unbleached or bread flour plus flour for dusting
> ¾ cup toasted walnuts (see page 108)

1. In a small bowl or measuring cup, stir yeast and honey into the water. Let rest until bubbly (5 to 10 minutes).

2. In a large mixing bowl or the bowl of a heavy-duty mixer, combine milk, oil, salt, and whole wheat flour. Mix onion with ingredients in mixing bowl. Add yeast mixture and mix well. Add enough unbleached flour to form a stiff dough.

3. Lightly dust work surface with flour, and knead dough vigorously until it is smooth and springy, and does not stick to hands. Place kneaded dough into a lightly oiled bowl, and let rise in a draft-free place for 2 hours.

4. Lightly oil two 5- by 9-inch loaf pans. Remove dough from bowl after it has risen and punch down. Knead walnuts into dough and shape into 2 loaves. Place bread into prepared baking pans, and let rise in a cool, draft-free place for 45 minutes.

5. Preheat oven to 400° F. Bake loaves for about 55 minutes. Remove loaves from pans. Tap bottom. If they sound hollow they are done. If not, return to oven for additional baking. Cool on racks.

Makes 2 loaves.

CURRIED VEGETABLE STEW

In India traditional curry powder is a personal, specially made blend rather than the ready-mixed spice available in this country. This recipe is a mix of complex flavors that can be adjusted to taste. Four tablespoons of packaged curry powder may be substituted for the variety of spices.

    3 zucchini
    2 Japanese eggplant
    1 red bell pepper
    1 pound cauliflower
    1 pound broccoli
    2 carrots, peeled
    1 teaspoon coriander seed
    2 tablespoons oil
    1 tablespoon butter
    2 onions, diced
    2 cloves garlic, diced
    1½ tablespoons minced fresh
       ginger
    ½ teaspoon cayenne pepper
    2 teaspoons cumin
    1 teaspoon turmeric
    1 teaspoon kosher salt
    2 cups Vegetable Broth
       (see page 15)
       Cilantro sprigs, for garnish

1. Cut zucchini into 2-inch pieces. Slice eggplant into ½-inch-thick disks. Cut bell pepper into 2-inch cubes. Cut florets from cauliflower and broccoli and cut stems into ½-inch-thick disks. Cut carrots into 1-inch-thick pieces. Crack open coriander seed.

2. Heat oil and butter together in a large, shallow 5-quart skillet. Add onion, garlic, and ginger, and cook together over medium heat for about 10 minutes. When onions are translucent, add coriander, cayenne, cumin, turmeric, and salt. Stir to mix well and cook for 5 minutes. Add Vegetable Broth, mixing thoroughly.

3. Add eggplant and carrots. Cover and cook for 15 minutes. Add broccoli, cauliflower, and red bell pepper. Stir to mix well. Cover and cook for 5 minutes. Add zucchini and cook uncovered for 5 minutes. Garnish with sprigs of cilantro.

CINNAMON BROWN RICE

Almonds, which provide texture in this rice dish, are high in carbohydrates, protein, and calcium.

    1 recipe Perfect Brown Rice
       (see page 16)
    ½ cup dried currants
    ½ cup slivered almonds, toasted
       (see page 108)
    1½ teaspoons ground cinnamon

When the rice has finished cooking, stir in currants, almonds, and cinnamon. Serve immediately, or keep warm in the pan on the stove for up to 20 minutes.

APPLE AND CHEDDAR CHEESE CRUMBLE

This is an old-fashioned apple dessert, best served warm from the oven. Tart pippin or Granny Smith apples best complement the sweet and pungent crumb topping. If using a sweeter apple, you may want to lessen the amount of sugar.

       Butter for baking dish
    5 large apples
    1 tablespoon ground cinnamon
    ½ cup brown sugar
    ½ pound Cheddar cheese, grated
    ½ cup flour
    ½ cup rolled oats
    ½ cup granulated sugar
    ½ cup unsalted butter

1. Preheat oven to 375° F. Butter a 10-inch-square baking dish.

2. Peel and core apples. Cut each into 8 pieces. In a 2-quart mixing bowl, toss together apples, cinnamon, and brown sugar. Place in baking dish.

3. In a 2-quart mixing bowl, combine cheese, flour, oats, and granulated sugar. Cut unsalted butter into small pieces and rub into dry ingredients. Combine until mixture holds together in large crumbs. Cover apples with crumb mixture. Bake until apples are tender and topping is slightly browned (35 minutes).

AUTUMN SIDE DISHES

The bright profusion of fresh autumn produce begs to be used in eclectic combinations before the season ends. Besides adding visual appeal to a meal, seasonal side dishes help complete the amino-acid chain begun with the main dishes. For refresher information on protein balancing for vegetarians, see the discussion of good eating on page 6. You may also want to try serving several side dishes as a complete meal. Serving multiple side dishes is an excellent way to use smaller portions of ingredients in creative ways, and a good way to experiment with many new recipes.

POTATO PILLOWS

A variation on the traditional German potato pancake, this bright assortment of shredded vegetables is especially good with Lentil Ragout Printanier (see page 32).

    1 medium potato, peeled
    1 carrot, peeled
    1 yellow or green zucchini
    1 small onion, minced
    ¾ cup bread crumbs
    2 eggs
    1 teaspoon kosher salt
    ¼ teaspoon pepper
    2 tablespoons oil

1. Shred potato, carrot, and zucchini, using the largest-sized shredder.

2. In a large mixing bowl, combine potato, carrot, zucchini, and onion. Stir in bread crumbs, eggs, salt, and pepper. Mix together well.

3. Place oil in a shallow, 14-inch skillet over medium-high heat. Divide mixture into 6 portions. Place each into skillet. Slightly flatten each to about ⅓ inch thick. Cook over medium heat until lightly browned (10 to 12 minutes). Turn and cook the second side for 8 to 9 minutes. Serve immediately.

Serves 6.

SWEET POTATO SAUTÉ

Rich in vitamin A, sweet potatoes are wonderful prepared just about any way you would prepare other types of potatoes. In this sauté recipe the garlic and cream enhance the flavor.

   4 medium sweet potatoes, peeled
   4 tablespoons butter
   1 onion, minced
   3 cloves garlic, minced
1½ teaspoons kosher salt
   ¼ teaspoon freshly ground
        pepper
   5 tablespoons whipping cream

1. Cut potatoes into fine julienne strips about ⅛ inch thick by 2 inches long. In a 14-inch skillet over medium heat, melt butter and sauté onion and garlic. Add julienned sweet potato, and cook for 10 minutes, stirring constantly.

2. Stir in salt, pepper, and cream, and cook for 5 minutes more. Serve immediately.

Serves 6.

THAI EGGPLANT

Marinated in dried chiles and miso, a fermented soybean paste, Thai eggplant can be served warm or at room temperature. Cooked spinach is a fine alternative to eggplant.

12 medium Japanese eggplants
   ½ teaspoon kosher salt
   2 green onions, minced
   2 cloves garlic, minced
   1 teaspoon cilantro, minced
   1 teaspoon sesame oil
   3 tablespoons peanut butter
   2 tablespoons rice wine vinegar
   5 tablespoons water
   ½ teaspoon ground dried
        red chiles
   2 tablespoons miso

1. Preheat oven to 350° F. Slice eggplants in half lengthwise and sprinkle with salt. Let rest for 20 minutes. Rinse salt from eggplants and pat dry. Place eggplants on a baking sheet, cut side down, and bake for 25 minutes.

2. In a 1-quart mixing bowl, stir to combine thoroughly green onions, garlic, cilantro, sesame oil, peanut butter, rice wine vinegar, the water, red chiles, and miso.

3. Slice baked eggplant into ½-inch-thick strips and toss with sauce. Serve immediately.

Serves 6 to 8.

Serve two delicious side dishes—Harvest Stir-Fry (see page 86) and Thai Eggplant—to create one outstanding supper.

HARVEST STIR-FRY

Nothing displays the fresh tastes of autumn as simply as a stir-fry of available produce. Any favorite vegetables, such as spinach, carrots, or cauliflower, can be substituted for those used in the recipe, just let your imagination be your guide.

- ½ pound shiitake or domestic mushrooms
- 1 red bell pepper
- 1 head broccoli (about 1 lb)
- 5 baby bok choy or Swiss chard leaves
- 1 medium onion
- 2 cloves garlic
- Fresh ginger, 1-inch cube
- 1 tablespoon oil
- 2 tablespoons water
- 2 tablespoons soy sauce
- 1 teaspoon sesame oil
- 2 tablespoons sesame seed, toasted (see page 108)

1. Slice mushrooms and pepper into pieces about ½ inch thick. Trim the broccoli florets and cube the stems. Cut bok choy leaves in quarters lengthwise. Dice onion in large pieces. Slice garlic and ginger into quarters.

2. Heat oil in a wok or 14-inch skillet over medium-high heat. Add garlic and one half of the ginger to hot oil, and stir constantly to flavor oil (1 to 2 minutes). Discard garlic and ginger. Stir in broccoli. Add the water and cook for 3 minutes.

3. Add onion and stir constantly for 3 minutes. Add remaining ginger and bok choy, and cook for 2 minutes while stirring continuously. Stir in pepper and mushrooms, and cook for 2 minutes longer. Stir in soy sauce and sesame oil. Sprinkle with sesame seed and serve immediately.

Serves 6.

AUTUMN CEREALS AND AUTUMN BREADS

A good diet is only possible if each day starts with a healthy meal. Autumn, when children go back to school, seems the appropriate time to introduce morning cereal recipes, though they can be made throughout the year. Adjust to available ingredients and your taste.

The earthy flavors and textures of autumn breads harmonize well with the intense tastes of autumn produce. Prepare bread for the holidays by doubling a recipe and freezing half until you're ready to use it. Bread keeps for up to three months at 0° F.

TOASTED MULTIGRAIN CEREAL

On mornings when there is little time for breakfast, have this prepared cereal at the ready. Serve it with milk. Stored in a plastic bag or tin in a cool, dark place, this cereal keeps for up to 2 months.

- 2 cups (8 oz) rolled oats
- 2 cups (6 oz) rolled rye
- 2 cups (8 oz) rolled wheat
- 1 cup (3½ oz) shredded coconut
- 1 cup (6 oz) raisins
- 1 cup (6 oz) whole almonds
- 1 cup (5 oz) sunflower seed
- ½ cup (2 oz) wheat germ
- ½ cup (1 oz) bran
- ½ cup maple syrup
- ½ cup oil

1. Preheat oven to 300° F. Place oats, rye, wheat, coconut, raisins, almonds, sunflower seeds, wheat germ, and bran in a 3-quart mixing bowl. Toss well to combine.

2. Pour in syrup and oil, and stir to incorporate. Spread mixture on 2 jelly-roll pans and toast for 15 minutes. Remove from oven and stir. Spread again to cover pan and return to oven for 15 minutes. Remove a second time and stir. Spread again to cover pan. Bake 10 minutes. Remove from oven and cool. Store in an airtight tin or plastic bags.

Makes 12½ cups; 25 half-cup servings.

MORNING POLENTA

Cooked grains provide some of the best morning starters. Polenta, or coarse cornmeal, is a traditional food of northern Italy. It is often served speckled with Gorgonzola cheese for a light supper. Serve it for breakfast with your favorite syrup, jams, or fruit for a quickly made meal.

- 4 cups water
- 1½ teaspoons kosher salt
- 1 cup polenta
- Maple syrup, Spring Berry Jam (see page 37), or fresh fruit

In a 2½-quart saucepan, bring the water to a boil. Add salt. Gradually stir in polenta, a tablespoonful at a time, to prevent lumps from forming. Reduce heat to low and simmer for 20 minutes, stirring constantly to prevent sticking. Cool for 5 minutes, and serve in shallow bowls garnished with a swirl of maple syrup, a dollop of jam, or a selection of sliced fruit or berries.

Serves 4 to 6.

JALAPEÑO CORN BREAD

Spicy corn bread can be taken on a picnic with a thermos of Corn and Pepper Chowder (see page 71) or served with Three-Bean Chile (see page 38) for a fireside supper. When available, red jalapeño chiles are an attractive addition to this corn bread.

- 5 tablespoons butter
- 2 jalapeño chiles, minced
- 2 ears corn or 1 cup corn kernels
- 1 small red onion, minced
- 1 cup milk
- 2 eggs
- 1 cup flour
- 1½ teaspoons baking powder
- 1½ teaspoons kosher salt
- 1½ teaspoons sugar
- 1 cup cornmeal
- 2 ounces Cheddar cheese, grated (optional)

1. Preheat oven to 400° F. Using 1 tablespoon of the butter, grease an 8-inch-square pan, or line pan with baking parchment. Trim stems from chiles and discard. Slice kernels from ears of corn. In a 2-quart mixing bowl, combine chiles, corn, and onion. In a small bowl, combine milk, eggs, and remaining butter, then add to the chile-onion-corn mixture.

2. Sift together flour, baking powder, salt, and sugar. Stir in cornmeal. Gradually stir flour mixture and Cheddar cheese (if used) into the chile-corn-milk mixture until just combined and slightly lumpy. Do not stir until smooth or corn bread will be tough. Place mixture into prepared pan. Bake until top is golden brown and a skewer inserted about 2 inches from edge comes out dry (35 to 40 minutes). Cut into squares to serve.

Makes one 8-inch-square bread.

COTTAGE CHEESE AND HERB BREAD

Cottage cheese offers a low-fat, protein-rich base for this hearty bread. Cheddar or Swiss cheeses may be substituted, but increase the amount of milk by ½ cup because there is more moisture in cottage cheese than in firm cheese.

> 1 *package active dry yeast*
> 9 *tablespoons warm water*
> 2 *tablespoons honey*
> 1 *medium onion, minced*
> 1 *cup milk*
> 4 *tablespoons oil*
> 1¼ *cups cottage cheese*
> 3 *eggs*
> 5 *tablespoons dill weed*
> 4 *teaspoons kosher salt*
> 6½ *to 7 cups flour plus flour for dusting*

1. In a large mixing bowl, stir together yeast, 8 tablespoons of the water, and honey until yeast is dissolved.

2. Stir onion, milk, 3 tablespoons of oil, cottage cheese, and 2 eggs into yeast mixture. Gradually stir in dill, salt, and enough flour to form a soft dough. As dough becomes too stiff to stir, lightly flour work surface and place dough on it. Knead dough vigorously for approximately 5 minutes. Lightly oil a large mixing bowl, place dough in bowl, and cover with plastic wrap. Let rise for 1½ hours.

3. With remaining oil, lightly oil two 5- by 9-inch loaf pans. Beat remaining egg and water to form a glaze. Punch down dough and divide in half. Knead dough briefly (about 1 minute), and shape into loaves. Place into prepared pans. Let dough rise, in a draft-free area, for 45 to 60 minutes.

4. Near end of rising time, preheat oven to 350° F. Brush loaves with egg glaze. Bake for 55 to 60 minutes. Cool on racks for 10 to 20 minutes before serving.

Makes 2 loaves.

Fragrant Herb Butters (see page 26) can be shaped using candy molds or ice-cube trays to accompany autumn's homemade breads. Jalapeño Corn Bread is delicious with Green Chile Soufflé (see page 80) for a special brunch menu.

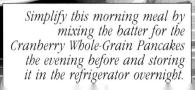

Simplify this morning meal by mixing the batter for the Cranberry Whole-Grain Pancakes the evening before and storing it in the refrigerator overnight.

FARM-STYLE BREAKFAST

Cranberry Whole-Grain Pancakes

Breakfast Nog

Peach Frappé

Pears and Pomegranate Seeds

Nutritionists find that at least one third of daily protein should be eaten in the morning, whatever your activity level. School children need protein for concentration and energy, adults to prevent midday slump. Pears and pomegranate seeds, or other fruits of the season, round out the meal. All recipes serve 4.

NUTRIENT BREAKDOWN	
Calories	850
Protein	26 gm
Fiber	6 gm
Cholesterol	330 mg
Vitamin C	230 mg
Calcium	220 mg
Sodium	740 mg

CRANBERRY WHOLE-GRAIN PANCAKES

Loaded with vitamin C, cranberries are readily available in the fall months. They are easily frozen whole in freezerproof plastic bags. You can mix them into the pancake batter while they are still frozen.

> 2 cups Whole-Grain Baking Mix (see page 17)
> 1 cup milk or water
> 1 egg
> 1 cup cranberries, coarsely chopped
> ½ cup pure maple syrup
> 1 to 2 teaspoons oil

1. In a medium-sized mixing bowl, stir together Whole-Grain Baking Mix, milk, and egg until dry ingredients are moistened. Let rest for 5 minutes. Stir in cranberries.

2. Place maple syrup in a 1-cup heat-proof pitcher. Bring 2 cups of water to a boil in a 1-quart saucepan. Turn heat to low and place heat-proof pitcher of syrup into hot water for about 20 minutes.

3. Heat a 10-inch skillet and brush with oil. Place ⅓ cup batter per pancake into skillet. Cook until surface appears dry and small bubbles appear at the edges. Turn over and cook second side for about 30 seconds. Pour warm maple syrup over each pancake.

BREAKFAST NOG

For those in a hurry, this pick-me-up shake can also be a completely satisfying meal for one. These portions make 4 small glasses of nog as part of a complete family breakfast.

> 6 to 8 strawberries
> 1 ripe banana
> 1 egg
> 1 cup plain yogurt
> 2 tablespoons wheat germ
> 1 tablespoon honey
> 1 teaspoon vanilla extract
> ½ cup crushed ice
> Nutmeg for dusting

Wash and hull strawberries. Slice strawberries and banana in half, and place in a blender jar. Add egg, yogurt, wheat germ, honey, vanilla, and ice. Purée until foamy. Dust with nutmeg. Serve immediately.

PEACH FRAPPÉ

This frappé can be prepared with a variety of fresh fruit and fruit juices. The unifying ingredients are the ice and the small amount of milk. For the vegetarian, vitamin D, which is found in egg yolks and milk, is especially important to promote the absorption of calcium and phosphorus necessary for bone formation.

> 3 ripe fresh peaches or 1 can (15 oz) peaches in juice
> 1 can undiluted raspberry juice
> 1 cup milk
> 1 cup crushed ice

1. Peel and pit peaches. Slice each peach into 6 to 8 pieces.

2. In a blender jar or food processor, combine peaches, raspberry juice, milk, and crushed ice. Hold lid securely and process for 3 minutes. Scrape down sides of container and process for another minute. Serve immediately.

AUTUMN DESSERTS

Fresh fruit, selected right from the tree, vine, or shrub, is the basis for many hearty autumn desserts. Apples, figs, pears, and quince, picked before the first frost, make delicious fruit butters, jams, cookies, and pie fillings. The aroma of freshly baked goodies is a pleasant treat for those returning home.

BAKED CRANBERRY APPLES

Baking apples is an old-fashioned preparation that works equally well with pears and quince. Cranberries and pecans add a festive touch. Granny Smith or pippins are the apples of choice in this recipe, but any tart apple will do.

8 large tart apples
1 orange
½ cup pecans, toasted
4 tablespoons butter, melted
1 cup cranberries
⅓ cup maple syrup or honey
1 teaspoon cinnamon

1. Preheat oven to 350° F. Slice tops from apples. Carefully remove cores, taking care not to cut through to bottoms.

2. Peel rind from orange, leaving the bitter white membrane. Dice orange rind. Juice orange. Discard membrane. Coarsely chop pecans. Drizzle 2 tablespoons of melted butter in the bottom of a 9- by 12-inch baking dish. In a 1-quart mixing bowl, combine cranberries, orange rind, orange juice, pecans, remaining butter, maple syrup, and cinnamon.

3. Place ⅛ of the mixture into each cored apple. Put apples into baking dish. Cover pan with aluminum foil. Bake for 20 minutes. Remove foil and bake until a knife inserted in the side of apples meets no resistance (5 minutes). Apples will be tender but should still hold their shape.

Serves 8.

FIG PINWHEEL COOKIES

The Fig and Walnut Preserves can be prepared in advance (see Basic on Preserving Fruits, page 61) as a preserve or cookie filling for gift giving later when figs are out of season. Rose water is available in gourmet sections of supermarkets and stores specializing in Mediterranean ingredients. Rolled wheat can be found in health-food stores, but if it is unavailable, rolled oats may be substituted.

½ cup butter, softened
6 tablespoons brown sugar
6 tablespoons granulated sugar
½ teaspoon vanilla extract
1 egg
1½ cups flour
½ teaspoon baking powder
½ teaspoon baking soda
¼ teaspoon kosher salt
1¼ cups rolled oats
½ cup rolled wheat

Fig and Walnut Preserves

1½ pounds figs
1 lemon, juiced
½ cup water
½ cup brown sugar
1 cup walnuts or pistachios, coarsely chopped
2 teaspoons rose water (optional)

1. In a 3-quart mixing bowl, cream butter, brown sugar, and granulated sugar. Stir in vanilla and egg. Sift in flour, baking powder, baking soda, and salt. Thoroughly mix oats and wheat into butter-sugar-flour mixture.

2. Preheat oven to 375° F. Place dough on a sheet of waxed paper, aluminum foil, or parchment about 16 inches long. Flatten dough into an 8-inch square. Cover dough with another sheet of waxed paper 16 inches long. Roll cookie dough to a rectangle about 8 inches wide by 14 inches long. Remove top sheet of waxed paper and discard.

3. Spread cookie dough with Fig and Walnut Preserves. Using the bottom sheet of waxed paper as a guide, roll dough jelly-roll fashion to enclose filling. Cut cookie roll into slices

about ½ inch thick. Place slices about 1 inch apart on a baking sheet. Bake until lightly browned (15 minutes). Cool for 10 minutes before serving. Store, completely cooled, in an airtight tin in the freezer for 1 month.

Makes 20 to 24 cookies.

Fig and Walnut Preserves

1. Wash figs and trim about ⅛ inch from stem. Dice figs and place in a 2-quart saucepan. Stir in lemon juice, the water, and brown sugar.

2. Bring fig-sugar solution to a boil, reduce heat to medium, and simmer for 15 minutes. Stir in walnuts. Cook over medium heat for 5 minutes more. Place in a mixing bowl to cool. When cool, stir in rose water.

Makes about 2½ cups.

GRAPES IN ORANGE SAUCE

Although any kind of grape mixes well with the subtle tartness of fresh orange juice, seedless grapes are simply easier to eat. Anne's Almond Shortbreads (see page 67) make a delicious complement. Bitter orange-flavored liqueur, and orange-flower water, an aromatic solution made from orange blossoms, add a delicate flavor to the sauce.

2 oranges, juiced
1 lemon, juiced
2 tablespoons honey
1 tablespoon bitter orange-flavored liqueur (optional)
1 tablespoon orange-flower water
1 pound Thompson seedless grapes
1½ pounds red flame seedless grapes

1. In a 2-quart mixing bowl, stir together orange juice, lemon juice, honey, bitter orange-flavored liqueur (if used), and orange-flower water.

2. Slice grapes in half. Place in bowl with juice mixture. Marinate for 2 hours. Serve in stemmed glasses.

Serves 8.

*Fresh Grapes in Orange Sauce
provides a simple finale to
a hearty meal. Keep Fig Pinwheel
Cookies on hand for the guest
with a sweet tooth.*

Create warmth in the kitchen
to buffer the chill outside
by simmering soups and
stews, preparing pasta,
and baking holiday treats.

Celebrating Winter's Bounty

Just a few years ago, the severity of winter was a major factor in the uninspired vegetarian menus of December, January, and February. Bleak offerings in the produce aisle taxed the imagination of even the most creative cooks. Today improvements in growing conditions and mass transportation bring a selection of winter produce that rivals the bounty of the other seasons. This welcome change offers a dramatic increase in cooking options. An understanding of this diversity and a dash of imagination allow your winter table to be alive with the colors and tastes of nature's garden.

BEAT WINTER BLAHS

The myth of the barren larder of winter is exploded by the abundance of citrus fruit, root vegetables, and specialty produce such as snow peas, pearl onions, and wild mushrooms. The family of dark leafy greens—key to the winter harvest—provides dishes that combine color and fiber with a treasure chest of vitamins.

Winter produce lends itself as well as the produce of any other season to the creation of menus with an international theme. Many of the recipes in this chapter draw from the heritages of other lands and peoples. What better time of year than gray and dreary winter to discover foods and spices from foreign lands. Vegetarians and nonvegetarians alike benefit from dishes that have evolved from the cultures of different countries or locales.

Hearty soups and stews, thick with steamy flavors and rich with nutrients, can be a trusted ally to combat vigorous winter weather. Nuts, a traditional holiday accent, provide just the right touch in conventional as well as novel dishes. Winter is also the time of year to master bread-making skills without the distractions of gardening or the heat of summer. Substantial pasta dishes are a pleasant pastime and are easily frozen to create future effortless meals.

In contrast to the cold and hibernating world outside, the winter kitchen can be a center of robust, comforting creativity and an oasis of tasty productivity.

WINTER SOUPS

Chilly winter days call for a pot of steamy soup accompanied by fresh homemade bread. Many soups improve in flavor when started one day and reheated the next. To take advantage of this—and to save yourself time—double a recipe and freeze half for a future meal.

BUDAPEST BORSCHT

Budapest Borscht is a combination soup and stew developed in Eastern Europe. It is a substantial winter food. Serve with homemade whole-grain bread as a colorful first course.

1½ pounds red cabbage
5 beets
5 small boiling potatoes
6 plum tomatoes
1½ tablespoons oil
1 onion, diced
2 cloves garlic, finely chopped
6 cups water
½ cup red wine vinegar
1 tablespoon honey
3 tablespoons parsley
1 teaspoon thyme
1 bay leaf
1½ teaspoons dried dill weed
1 tablespoon Hungarian paprika
2 teaspoons kosher salt
¼ teaspoon pepper
½ cup sour cream, for garnish
4 tablespoons fresh dill weed, for garnish

1. Slice cabbage into ¼-inch strips. Peel beets with a sharp knife and cut into julienne strips. Peel potatoes and cut in half. Peel and seed tomatoes. Cut into quarters.

2. In a 4-quart saucepan, heat oil. Add onion and garlic. Sauté for 5 minutes. Add cabbage, beets, potatoes, tomatoes, water, vinegar, honey, parsley, thyme, bay leaf, dill weed, paprika, salt, and pepper. Bring to boil and reduce heat. Simmer for 25 minutes. Serve with a dollop of sour cream and a garnish of chopped dill.

Makes 8 cups, 6 to 8 servings.

ALL-AMERICAN NAVY BEAN SOUP

One of the special treats of visiting Washington, D.C., is to taste the U.S. Senate Bean Soup in the Congressional Dining Room. This version uses the same small white beans as the base. Plan to make this soup a day ahead of serving; its flavor improves with a bit of aging.

1 pound small white beans
6 cups water
6 cloves garlic
3 onions
2 tablespoons olive oil
4 sprigs parsley
2 bay leaves
1½ tablespoons kosher salt
1 tablespoon basil
1½ teaspoons oregano
1 tomato
1 bell pepper
1 tablespoon chopped parsley, for garnish

1. Rinse beans under cold running water. Remove any stones or debris. Place beans in a 4-quart stockpot and cover with the water. Bring to boil. Turn off heat and let beans sit for 1 hour.

2. Preheat oven to 375° F. Separate cloves of garlic but do not peel. Peel onions and cut in half. Place onions and garlic in a small baking dish. Sprinkle with olive oil and cover loosely with aluminum foil. Bake for 45 minutes.

3. Bring pot of beans to boil, add baked onion and garlic, parsley sprigs, and bay leaves. Reduce heat to simmer and cook until beans are tender. This time will vary according to age of beans but is approximately 2½ hours. Remove and discard garlic and onion.

4. When beans are tender, add salt, basil, and oregano. Chop tomato and bell pepper into ½-inch chunks. Stir into soup and cook for 25 minutes. Sprinkle chopped parsley over individual servings.

Makes 8 cups, 6 to 8 servings.

LENTIL AND HERB SOUP

The pungent aroma of herbs permeates this simple country soup. Serve with bread, salad, and fruit for a satisfying hearth-side supper.

2   tablespoons butter
1   onion, finely chopped
2   carrots, finely chopped
2   large stalks celery, finely chopped
2   cups lentils
5   cups Vegetable Broth (see page 15)
1½ tablespoons herbes de Provence
2   teaspoons kosher salt

In a 3-quart saucepan, heat butter. Add chopped vegetables. Stir to coat with butter and cook over medium heat for 5 minutes. Add lentils, Vegetable Broth, herbes de Provence, and salt. Bring to boil and reduce heat. Cook for 35 minutes.

Makes 6 cups, 4 to 6 servings.

WINTER MUSHROOM SOUP

Chanterelle, shiitake, oyster, and hedgehog mushrooms are among the many types of "wild" mushrooms currently available in produce markets. Be careful that you purchase mushrooms picked by experts; do not attempt to pick your own mushrooms. Many inedible mushrooms are very similar in appearance to edible mushrooms but can be harmful if eaten. This elegant soup may be prepared with domestic mushrooms alone, but the addition of an assortment of "wild" mushrooms imparts an intense flavor.

2   pounds domestic mushrooms
8   ounces chanterelle, shiitake, oyster, or hedgehog mushrooms
3   tablespoons butter
3   large shallots, finely diced
2   cups Vegetable Broth (see page 15)
1   teaspoon kosher salt
1   cup cream
1   bunch chives, for garnish
½   cup plain yogurt, for garnish

1. Wash all of the mushrooms by rubbing gently with a damp towel. Wild mushrooms may also need to be brushed around gills (the part under cap) to dislodge some of the dirt.

2. Cut domestic mushrooms into ¼-inch cubes. Slice wild mushrooms.

3. In a 2-quart saucepan, heat butter and add domestic mushrooms, wild mushrooms, and shallots. Cook for 10 minutes over medium heat. Add Vegetable Broth and salt, and simmer for 20 minutes. Add cream and simmer just until cream is warm (8 to 10 minutes).

4. Cut chives into ½-inch lengths. Pour soup into individual bowls. Garnish with a swirl of yogurt in the center of each serving, and sprinkle with cut chives.

Makes 5 cups, 4 to 6 servings.

Shiitake mushrooms (from the Japanese for "oak fungus") provide calcium, iron, and vitamin D, and may even fend off the flu. Enjoy their rich flavor in Winter Mushroom Soup.

Ancient Greeks ate garlic for strength before athletic contests. Sweet Garlic Soup, too, can fortify us for winter; red bell pepper is rich in vitamin A.

WINTER FRESH PRODUCE

FRUITS	Purchase	Storage	Special Notes
Grapefruits	Oct.–June. Look for firmness, springy surface, medium size, heaviness (indicates thin skin and more juice than thick-skinned varieties).	Will keep in refrigerator for 3 to 5 days.	Moderate source of vitamins A and C.
Tangerines	Nov.–Mar. Look for deep-orange or almost red color and heaviness. Puffiness is normal; skin is easily removed. Avoid soft, water-soaked areas.	Will keep for 3 to 5 days in coldest part of refrigerator, high humidity.	Moderate source of vitamins A and C. Many varieties. Also called mandarins. Tangelo is a grapefruit-tangerine cross.

VEGETABLES			
Celery Root (Celeriac)	A celery grown for its knobby root, which is somewhat turniplike and the only edible part. Look for smooth, firm flesh.	Keep at 32° F, high humidity.	May be served raw or cooked.
Mushrooms	Nov.–Apr. White field mushroom is most common variety; the morel, often dried, is a favorite in French cuisine. Look for firm, clean, well-shaped mushrooms with no gills showing. Avoid open caps, dark discoloration, wilting, or injury. When buying packaged mushrooms, avoid those coated with the preservative sodium bisulfite, which changes flavor and occasionally causes allergic reaction.	Will keep in paper bag in refrigerator up to 2 days. To use, wipe with damp cloth or paper towel rather than rinsing under water; however, morels should be washed carefully with water or recipe liquid to remove any sand or insects.	High in potassium and niacin. Will reduce to about one third when cooked. Many wild mushrooms (chanterelle, hedgehog, morel, oyster, shiitake) are similar in appearance to poisonous mushrooms and should be purchased from a reputable dealer.
Parsnips	Oct.–Apr. Look for small to medium size; firm, smoothly shaped roots.	Will keep in plastic in refrigerator for several weeks.	Excellent source of potassium.
Sorrel	Buckwheat family member. Usually cooked as a green. Look for arrow-shaped leaves. See Spinach.		
Spinach	Jan.–May. Look for large, fresh, green leaves. Both the crinkly-leaf and flat-leaf types are good for cooking. Avoid wilted, yellowed, or slimy leaves.	Keep at 32° F, relative humidity 90 percent. Crushed-ice packages help keep greens fresh.	When washing spinach add a little salt to rinse water to help remove soil from leaves. Excellent source of vitamins A and C; good source of iron and calcium.

SWEET GARLIC SOUP WITH ROUILLE

Rouille is a spicy pepper and almond spread for toast, which floats on top of this French soup. Serve this dish as a savory prelude to Brown Rice Casserole (see page 110). The long, slow cooking removes the bite of the garlic but leaves the essential flavor.

- 8 heads of garlic
- 10 cups Vegetable Broth (see page 15)
- 1 tablespoon kosher salt
- 1 small baguette
  Parsley, for garnish

Rouille

- 1 red bell pepper
- ¼ cup almonds
- 1 large clove garlic
- 1 egg yolk
- ¼ teaspoon cayenne pepper
- ½ teaspoon kosher salt
- 2 tablespoons olive oil

1. Separate cloves of garlic. It is not necessary to remove papery husks. In a 3-quart saucepan, bring Vegetable Broth to a boil. Add garlic cloves and salt. Reduce heat and simmer 45 minutes.

2. Place a food mill over a 3-quart bowl. Place some of the cooked garlic cloves into the food mill with the broth. Purée garlic. Papery husks will stay in the mill while garlic purée flavors broth. Repeat with remaining garlic and broth.

3. Slice baguette, lightly toast, and spread with Rouille. Serve soup in shallow bowls with a Rouille-covered toast floating on top. Sprinkle with parsley.

Makes 6 cups, 4 to 6 servings.

Rouille Roast, peel, and seed red pepper as you would chiles (see directions for Grilled Chile Rellenos, page 50). Place pepper in food processor or blender with almonds, garlic, egg yolk, cayenne, and salt. With food processor or blender running, add oil in a thin stream until purée thickens.

Makes ⅔ cup.

CREAMY CELERY SOUP

The flavor of celery is subtle in this pale green soup. Serve with crackers.

- 2 tablespoons butter
- 1 onion, chopped
- 1 clove garlic, chopped
- 3 or 4 stalks celery, diced
- 2½ cups Vegetable Broth (see page 15)
- 1½ teaspoons kosher salt
- ¼ teaspoon white pepper
- ⅛ teaspoon cayenne pepper
- ½ teaspoon dry mustard
- ½ cup cream (optional)
- 2 ounces blue cheese

1. In a 3-quart saucepan, melt butter. Add onions, garlic, and celery. Cook for 10 minutes. Add Vegetable Broth, salt, white pepper, cayenne, and mustard, and cook for 25 minutes more.

2. Purée in a food processor or blender for 1 to 2 minutes until evenly puréed. The mixture will not be completely smooth. Reheat in same saucepan. Whisk in cream (if used), crumble in blue cheese, and stir to mix well. Simmer soup until heated through.

Makes 4½ cups, 4 servings.

Serve this elegant assortment of bite-sized hors d'oeurves at a New Year's party that your friends will remember the whole year.

menu

WINTER COCKTAIL PARTY

Stilton Snow Peas

Stuffed Cherry Tomatoes

Quail Eggs

Leek and Apple Tartlets

Raw Vegetables With Cilantro Raita

Bran Muffins With Ginger-Chutney Spread

Tabbouleh Salad in Romaine Leaves

Sliced Apples and Bouquets of Grapes

Mulled Apple Cider

Cocktail parties, with or without alcohol, are a good way to entertain groups of friends. Serving finger food reduces cleanup while guests are present, so the hosts can enjoy the party too. Each recipe makes about 40 appetizers. This menu is planned for 20 guests.

MULLED APPLE CIDER

Serve this fragrant punch from a pot on top of the stove or from an electric slow cooker on a buffet table.

　4 *quarts apple cider*
　4 *oranges*
　6 *sticks cinnamon*
　12 *whole cloves*
　12 *whole allspice berries*
　2 *bottles white wine (optional)*

Heat apple cider in an 8-quart sauce-pan. Peel oranges with a vegetable peeler in long strips, removing only the orange rind and none of the white membrane underneath. Add the orange rind, cinnamon sticks, cloves, allspice, and wine (if used).

STILTON SNOW PEAS

A quick blanching highlights the color and flavor of the snow peas while retaining their crispness. The filled snow peas will hold in the refrigerator for several hours if loosely covered with plastic wrap to prevent drying out.

　40 *snow peas*
　3 *ounces Stilton cheese, at room temperature*
　3 *ounces cream cheese*
　1 *teaspoon chopped parsley*

1. Remove stems from snow peas. Bring 3 quarts of water to a boil. Drop in snow peas and blanch for 30 seconds. Remove with slotted spoon and immediately place in ice-cold water to stop cooking. Remove from water and pat dry with paper towels. Carefully cut a 1- to 1½-inch slit in the center of the curved side of the snow pea with a sharp paring knife.

2. In a small mixing bowl, mix Stilton cheese, cream cheese, and parsley. Fill snow peas through the slit, using two spoons or a pastry bag fitted with a small star tip. Chill until serving time on paper towel-lined baking sheets covered loosely with plastic wrap.

3. To serve, arrange alternately with the Stuffed Cherry Tomotoes described below.

STUFFED CHERRY TOMATOES

Bright red cherry tomatoes and tart lentil salad are a colorful and tasty combination. The cherry tomatoes can be hollowed out early in the day of the party, and the lentil salad can be made a few hours ahead, covered well and chilled in the refrigerator.

　1 *bunch parsley*
　40 *to 48 cherry tomatoes (about 3 pints)*
　　Brown Lentil Salad (see page 21)
　2 *ounces feta cheese*

1. Wash and dry parsley. Remove some of the larger stems and discard. Line a serving tray with the parsley. This will form a nest for the tomatoes so they will not tip over after filling.

2. Wash and dry cherry tomatoes. Remove stem end by slicing horizontally across top. Hold tomato upside down over the sink, and gently squeeze out the seeds. A membrane in the center will remain. Carefully slice one side of membrane and push against side of tomato to make room for the Lentil Salad. Place tomatoes upside down on a baking rack over a baking sheet pan to drain for about 30 minutes.

3. Using two spoons, fill tomatoes with salad. Sprinkle with feta cheese. Nest on the parsley-lined tray alternating cherry tomatoes and Stilton Snow Peas. Chill until serving time.

99

QUAIL EGGS

Hard-cooked quail eggs dipped in a béarnaise sauce make quite a spectacular presentation. If quail eggs are unavailable, you may substitute quartered, hard-cooked chicken eggs. Tiny quail eggs are usually available in health-food stores and are easily identified by their blue and brown speckled shells.

    40 quail eggs
     1 large shallot, minced
     1 teaspoon tarragon
     2 tablespoons white wine
        vinegar
     2 tablespoons white wine
        or water
     2 chicken egg yolks
    ¾   cup oil
     2 tablespoons lemon juice
    ½   teaspoon kosher salt
    12 ounces dry beet pasta,
        for garnish (optional)
        Green bell pepper, for garnish
        (optional)
        Watercress, for garnish

1. Bring 3 quarts of water to a boil. Add quail eggs and reduce heat to medium high. Cook eggs exactly 8 minutes, remove with a slotted spoon and place in cold water to stop cooking. Chill if not serving immediately. Remove shells just before serving. Eggs will be bright yellow in the center, creamy and just barely moist.

2. In a 1-quart saucepan over medium heat, combine shallot, tarragon, wine vinegar, and wine. Cook until amount is reduced by half. Place into food processor or blender with chicken egg yolks. Process until pale yellow, about 1 minute. With machine on, add oil in a thin stream. Egg yolks will thicken. Add lemon juice and salt.

3. To serve, shape dry beet pasta (if used) into a nest in the center of a serving dish. Remove shells from quail eggs and place into nest. Hollow out green bell pepper (if used), and fill with béarnaise dip. Place next to nest. Garnish tray with watercress.

LEEK AND APPLE TARTLETS

Leeks are a delicate and flavorful winter vegetable. The tart green apple enhances their subtle taste. If you do not have small tartlet tins, this recipe can be prepared in a large removable-bottom quiche pan. In that case bake the shell for 25 minutes, place filling in shell, and return to oven for 8 to 10 minutes.

     1 cup flour, plus flour
        for dusting
    ¾   teaspoon plus a pinch
        kosher salt
    ½   cup cold unsalted butter
     1 egg
     1 to 2 tablespoons cold water
     5 leeks
     2 pippin apples
     3 tablespoons butter
     3 tablespoons cream
    ½   teaspoons white pepper
    ⅛   teaspoon nutmeg
    ⅛   teaspoon cayenne pepper

1. *To prepare by hand:* Place flour and a pinch of salt in a 2-quart mixing bowl. Cut butter into 16 pieces, and rub into flour and salt with your fingertips, two knives, or a pastry cutter. Beat egg in a small bowl with the cold water. Gently stir egg and water mixture into flour and butter to incorporate. Be careful not to overwork. Mix just until combined. *To prepare in a food processor:* Cube butter. Place flour, butter, and a pinch of salt in bowl of food processor. Turn the processor on and off 2 or 3 times to cut butter into flour. Small pieces of butter should be visible. Add egg, and again turn machine on and off to incorporate. Turn machine on while adding the water by the teaspoonful. Turn machine off as soon as water is added and dough just begins to hold together.

2. Flatten dough into a disk about 6 inches in diameter, and wrap it in aluminum foil. Chill in refrigerator for 30 to 60 minutes. Dough may be frozen at this point; to use later, defrost overnight in refrigerator.

3. Remove chilled dough from refrigerator and let rest for 10 to 15 minutes. Lightly dust work surface with flour. Roll dough to ¼ inch thick. Cut dough into ovals slightly larger than the 2½-inch tartlet tins. This recipe makes 36 tartlets. Press dough into tins. Place tartlet tins on a baking sheet as they are filled. Prick shells in 2 or 3 places with a fork, and chill for 1 hour. Repeat with the remaining 35 tartlet tins. (If you do not have enough tins, you may prepare half the shells, bake them, and repeat procedure with cooled tins.)

4. Preheat oven to 400° F.

5. Clean leeks (see page 15) and dice into small pieces. Dice washed but unpeeled apples. In a 2-quart saucepan, heat butter. Add leeks and apples. Cook for 8 to 10 minutes. Add cream, the ¾ teaspoon salt, the pepper, nutmeg, and cayenne. Cook for 5 minutes more.

6. If serving immediately, bake chilled tartlet shells for 12 minutes. Remove shells from tins and return to baking sheet. Place 1 rounded teaspoon of filling on each tartlet shell and return to the oven for 3 minutes. Serve warm.

7. If you prefer to prebake shells, bake them for 15 minutes. Remove from tins and cool. They may be kept at room temperature in a tightly closed tin for one day or frozen for up to 1 month. To serve, preheat oven to 400° F, place 1 rounded teaspoon of filling on each shell, and bake until heated through (7 to 8 minutes). Serve warm.

RAW VEGETABLES WITH CILANTRO RAITA

Every guest appreciates the fresh taste of simple sliced vegetables. Jicama, a crunchy root vegetable, is especially good with this spicy dip. The *raita* dipping sauce can be made without the chiles, but the added zest is delicious.

>   6 *medium boiling potatoes*
>   4 *carrots*
>   1 *large head broccoli*
>   1 *medium jicama*
>   2 *large red bell peppers*
>   3 *yellow crookneck squash*
> 12 *large spinach leaves, for garnish (optional)*

Cilantro Raita

>   8 *tablespoons cilantro*
>   1 *clove garlic*
>   ½ *jalapeño chile*
>   1 *teaspoon kosher salt*
>   1 *cup plain yogurt*

1. Bring 4 quarts of water to a boil. Wash potatoes and place in water. Reduce the heat to simmer, and cook for 25 to 30 minutes depending on size of potatoes. They are done when a knife easily pierces the center. Remove from water with a slotted spoon. Place immediately in cold water to stop cooking. When potatoes are cooled, cut into ½-inch-thick slices.

2. Peel carrots. Slice on the diagonal, about ½ inch thick, with a decorative knife. Place into the boiling water for 2 to 3 minutes to enhance flavor and color. Remove with a slotted spoon, and place in ice water to stop cooking and set color. Wash broccoli. Cut florets into bite-sized pieces and peel stems. Slice stems into rounds about ½ inch thick.

3. Peel brown skin from jicama. Slice into sticks about ½ inch by 4 inches long. Slice bell peppers in half; remove and discard seeds. Slice squash on the diagonal with the decorative cutting knife. Arrange vegetables in a basket lined with washed and dried spinach leaves (if used). Serve with Cilantro Raita.

Cilantro Raita Mince cilantro, garlic, and chile. Stir this mixture and salt into yogurt. Chill.

Makes 1¼ cups.

BRAN MUFFINS WITH GINGER-CHUTNEY SPREAD

This recipe makes 24 miniature muffins. These are equally good for breakfast baked in larger muffin cups for 25 minutes.

>   *Butter for preparing pan*
>   1 *cup bran cereal*
>   ½ *cup milk*
>   ¼ *cup honey*
>   1 *egg*
>   3 *tablespoons oil*
>   2 *teaspoons baking powder*
>   ½ *teaspoon kosher salt*
>   ½ *teaspoon baking soda*
>   ½ *cup unbleached flour, plus flour for dusting*
>   ½ *cup whole wheat flour*
>   ½ *cup chopped dates*

Ginger-Chutney Spread

>   3 *tablespoons candied ginger*
>   8 *ounces cream cheese, at room temperature*
>   3 *tablespoons Pecan-Nectarine Chutney (see page 75)*
>   2 *tablespoons shredded coconut (optional)*

1. Preheat oven to 400° F. Butter and flour 2 miniature muffin pans, each with 12 individual muffins about 1½ inches across.

2. Place bran cereal in a mixing bowl. Add milk, honey, egg, and oil. Sift in baking powder, salt, baking soda, and flours. Stir in dates, using just a few strokes. Do not overmix.

3. Fill prepared muffin pans and bake for 15 minutes. Unmold and cool. Serve with Ginger-Chutney Spread.

Ginger-Chutney Spread Mince ginger and combine with cream cheese, Pecan-Nectarine Chutney, and coconut (if used). Serve at room temperature.

Makes 1 cup.

TABBOULEH SALAD IN ROMAINE LEAVES

Tabbouleh is a popular salad on hors d'oeuvre tables in the Middle East. This variation combines the customary bulgur wheat with radishes and red bell peppers for a bright presentation.

>   1½ *cups bulgur*
>   2 *cups boiling water*
>   1 *bunch radishes*
>   1 *cucumber*
>   2 *bunches green onions*
>   1 *large red bell pepper*
>   1 *bunch parsley, minced*
>   ¾ *cup lemon juice*
>   3 *tablespoons rice wine vinegar*
>   1 *teaspoon kosher salt*
>   *Pepper, to taste*
> 40 *small inner leaves from 2 heads romaine lettuce*
>   1 *tablespoon chopped parsley*

1. Place bulgur in a 2-quart mixing bowl. Add the boiling water, and let rest for 20 to 30 minutes.

2. Slice radishes in half lengthwise and then into ¼-inch-thick half circles. Peel cucumber, quarter, and remove seeds. Slice into ¼-inch-thick pieces. Trim green onions and slice crosswise into thin rounds. Dice bell pepper into ½-inch-square pieces.

3. Drain wheat, and stir in the radishes, cucumber, green onions, bell pepper, parsley, lemon juice, vinegar, and salt. Stir to combine. This may be covered and refrigerated until serving time.

4. Before serving, reseason tabbouleh with salt, pepper, and vinegar as needed, and place in the center of a medium-sized serving dish. Wash lettuce leaves and pat dry. Arrange leaves on dish. Sprinkle salad with parsley. Guests serve themselves by spooning some of the tabbouleh onto the lettuce leaves.

PERFECT PURÉE

A purée is a thick liquid made from finely ground, cooked vegetables, fruits, grains, or legumes. Familiar purées include applesauce, mashed potatoes, and pumpkin pie filling. Purées add nutrition rather than flour, fat, or dairy products to thicken a soup or sauce.

Prepare food for puréeing by washing, trimming blemishes, and removing seeds. Skins should be scrubbed but do not always have to be removed. Hard-skinned vegetables, however, such as pumpkins and winter squash should peeled; peeling most other foods is a matter of personal taste. Cook food until tender. Most fruits and vegetables will purée best when still warm. Mash food with a potato masher, then press through a fine strainer. Blenders or food processors are helpful, but not neccessary. A food mill is also useful, especially for unpeeled foods.

Different foods can be cooked separately or combined for purées. Non-starch food such as beans and tomatoes produce very liquid purées, which are good for sauces. Starchy vegetables such as carrots, potatoes, or parsnips produce thicker purées.

Serve purées immediately, or store them refrigerated for up to four days or frozen for up to a month. Reheat in a double boiler.

In general, 1 pound of trimmed and cleaned raw fruits and vegetables makes about 2 cups of purée. Thick-skinned vegetables and pitted fruits are an exception. For these foods, about 1 pound of raw food yields 1 cup of purée. One-half pound of beans makes 2½ cups of purée. When using purée as a thickener, 1 cup of puréed potato, or a similar starchy vegetable, is enough to thicken 2 quarts of vegetable soup.

WINTER SALADS

Winter salads take advantage of seasonally fresh greens such as endive, watercress, romaine lettuce, curly endive, and spinach. These flavorful greens support the aromatic walnut and hazelnut oils and the robust balsamic vinegar. Many winter salads can be enhanced with artichoke hearts, Brussels sprouts, celery root, and fennel. Toasted nuts and seeds (see page 108) make a tasty addition.

CAULIFLOWER AND BROCCOLI SALAD

One-half cup of broccoli has about the same amount of vitamin C as one-half cup of orange juice and as much calcium as one-half cup of milk. This salad of readily available ingredients is as lovely to look at as it is nutritious.

1 head cauliflower
1 bunch broccoli

Creamy Garlic Dressing

4 cloves garlic
1 egg
1 tablespoon Dijon mustard
¾ cup oil
1 tablespoon lemon juice
1 tablespoon white wine vinegar
1 teaspoon kosher salt
⅛ teaspoon white pepper

Separate cauliflower and broccoli flowers from stems. Peel stems and cut into 1-inch pieces. Place florets and stems in basket over boiling water. Steam until a knife inserted will easily pierce vegetable (6 to 8 minutes). Remove from steamer and cool. Toss with Creamy Garlic Dressing and serve.

Serves 6 to 8.

Creamy Garlic Dressing With a food processor or blender running, drop in garlic to purée. Add egg and mustard. With machine still running, add oil in a thin stream until mixture is slightly thickened. Season with lemon juice, vinegar, salt, and pepper.

Makes about ¾ cup.

GREEN SALAD WITH WINTER VINAIGRETTE

Even simple greens are especially delicious with Winter Vinaigrette.

1 orange
1 clove garlic
½ cup walnut oil
1 teaspoon kosher salt
3 tablespoons orange juice
2 tablespoons red wine vinegar
Pinch white pepper
8 cups mixed winter greens (romaine lettuce, spinach, and watercress)

1. Remove rind from orange, taking care to peel away only the orange part and none of the white membrane. Reserve peel. Remove membrane from orange and discard. Section orange and reserve for salad. Purée garlic through garlic press. Marinate orange peel and garlic in walnut oil for 24 hours.

2. Strain rind and garlic from oil. Add salt, juice, vinegar, and white pepper to oil. Clean and tear greens. Toss greens, orange sections, and dressing. Serve immediately.

Serves 8.

GEORGIA PECAN AND PEAR SALAD

Serve as a substitute for the cheese course at a formal dinner party.

1 cup pecans (about 30), shelled
1 head curly endive
12 leaves romaine lettuce
1 comice pear

Blue Cheese Vinaigrette

1 clove garlic
4 ounces blue cheese
4 tablespoons red wine vinegar
8 tablespoons oil
½ teaspoon kosher salt
¼ teaspoon black pepper

Toast pecans as directed on page 108. Wash curly endive and lettuce. Tear into small pieces. Wash but do not peel pear. Slice into paper-thin pieces. Toss greens, pear, and pecans with Blue Cheese Vinaigrette.

Serves 6 to 8.

Blue Cheese Vinaigrette Squeeze garlic through garlic press into a small jar or mixing bowl. Crumble in blue cheese. Add vinegar, oil, salt, and pepper. Stir to mix thoroughly.

Makes about ¾ cup.

WILD-RICE SALAD

Wild rice is not really a rice but the seeds of a swamp-growing grass. For centuries it has been harvested by hand from semiwild conditions on the northern lakes of Minnesota. Now however, growers in California, which has recently become the leading wild rice-producing state, plant it annually.

    ½ cup almonds, slivered
    12 dried apricots
    2 tablespoons oil
    1 onion, chopped
    ½ cup wild rice
    1 cup brown rice
    ½ cup rye berries
    3½ cups Vegetable Broth (see
       page 15) or water
    1 bunch green onions
    ⅓ cup orange juice
    2 tablespoons lemon juice
    ½ cup oil
    2 teaspoons kosher salt
    ½ teaspoon pepper
    3 small persimmons
    8 romaine lettuce leaves

1. Toast almonds as described on page 108. Cut each apricot into four pieces. Heat 2 tablespoons oil in a heavy 4-quart saucepan. Add onion and cook until lightly browned. Add wild rice, brown rice, rye berries, and apricots. Stir to coat with oil and cook for 1 minute. Add Vegetable Broth. Bring to boil and reduce heat. Simmer, covered, for 40 minutes.

2. Remove and cool. While rice is cooling, slice green onions across width into ⅛-inch-thick circles. Mix orange juice, lemon juice, ½ cup oil, salt, and pepper. Add green onions.

3. Remove cooked wild-rice mixture from pan to shallow bowl or platter to cool. Pour in juice mixture and toss well to combine.

4. Peel persimmons and cut each into eight pieces. Line eight individual plates with romaine leaves. Place approximately ½ cup rice mixture on each plate. Top with persimmon slices and almonds.

Serves 8.

SPICY CARROT SALAD

This vitamin-packed salad is delicious by itself but is the traditional accompaniment to Vietnamese Rolls (see page 116).

    2 carrots, shredded
    2 cloves garlic, minced
    ¼ teaspoon dried red chiles
    3 tablespoons vinegar
    2 tablespoons honey
    2 tablespoons water

1. In a mixing bowl, combine carrots and garlic.

2. In a small saucepan, combine chiles, vinegar, honey, and water, and bring to boil. Pour mixture over carrots. Let stand for 20 minutes. Servings of this spicy salad are traditionally quite small.

Serves 6.

Naturally sweet carrots, enhanced by vinegar and dried red chiles, make a Spicy Carrot Salad that complements the vegetable- and tofu-filled Vietnamese Rolls (see page 116).

Pomegranate, used as a symbol of fertility in ancient rites, adds edible rubies to orange, grapefruit, and watercress in the Tricolor Salad.

TRICOLOR SALAD

Vitamin C-rich oranges and grapefruits are flavorful enough to complement the hearty Herb and Garlic Vinaigrette. Watercress and endive lend their peppery and slightly bitter flavor to this composed salad. For an alternative presentation simply toss the vinaigrette, greens, and fruits.

> 1 *pomegranate*
> 2 *oranges*
> 1 *grapefruit*
> 2 *heads Belgian endive*
> 2 *bunches watercress*

Herb and Garlic Vinaigrette

> 3 *cloves garlic, minced*
> 1 *tablespoon Dijon mustard*
> 1 *teaspoon kosher salt*
> 3 *tablespoons balsamic vinegar*
> 7 *tablespoons oil*
> 1 *tablespoon parsley*
> 1 *tablespoon chives*
> 3 *to 4 leaves fresh basil*
>   *Freshly ground black pepper*

Pull open pomegranate and remove seeds. Peel and section oranges and grapefruit. Separate endive leaves. Arrange watercress in center of a 12- to 15-inch platter. Place endive leaves around perimeter like spokes in a wheel. Place a section of grapefruit and a section of orange between endive spokes. Drizzle Herb and Garlic Vinaigrette over salad and dot with pomegranate seeds.

Serves 6.

Herb and Garlic Vinaigrette

Whisk all ingredients together. Serve immediately or chill and whisk again before serving.

Makes about ½ cup.

WINTER MAIN DISHES

The main dishes of winter are deeply satisfying fare. Inclement weather calls for robust food: aromatic pots of stew and hearty casseroles.

CORNMEAL LOAF WITH AUBERGINE SAUCE

The Cornmeal Loaf is an earthy Italian polenta molded in a loaf pan to be reheated at serving time. The eggplant sauce benefits from being made the day before, which allows the flavors to mellow overnight. This dish is an attractive presentation of golden cornmeal, purple eggplant, red and green peppers. Watercress and curly endive salad with orange sections makes a good counterpoint to this main course.

>   2 tablespoons butter
> 2½ cups water or Vegetable Broth
>   (see page 15)
>   1 cup polenta or coarse
>   cornmeal
>   1 teaspoon kosher salt
>   ½ cup grated Parmesan or
>   Asiago cheese

Aubergine Sauce

>   1 to 1½ pounds eggplant
>   3 teaspoons kosher salt
>   3 tablespoons olive oil
> 2½ pounds tomatoes
>   1 red bell pepper
>   1 green bell pepper
>   1 onion, finely diced
>   1 tablespoon fresh or 1 teaspoon
>   dried oregano
>   1 tablespoon fresh or 1 teaspoon
>   dried basil
>   2 or 3 drops red pepper sauce,
>   or to taste
>   12 to 16 black olives, for garnish

1. Butter an 8- by 8-inch baking pan with 1 tablespoon of the butter. Preheat oven to 375° F.

2. In a 3-quart saucepan, bring the water Broth to a boil. Reduce to medium heat. Add polenta by the tablespoon while stirring constantly to prevent lumps from forming. Continue stirring while mixture cooks for 20 minutes. Add salt and remaining 1 tablespoon butter. Remove from heat and pour into prepared pan. Cover with plastic wrap and cool if not serving immediately.

3. When ready to serve, sprinkle with grated cheese and heat in oven for 10 to 15 minutes. Slice polenta into ½-inch-thick by 4-inch-long strips. Place 3 slices on each dinner plate. Serve with Aubergine Sauce garnished with black olives.

Serves 6.

Aubergine Sauce

1. Cut eggplant into ½-inch cubes. Place in a colander and sprinkle with 2 teaspoons salt. Let rest 30 minutes with a plate or towel under colander to catch any drips. Rinse and pat dry.

2. Heat 1 tablespoon of the oil in a large sauté pan. Cook one half of the eggplant, one layer at a time, over medium-high heat for 8 to 10 minutes. Remove with slotted spoon and reserve. Heat another tablespoon of oil and add remaining eggplant cubes. Cook until tender. Reserve with first half.

3. Seed tomatoes by cutting in half crosswise and gently squeezing. Most of the seeds should come out easily. Cut peppers into ½-inch cubes.

4. In the same pan used for eggplant, heat last tablespoon of olive oil at a low temperature and add onion and bell peppers. Sauté onion and peppers for 10 minutes until onion is translucent. Add tomatoes, reserved eggplant, oregano, basil, 1 teaspoon salt, and red pepper sauce. Cook for 25 minutes over low heat.

Makes 4 cups.

EGGPLANT MOUSSAKA

Moussaka—a hearty dish with the pungent seasonings of the Mediterranean—is excellent when prepared one day and served the next as the flavors only improve. Serve with Greek Salad (see page 55) and Stuffed Grapevine Leaves (see page 76) to create an exotic menu.

> 1½ to 2 pounds eggplant
>   1 tablespoon kosher salt
>   ¼ cup olive oil
>   2 cups Béchamel Sauce
>   (see page 13)
>   2 eggs
>   1 tablespoon cinnamon
>   1 cup ricotta cheese
> 1½ cups grated Parmesan cheese
>   6 to 8 springs parsley
>   ¼ teaspoon cayenne pepper
> 1½ cups Fresh Tomato Sauce
>   (see page 15)

1. Slice eggplant across diameter into ¼-inch-thick rounds. Arrange slices on paper towel–lined baking sheets and sprinkle with salt. Let rest for 30 minutes.

2. After 30 minutes rinse eggplant and pat dry. Preheat oven to 375° F.

3. Lightly brush two cookie sheets with olive oil. Brush eggplant slices with olive oil and place on cookie sheets. Bake for 20 minutes until golden brown, turn over, and bake underside 15 minutes more.

4. In a 1-quart mixing bowl, combine Béchamel Sauce, eggs, cinnamon, ricotta, 1 cup Parmesan, parsley, and cayenne.

5. In an 8-inch baking dish or 6- to 8-cup mold, layer ½ cup Fresh Tomato Sauce, one third of the Béchamel Sauce mixture, and one third of the cooked eggplant slices sprinkled with 2 tablespoons Parmesan cheese. Repeat until all ingredients are used.

6. Cook for 50 to 60 minutes until golden brown on top. Let rest 10 minutes before serving.

Serves 6 as a main course, 8 as a first course.

PIROSHKI

These little dumplings are from Eastern Europe. The piroshki are similar to the ravioli of Italy and the potstickers of China. You have a choice of two fillings—a traditional cabbage and potato or sauerkraut, Cheddar, and spinach.

2½ cups flour, plus flour
    for dusting
¼ cup oil
⅔ cup water
4 cups Vegetable Broth
    (see page 15) or water
    Chopped parsley, for garnish

Sauerkraut Filling

1 tablespoon oil
1 small onion, finely diced
1 bunch spinach, chopped
½ cup sauerkraut
2 cups shredded Cheddar cheese
    (about 6 oz)
½ cup sour cream or plain
    yogurt
1 teaspoon dill weed
½ teaspoon kosher salt
    (optional)
⅛ teaspoon pepper
⅛ teaspoon paprika
    Pinch nutmeg

Cabbage-Potato Filling

½ small cabbage (2 c shredded)
1½ teaspoons kosher salt
2 tablespoons oil
1 onion, minced
1 large potato, peeled and diced
1 cup Vegetable Broth (see
    page 15) or water
¼ teaspoon pepper
⅛ teaspoon nutmeg

Dill Sauce

2 green onions, minced
1 cup sour cream or plain
    yogurt
1 tablespoon dill weed
2 teaspoons lemon juice
¼ teaspoon kosher salt
2 tablespoons milk

1. Prepare dough by placing flour in a food processor or a large mixing bowl. In a separate bowl, stir together oil and the water, then mix with flour. Cover and let dough rest 1 hour. After 1 hour, lightly flour the work surface. Roll out dough paper-thin, about ⅛ inch thick. Using a 3-inch diameter cutter, press circles from dough. The recipe makes about 36. Place a rounded teaspoonful of filling in the center of each circle. Brush edges of each circle with water. Fold each circle in half and press to seal.

2. Bring Vegetable Broth or the water to a boil. Add piroshki a few at a time to maintain temperature of broth. Cook for 7 to 8 minutes. Remove from broth with slotted spoon. Serve in shallow bowls. Add a little of the broth if desired. Top with Dill Sauce and a sprinkling of parsley.

Serves 6.

Sauerkraut Filling Heat oil in a 10-inch skillet and add onion and spinach. Cook for 5 to 7 minutes until onion is translucent and spinach is wilted. Place in a mixing bowl to cool. While onion-spinach is cooking, rinse sauerkraut and pat dry. Add to cooled mixture with cheese, sour cream, dill, salt if used, pepper, paprika, and nutmeg.

Makes 2½ cups of filling, enough for 36 piroshki.

Cabbage-Potato Filling Slice cabbage, place in a colander, and sprinkle with 1 teaspoon salt. Let rest 1 hour. Rinse and pat dry. Heat oil in a 10-inch skillet and sauté onion. Add cabbage, potato, and Vegetable Broth to onion. Cover and cook over low heat for 8 to 10 minutes. Place in a 2-quart mixing bowl to cool. Add remaining salt, pepper, and nutmeg.

Makes 2¼ cups of filling, enough for 36 piroshki.

Dill Sauce Combine green onions, sour cream, dill, lemon juice, salt, and milk.

Makes 1¼ cups.

BEET RAVIOLI WITH SWISS CHARD SAUCE

The pale pink ravioli look lovely mixed with the rich green Swiss chard. If you are able to find red Swiss chard, the contrast is even more striking; the red color complements the green leaves as well as the pink ravioli.

Cheese Filling

2½ ounces Parmesan cheese
2 green onions, finely chopped
1 cup ricotta cheese
3 ounces French goat cheese
1 egg yolk
½ teaspoon kosher salt
½ teaspoon nutmeg
¼ teaspoon white pepper

Pasta

1 bunch red beets (12 oz with
    stems, 6 oz without stems) or
    ½ cup puréed red beets
1¾ cups flour
1 egg

Swiss Chard Sauce

1 bunch red Swiss chard
    (12 oz)
1 tablespoon olive oil
1 tablespoon butter
1 onion, finely diced
2 cloves garlic, finely diced
4 cups Vegetable Broth
    (see page 15)
2½ ounces grated Parmesan
    cheese
1 tablespoon pine nuts, toasted

1. *To prepare filling:* Grate Parmesan cheese using medium-sized grater. In a small mixing bowl, stir together onions, Parmesan, ricotta, goat cheese, egg yolk, salt, nutmeg, and pepper.

2. *To prepare pasta:* Trim leaves from beets, leaving an inch of stem on each. If beets are small, they may be cooked whole; if they are large, they should be cut in half. It is not necessary to peel beets, as skin slips off easily after cooking. You may want to wear rubber gloves because beets stain hands.

3. Bring two quarts of water to a boil and add beets. Reduce heat to medium and cook beets 15 to 20 minutes, depending on size. Beets are done when a knife inserted in center pierces beet easily.

4. Cool beets 10 minutes until they are easily handled. Slip skin from beets under running water.

5. Place beets in a food processor and purée. Add flour and egg, and process until dough forms a ball (about 2 minutes).

6. Prepare sheets of dough using a pasta machine (see Making Fresh Pasta By Hand, page 80). Roll to second thinnest setting.

7. Place a sheet of dough about 4½ inches wide by 20 inches long on work surface. Place 1 teaspoon of filling along left side of sheet about 1 inch from edge. Continue to place teaspoons of filling along left side about 1½ inches apart.

8. Lightly spray right side with water using an atomizer. Gently fold right side of dough over left and press around each ravioli with the side of your hand, a ravioli cutter, or a pastry crimper. The pastry crimper and the ravioli cutter will cut as they seal. If you seal ravioli with the side of your hand, cut them into squares with a sharp knife.

9. Place ravioli on a rack to dry if you are not using them immediately. They may be refrigerated several hours or frozen 1 month.

10. *To prepare sauce:* Cut stems of Swiss chard into ½-inch pieces. Cut leaves into 1-inch strips and reserve.

11. In a large sauté pan with 3-inch-deep sides, heat oil and butter. Add onion and cook 5 minutes, then add garlic and cook 2 minutes more. Stir in stems and cook an additional 10 minutes. Add leaves and cook again for 10 minutes.

12. Add Vegetable Broth. Bring to a boil and add ravioli. Turn heat down to medium and cook ravioli about 2 minutes. They are done when they float to surface.

13. To serve, place five or six ravioli on each plate, cover with some of the Swiss chard, and sprinkle with Parmesan cheese and pine nuts.

Makes 40 ravioli, 2 inches by 2 inches; serves 6 to 8.

This beautiful dish is also beautifully nutritious. Beets, native to Italy, and chard provide vitamins A and C, riboflavin, and iron in Beet Ravioli With Swiss Chard Sauce.

Basics

NUTS TO YOU

Many foods called nuts are actually legumes (peanuts) and seeds (Brazil nuts and almonds). For our purposes *nut* includes any edible fruit or seed contained in a separable shell. Nuts contain protein, carbohydrates, fats, and oils. The fats and oils make them highly perishable, but if stored properly you can use nuts in recipes throughout the year. For more information on purchasing and storing nuts, see the All Seasons Produce Chart on page 11.

Cooking oils made from nuts are also highly perishable and are best purchased in quantities that can be used in a relatively short time.

Toasting Nuts and Seeds

Toasting heats the oils in nuts and seeds and brings out their flavors. *Toasting in the oven:* Preheat oven to 350° F. Place whole nuts in one layer on a baking sheet with sides, such as a jelly-roll or other shallow pan. Place into preheated oven for 8 to 10 minutes until nuts begin to color and crisp. Stir once, and replace in oven for another 3 to 5 minutes. The actual toasting time depends on the size of the nuts. Nuts will continue to cook for a few seconds as they cool. Remove nuts to another pan to cool more quickly. Wait to chop or pulverize until they have cooled completely. *Toasting in a dry skillet:* When a recipe requires only 1 or 2 tablespoons of toasted nuts, the preferred toasting method is to place whole or ground seeds in a dry skillet over low heat. Stir constantly until aromatic oils are released and seeds color slightly, about 2 to 4 minutes depending on size of seeds. Remove from pan to cool.

HONEY PEANUT BUTTER

Displayed at the 1904 St. Louis World's Fair as a nutritious protein-rich food, peanut butter has become an American staple. Almonds, cashews, or hazelnuts may be substituted for peanuts.

> ½ *pound raw peanuts, toasted*
> ¼ *teaspoon kosher salt*
> ¼ *teaspoon honey*
> 1 *tablespoon oil*

In a blender or food processor, purée peanuts, salt, honey, and oil until desired consistency is reached (about 3 minutes). Scrape sides of blender from time to time so that peanuts are well puréed. Keep refrigerated to prevent oils from separating.

Makes about ¾ cup.

MEDITERRANEAN CARROT ROTOLO

Vitamin A is only one of the benefits of this rolled carrot pasta. The pasta and filling, once assembled, will keep in the refrigerator two days or in the freezer one month so that you can serve this delicious dish when you are short on time. John's Cinnamon Buttermilk Cake (see page 121) would make a great finish to the dinner.

> 6 *ounces raw carrots*
> 1¾ *cups flour, plus enough to cover work surface*
> 1 *egg*
> 1 *egg beaten with 1 tablespoon water*

Mediterranean Filling

> 1 *cup dried currants*
> 2 *lemons, juiced*
> 4 *ounces almonds*
> 1 *pound romaine lettuce, spinach, or Swiss chard*
> 1 *leek*
> 3 *tablespoons butter*
> 1 *onion, diced*
> 4 *cloves garlic, diced*
> 2 *pounds ricotta cheese*
> ½ *cup Parmesan cheese*
> 1 *teaspoon kosher salt*
> ¼ *teaspoon pepper*
> ½ *teaspoon nutmeg*

Lemon Mint Sauce

> 1 *bunch chives*
> 3 *tablespoons butter*
> 2 *lemons, juiced*
> 1 *tablespoon mint*
> ½ *cup plain yogurt*

1. Peel carrots and cut into 2-inch pieces. Cook carrots in boiling water for 7 to 8 minutes. *If using a food processor:* Purée carrot. Add flour and egg, and whirl until dough forms a ball. *If using a food mill:* Purée carrot into 2-quart mixing bowl; add egg. Add flour and mix to form a firm dough. Knead dough on lightly floured work surface until smooth.

2. Prepare pasta as described on page 80. Roll sheets 16 inches long.

3. Place a larger than 16-inch-square cheesecloth on work surface. Place sheets of dough on towel one at a time, first brushing 1 long edge with beaten egg. Place second sheet of dough slightly overlapping first, and press length to seal. Repeat this procedure to create a square of dough that is approximately 16 inches by 16 inches.

4. Spread prepared Mediterranean Filling on pasta. Roll jelly-roll fashion. Wrap cheesecloth around pasta roll. Tie ends of cheesecloth with string.

5. Bring 6 quarts of water to boil. Place cheesecloth-covered pasta roll in water. Reduce heat to medium and cook for 25 to 30 minutes. Remove from water. Unwrap. Cut roll into sixteen 1-inch-thick slices.

Serves 8.

Mediterranean Filling

1. Macerate currants in lemon juice 15 to 20 minutes. Toast almonds as described in Basics of Toasting Nuts and Seeds (see opposite page). Cool for 10 minutes and chop coarsely. Reserve.

2. Chop greens into ½-inch strips. Clean (see page 15) and slice leek. Heat butter in a large skillet and add leek, onions, and garlic. Cook for 5 minutes and add greens. Remove from heat and cool slightly.

3. Stir in ricotta, Parmesan, macerated currants, almonds, salt, pepper, and nutmeg.

Makes 5 cups.

Lemon Mint Sauce Cut chives into 1-inch strips. Heat butter in an 8-inch skillet; add lemon juice, mint, chives, and yogurt. Whisk to combine and serve next to pasta roll.

Makes ½ cup.

CANTONESE SWEET AND SOUR WALNUTS

Stir-frying takes only a few minutes. If you have prepared the walnuts and sauce ahead, the walnuts can be stored overnight in an airtight tin, and the sauce can be stored in the refrigerator for up to two weeks. The vegetables, cut, sliced, and covered with plastic wrap, can be kept in the refrigerator for several hours to await cooking. Serve with steamed brown rice and Vietnamese Rolls (see page 116) to continue the Asian theme. Cantonese Sweet and Sour Walnuts are best served as part of a multi-course meal.

> 1 *small onion*
> 2 *carrots*
> 1 *tablespoon soy sauce*
> 1 *tablespoon water*
> 1 *teaspoon red wine vinegar*
> 1 *teaspoon cornstarch*
> 1 *tablespoon oil*
> 1 *slice fresh ginger*
> 1 *clove garlic*
> 1 *green bell pepper, cubed*
> ¼ *cup chopped pineapple, lichee nuts, or sliced kumquats*
> 12 *ears baby corn, husked*

Deep-Fried Walnuts

> 2 *cups whole walnuts (about 35)*
> ¼ *cup rice cream (pulverized brown rice)*
> ¼ *cup whole wheat or unbleached flour*
> 1 *tablespoon baking powder*
> 7 *tablespoons cold water*
>   *Oil for deep-frying*

Sweet and Sour Sauce

> 1 *clove garlic*
> 4 *tablespoons honey*
> 4 *tablespoons red wine vinegar*
> 3 *tablespoons Fresh Tomato Sauce (see page 15)*
> 1 *tablespoon soy sauce*
> 1 *tablespoon dry sherry*
> ½ *teaspoon kosher salt*
> ⅓ *cup water*

1. Slice onion into 1-inch pieces, and slice carrots into ¼-inch-thick rounds. Mix soy sauce, the water, vinegar, and cornstarch.

2. Heat oil in a wok or large skillet over high heat. Add ginger and garlic to flavor oil. Cook for 1 to 2 minutes, stirring constantly. Remove with slotted spoon and discard. Still over high heat, add pepper, onion, carrots, pineapple, and baby corn. Toss to keep from sticking, for about 1 minute. Add Deep-Fried Walnuts and Sweet and Sour Sauce, and toss to combine while cooking. Stir in cornstarch mixture. Cook another 30 seconds and serve.

Serves 6.

Deep-Fried Walnuts

1. Toast walnuts as described on the opposite page.

2. To prepare batter, sift together rice cream, flour, and baking powder. Stir in cold water.

3. Pour oil into a wok or deep saucepan to a depth of 3 inches and heat to 370° F. Coat toasted nuts with batter a few at a time. Carefully put coated nuts into hot oil using fork or slotted spoon. Fry for 1 minute and turn over. Cook second side for 30 seconds. Remove with slotted spoon and drain on paper towels.

Sweet and Sour Sauce Squeeze garlic through a garlic press. Mix all ingredients in a 1-quart saucepan and heat over low heat. Reserve. Sauce may be prepared and refrigerated until needed.

SUPPLI AL TELÈFONO

The center of each ball of herbed rice contains strings of melted provolone that resemble telephone wires. The Fresh Tomato Sauce complements the flavor and visual appeal of the dish.

  2 cups cooked long-grain white
     rice or arborio rice
  1 teaspoon kosher salt (if there
     is none in the cooked rice)
  ½ cup Parmesan cheese
  1 tablespoon chopped parsley
  2 tablespoons chopped basil
  3 eggs
  4 ounces provolone cheese
  ½ cup flour
  ½ cup cracker crumbs
  ¼ cup almonds, finely chopped
     Oil for deep-frying
  3 cups Fresh Tomato Sauce
     (see page 15)

1. In a 2-quart mixing bowl, combine rice, salt if used, Parmesan, parsley, basil, and one egg. Cube provolone into ½-inch pieces. Place flour in a small bowl. Beat remaining 2 eggs with 1 tablespoon water. Mix cracker crumbs with chopped almonds in a small bowl.

2. Wet your hands with cold water to prevent rice from sticking. Place about ¼ cup rice mixture in the palm of your hand. Put one cube of provolone into the center of the rice and enclose to form a ball of rice. Carefully roll each ball in flour, then in beaten egg, then in crumb-nut mixture. Place coated rice balls on a baking sheet and chill for 2 hours.

3. Heat oil to 365° F. Add rice balls and cook for 4 minutes on one side. Turn to cook 2 minutes on opposite side. The secret of deep-frying is to seal flavors into food. Therefore the temperature of the oil must be carefully watched. Only cook 2 or 3 at a time to avoid crowding rice balls in pan, which would reduce temperature of oil and allow rice to absorb oil. Keep balls warm in a 200° F oven until serving time (no more than 40 minutes) or reheat in a 350° F oven until hot (10 to 15 minutes).

4. To serve, ladle ½ cup heated Fresh Tomato Sauce on individual plates. Place two warm Suppli al Telèfono on each plate beside the sauce.

Serves 6.

BROWN RICE CASSEROLE WITH TOFU AND VEGETABLES

The nutty taste of brown rice is an excellent foil for the steamed vegetables. Tofu provides plenty of protein and carries the herb flavors.

  2¾ cups water
  1½ teaspoons kosher salt
    1 cup brown rice
    8 ounces firm tofu
    2 tablespoons soy sauce
    1 teaspoon oregano
    1 teaspoon marjoram
    1 teaspoon basil
    2 carrots
    1 bunch broccoli
    2 zucchini
   ½ pound mushrooms
    2 tablespoons oil
    1 small red onion, sliced
    2 cloves garlic, sliced
   ¼ teaspoon pepper
      Butter for preparing pan

1. In a 2-quart saucepan, bring 2½ cups water to a boil. Add 1 teaspoon salt and rice. Cover and cook for 40 to 45 minutes. Dice tofu into 1-inch cubes. Mix soy sauce, oregano, marjoram, and basil, and toss with tofu. Peel carrots and cut into ½-inch rounds. Trim broccoli florets; peel stems and cut in cubes. Cut zucchini into ½-inch slices. Wash and quarter mushrooms.

2. Preheat oven to 350° F. Heat oil in a large skillet. Add onion and garlic, and sauté for 3 to 5 minutes. Add carrots, broccoli, and remaining water. Cover and cook for 4 minutes. Stir in zucchini and mushrooms, and cook for 2 minutes.

3. Toss rice with marinated tofu, vegetables, remaining salt, and pepper. Place combination in a lightly buttered 1½-quart soufflé dish. Bake, covered, for 20 minutes. Serve immediately.

Serves 6 to 8.

BEIJING MU SHU VEGETABLES

People in the northern provinces of China plan their menus around wheat noodles and breads rather than rice. In this version of a Beijing classic, Mandarin pancakes wrap the stir-fried vegetables in much the same way as a Mexican burrito is made. In fact, packaged flour tortillas may be substituted for pancakes. Cloud ear fungus is a type of dried mushroom, and dried lily buds are the buds from the tiger lily plant. Both are available in Asian markets. Oriental sesame oil is made from toasted sesame seeds and imparts a nutty flavor not found in most supermarket oils.

  1 large carrot, peeled
  2 zucchini
  1 can (8 oz) whole bamboo
     shoots
  ¼ cup dried lily buds
  ¼ cup cloud ear dried fungus
  6 green onions
  4 leaves Napa cabbage
  4 ounces firm tofu
  ½ teaspoon kosher salt
  2 tablespoons soy sauce
  1 teaspoon sugar
  1 tablespoon sherry
  1 teaspoon Oriental sesame oil
  2 tablespoons oil
  2 eggs
  2 slices fresh ginger
  2 cloves garlic, sliced
  ½ cup minced green onions,
     for garnish
  ½ cup hoisin sauce

Mandarin Pancakes
  2 cups flour plus flour for
     dusting work surface
  ½ teaspoon kosher salt
  1 cup boiling water
     Oriental sesame oil

1. Julienne peeled carrot by slicing in ⅛- by 2-inch strips. Cut zucchini in the same way, leaving on skin. Rinse whole bamboo shoots and slice the same way. Soak lily buds and cloud ear fungus separately in ½ cup water each for 10 minutes. Trim hard ends from lily buds after soaking. Drain cloud ear fungus. Chop both into bite-sized pieces. Slice green onions

on diagonal into long, thin strips. Reserve half for garnish. Julienne leaves of Napa cabbage. Cube tofu. Mix salt, soy sauce, sugar, sherry, and sesame oil, and toss with tofu.

2. Heat 1 tablespoon of the oil in a wok. Whisk eggs in a bowl and stir into wok. Stir constantly and cook only long enough to set eggs as they will cook again. Remove from wok and reserve.

3. Heat remaining tablespoon of oil. Add sliced ginger and garlic to flavor hot oil. Cook for 1 or 2 minutes, stirring constantly. Remove from wok with slotted spoon and discard. Add carrots, zucchini, bamboo shoots, lily buds, cloud ear fungus, one half of the minced green onions, and the cabbage. Cook, stirring constantly, for about 2 minutes. Add reserved egg and tofu. Stir to mix well and cook another minute.

4. To serve, place about 2 rounded tablespoons of vegetable mixture in the center of each pancake. Sprinkle with minced green onions; drizzle with hoisin sauce. Fold to form an envelope that can be picked up and eaten. Tie with reserved onions.

Serves 8.

Mandarin Pancakes

1. Place flour and salt in a bowl. Stir in the boiling water. Mix to form a firm dough. Place dough on dusted work surface. Knead briefly. Cover with an inverted bowl for 5 minutes to cool.

2. Roll dough into a rope approximately 1½ inches in diameter. Cut rope into 16 pieces. Working with two pieces of dough at a time, flatten each piece into a small disk about 3 inches in diameter. While rolling each pancake, cover remaining dough with a towel to prevent drying. Drizzle a small amount of sesame oil on top of one disk. Place second disk over oil and press disks together. Roll layered disks into a 6-inch circle.

3. Heat an ungreased 8-inch skillet. Add layered pancakes. Cook for 3 minutes and turn over. Cook for 1 minute on second side. When properly cooked, pancakes will appear dry but not brown. Remove from pan and gently pull apart the two pancakes. Wrap in foil and place in 200° F oven to warm while you prepare remaining pancakes.

Makes 16 pancakes.

Beijing Mu Shu Vegetables are traditionally wrapped in a thin, soft Mandarin Pancake. Place stuffing, condiments, and pancakes on the table, and let diners try their hand in rolling these Asian favorites.

DIRTY RICE GUMBO

Gumbo is a peppery stew from New Orleans served over Dirty Rice. The vegetables can be varied to suit availability and your tastes but okra is traditionally included.

- 4 tomatoes
- 2 red bell peppers
- 3 carrots
- 4 small kohlrabies
- 1 head broccoli
- 8 small okra
- 2 zucchini
- 3 tablespoons oil
- 1 large onion, diced
- 2 large stalks celery, diced
- 1 small green bell pepper, diced
- 4 tablespoons flour
- 2 cups Vegetable Broth (see page 15) or water
- 1 teaspoon thyme
- 1 teaspoon oregano
- 1 cup corn kernels
- 2 cups cooked black-eyed peas

Dirty Rice

- 2½ cups long-grain white rice
- 2½ teaspoons salt
- ⅔ cup Italian parsley
- 2½ teaspoons thyme
- 1¼ teaspoons paprika
- 2½ tablespoons butter

1. Place tomatoes and red peppers under broiler or on flame of gas stove. Turn after 2 to 3 minutes, slightly charring on all sides. Dice tomatoes and peppers after they are cool enough to handle. Reserve.

2. Peel carrots and kohlrabies. Cut into 2-inch pieces. Trim broccoli, cut stems into 2-inch pieces, and separate florets. Trim ends from okra. Cut zucchini into 2-inch sections. Reserve.

3. In a large skillet, heat oil. Add diced onion, celery, and green pepper, and cook until they start to brown lightly (8 to 10 minutes). Stir in flour and cook over low heat until flour turns golden brown. Add Vegetable Broth, thyme, and oregano, stirring constantly to avoid lumps, and cook for 5 minutes.

4. Add tomatoes, red peppers, carrots, kohlrabies, and okra. Stir to combine and cook for 20 minutes. Add broccoli and cook for 5 minutes more. Add zucchini, corn kernels, and black-eyed peas, and cook another 5 to 8 minutes until heated through. Serve over Dirty Rice.

Serves 8.

Dirty Rice Bring 5 cups water to a boil in a 1½-quart saucepan. Add rice and salt. Reduce heat to simmer and cover. Cook rice for 18 minutes. Stir in parsley, thyme, paprika, and butter. Serve with gumbo.

SPINACH AND FETA CHEESE TART

The Whole Wheat Yeast Crust for this tart can be made in the morning, chilled in the refrigerator all day, and rolled out and baked for the evening meal. The strong flavors of spinach and feta complement the nuttiness of the crust.

- 2 bunches spinach (about 1 lb cleaned and stemmed)
- 8 ounces fontina cheese
- 8 ounces feta cheese
- 8 green onions, minced
- 2 eggs
- ½ cup cream
- 2 tablespoons fresh or 1 tablespoon dried mint
- ½ teaspoon kosher salt
- ¼ teaspoon pepper
- ¼ teaspoon nutmeg
- ½ cup sliced almonds (optional)

Whole Wheat Yeast Crust

- 1 package active dry yeast
- 1 tablespoon honey
- ¾ cup warm water
- 1 teaspoon kosher salt
- 6 tablespoons oil
- ¾ to 1 cup whole wheat flour
- 1 cup unbleached flour

1. Preheat the oven to 375° F.

2. Wilt spinach in a 4-quart Dutch oven or skillet by cooking 4 to 5 minutes over low heat using only water remaining on leaves after washing. Chop coarsely. Place in a 2-quart mixing bowl when cooked.

3. Shred fontina cheese using the medium shredding disk of a food processor or largest holes in a hand shredder. Add one half (about 1 cup) to spinach. Reserve remaining half.

4. Crumble feta cheese into spinach mixture. Add green onions, eggs, cream, mint, salt, pepper, and nutmeg. Stir to combine thoroughly.

5. Roll Whole Wheat Yeast Crust into a 14-inch circle. Place into an 11-inch flan ring, pushing up sides as needed.

6. Pour spinach filling into unbaked crust. Sprinkle with reserved fontina cheese. Bake for 50 to 55 minutes until top is lightly browned. Sprinkle with almonds halfway through baking time if desired.

Serves 6 as a main dish, 8 as a side dish.

Whole Wheat Yeast Crust

1. In large mixing bowl or bowl of a heavy-duty mixer, dissolve yeast with honey in ¼ cup of the water. Let rest until bubbly, about 10 minutes.

2. Add remaining water, salt, oil, whole wheat flour, and ½ cup of unbleached flour.

3. Stir by hand or knead in mixer, adding remaining flour as needed. When dough is too stiff to knead in bowl, place on well-floured work surface and knead 10 minutes by hand. If you are using a heavy-duty mixer, 5 minutes will be sufficient. Place dough in an oiled bowl and cover with plastic wrap. Let rise 2 hours at room temperature or 8 hours in refrigerator if you make dough in advance. Continue with Step 5 above.

HUEVOS RANCHEROS

Corn and beans are traditional favorites in Mexican cuisine. For centuries they have provided the complementary nutrients required for a balanced diet. The sauce may be refrigerated or frozen and warmed before serving.

1¼ cup boiling water
 1 red dried New Mexico chile
 1 green bell pepper
 2 tablespoons oil
 1 onion, finely diced
 2 cloves garlic, finely diced
 2 large tomatoes, finely diced
 ½ small jalapeño chile, minced
 1 teaspoon parsley
 1 teaspoon kosher salt
 1 tablespoon tomato paste
 3 cups Three-Bean Chile (see page 38) or one 30-oz can refried beans
 6 large flour tortillas
 6 eggs
 2 tablespoons butter
 Guacamole (optional) (see page 74)
 Cilantro, for garnish

1. Pour boiling water over New Mexico chile. Let sit for 10 to 15 minutes.

2. Slice bell pepper into strips approximately ½ inch by 2 inches. Drain water from New Mexico chile, reserving liquid, and dice.

3. In a 10-inch skillet, heat oil. Add onion and garlic, and cook briefly (about 5 minutes) before adding tomatoes, bell pepper, chiles, parsley, salt, and tomato paste. Cook sauce for 10 minutes, stirring constantly. Stir in reserved liquid from soaking New Mexico chile and simmer until sauce is heated through.

4. Preheat oven to 375° F. Heat Three-Bean Chile.

5. *To prepare tortillas:* Press each tortilla one at a time into an 8-inch-round cake pan so that the bottom of the tortilla is shaped like the pan and resembles a shallow bowl. Place into the preheated oven until slightly crisp, 6 to 8 minutes. Carefully slide from the pan onto a serving dish. Repeat with the remaining tortillas.

6. *To prepare eggs:* Eggs are traditionally cooked sunny-side up. Heat 2 tablespoons butter in a 12-inch skillet. Carefully break eggs in one at a time. Cook slowly, basting with butter, until white is barely set and yolk is still bright yellow.

7. Serve on individual plates. Layer a tortilla, ½ cup chile, a cooked egg, and ½ cup sauce. Add Guacamole if desired. Garnish with cilantro sprigs.

Serves 6.

Originally cooked by Mexican cowboys, Huevos Rancheros would make a hearty breakfast on a camping trip. Prepare the beans and sauce at home. The tortillas can be crisped, the eggs fried, and the beans and sauce reheated over a campfire.

113

The pumpkin used in Pumpkin Chile Verde can be the traditional Halloween jack-o'-lantern or a more sophisticated Perfection squash, which has a dark greenish skin and delightfully firm flesh. Store pumpkins in a cool, dark room so that you can make this recipe long after the harvest.

PUMPKIN CHILE VERDE

This sauce is an untraditional green (*verde* in Spanish) one. The spice comes from the tiny green *serrano* chile, so adjust amount to suit your palate.

  12 *fresh tomatillos* or *two 13-oz cans tomatillos*
    4 *whole poblano chiles* or *two 7-oz cans poblano chiles*
    1 *serrano chile*
 2½ *pounds fresh pumpkin or winter squash*
    2 *tablespoons oil*
    4 *cloves garlic, diced*
    2 *onions, diced*
    1 *teaspoon cumin*
    1 *teaspoon oregano*
    1 *teaspoon kosher salt*
    8 *plum tomatoes, peeled and seeded* or *one 28-oz can plum tomatoes*
    2 *cups corn kernels*
 1½ *cups kidney beans*
    2 *tablespoons cilantro, for garnish*
  ¼ *cup green pumpkin seeds, for garnish*

1. If using fresh tomatillos, remove papery husk, toast in dry skillet to slightly char. Roast and peel chiles according to instructions for Grilled Chiles Rellenos on page 50. Place tomatillos and both types of chiles in a food processor and purée. Reserve.

2. Peel and remove seeds from pumpkin and cut into 1-inch cubes. In a 4-quart saucepan or Dutch oven, heat oil and add garlic and onions. Cook for 10 minutes over low heat. Add cubes of pumpkin.

3. Stir in reserved tomatillo-chile sauce, and add cumin, oregano, and salt. Cook for 20 to 25 minutes until pumpkin is tender.

4. Drain and quarter tomatoes. Add tomatoes, corn, and kidney beans. Cook for 10 minutes more. Garnish with cilantro and pumpkin seeds.

Serves 8.

WINTER SIDE DISHES

In vegetarian cuisine, side dishes may be similar to main dishes. Try these recipes as simple luncheon entrées; serve them as first courses of multi-course meals; or use them to bolster winter main dishes when more substantial fare is required.

MUSHROOM SOUFFLÉ

This soufflé is delicious as a side dish or simple supper accompanied by a salad and fresh fruit.

    8 ounces Gruyère cheese
    5 tablespoons butter
    2 shallots, diced
    ½ onion, diced
    1 pound mushrooms, sliced
    ½ cup flour
    2 cups Vegetable Broth
      (see page 15)
    1 teaspoon kosher salt
    ½ teaspoon pepper
    ¼ teaspoon nutmeg
    ¼ cup chopped Italian parsley
    6 egg whites

1. Preheat the oven to 375° F. Using a medium shredding blade, shred Gruyère cheese. Butter a 2-quart soufflé dish using 1 tablespoon butter.

2. Melt 2 tablespoons butter in a 2-quart saucepan. Add shallots, onion, and mushrooms. Cook until softened (10 to 12 minutes). Remove from pan and reserve.

3. Using the same pan, add remaining 2 tablespoons butter and melt over medium heat. Whisk in flour and cook for 3 to 4 minutes. Add Vegetable Broth and stir until sauce thickens. Return mushroom mixture to pan. Season with salt, pepper, nutmeg, parsley, and cheese. Let cool slightly.

4. In large mixing bowl, beat egg whites until stiff. Stir one third of the whites into mushroom mixture. Using a rubber spatula, fold remaining two thirds of the whites into mushroom

mixture. Pour carefully into prepared soufflé dish. Bake for 35 to 40 minutes. Serve immediately.

Serves 8.

SPICY MOROCCAN CARROTS

These carrots taste wonderful served either hot or at room temperature.

    4 carrots
    1 teaspoon cumin
    ⅛ teaspoon dried red chiles
    2 tablespoons olive oil
    ¼ cup water
    ½ teaspoon kosher salt
    3 tablespoons vinegar
    1 teaspoon dried mint

Peel and cut carrots into 1½-inch slices. In an 8-inch skillet, toast cumin seeds for 2 to 3 minutes over medium heat. Add carrots, chiles, oil, the water, salt, vinegar, and mint. Reduce heat, cover, and cook for 10 to 12 minutes.

Serves 6 to 8.

ROASTED ONIONS WITH BALSAMIC VINEGAR

Balsamic vinegar is a pungent, almost sweet, aged vinegar. It adds a special flavor to the roasted onions. Serve with pasta dishes.

    3 red onions
    1 clove garlic, minced
    4 tablespoons balsamic vinegar
    4 tablespoons olive oil
    ¼ teaspoon kosher salt
    ⅛ teaspoon pepper

1. Leaving root end attached, slice onions in half lengthwise. Peel papery skin off onion. In 9- by 12-inch baking pan, mix garlic with 2 tablespoons of the vinegar, oil, salt, and pepper to make a marinade. Add onions. Toss marinade with onions. Let sit for 1 hour.

2. Preheat oven to 350° F. Bake onions in marinade for 1¼ hours. Onions are done when a knife inserted into center meets no resistance. Remove from oven to a serving dish and sprinkle with remaining vinegar.

Serves 6.

ACORN SQUASH AND CREAMED SPINACH

Creamed spinach, nestled in an acorn-squash shell, is an eye-appealing presentation. The creamed spinach can be prepared early in the day and stored in the refrigerator. Cut, clean, and bake the acorn squash about an hour before serving. At the last minute simply combine for an elegant side dish.

    1 large acorn squash
    1 bunch spinach
    1 tablespoon butter
    1 onion, finely diced
    1 teaspoon kosher salt
    ¼ teaspoon pepper
    ½ teaspoon nutmeg
    1 cup cream

1. Preheat oven to 350° F. Cut squash in half and scoop out seeds. Seeds may be washed and dried in oven for 30 minutes to serve as a snack. Place squash cut side down on a foil-lined baking sheet and bake for 50 to 60 minutes.

2. Clean spinach and place in a salad spinner or paper towels to dry.

3. Heat butter in a 3-quart saucepan on medium heat. Add onion and cook for 8 minutes, stirring to prevent burning. Add spinach, salt, pepper, and half of the nutmeg. Stir to combine well and add cream. Reduce heat to a simmer and cook for 15 minutes.

4. Squash should be done when a knife inserted into flesh meets no resistance. Cut each piece in thirds and place some of the creamed spinach over each piece. Dust with reserved nutmeg.

Serves 6.

VIETNAMESE ROLLS

Wrappers made of rice flour are one feature that distinguishes these Vietnamese Rolls from other kinds of egg rolls. If rice-flour wrappers are not available, traditional wrappers made of wheat flour may be substituted. Vietnamese Rolls make a delicious luncheon dish when served with Spicy Carrot Salad (see page 103), or they may be used as a first course to any meal.

> 2 cups Chinese cabbage, thinly sliced
> ½ teaspoon kosher salt
> ½ cup tree ear fungus
> ½ pound bean sprouts
> 2 tablespoons soy sauce
> 2 tablespoons water
> 2 teaspoons cornstarch
> 8 ounces firm tofu
> 1 tablespoon oil
> 2 carrots, peeled and julienned
> 1 small onion, thinly sliced
> 1 cup bamboo shoots, julienned
> 4 large rice-flour wrappers
>   or 16 wheat-flour wrappers
>   Oil for deep-frying
> 16 small lettuce leaves

1. Place cabbage in a colander, and sprinkle with salt. Leave for 20 minutes, then rinse, drain, and pat dry. Soak tree ear fungus in water for 10 minutes to rehydrate. Remove string-like tails from bean sprouts. Mix together soy sauce, the water, and cornstarch. Slice tofu into strips ½ inch by 2 inches.

2. Heat oil in a wok or large skillet. Add carrots, cabbage, tree ear fungus, onion, bean sprouts, and bamboo shoots. Toss and cook over high heat for 1 to 2 minutes. Add soy-cornstarch mixture and tofu, and stir to cook for another 30 seconds. Remove to a bowl and cool.

3. Quarter rice-flour wrappers or use whole spring roll wrapper. Place a rounded tablespoon of filling on each wrapper. Roll wrapper to enclose filling, tucking in ends as you roll. Brush edge with water and press to seal. Reserve until all are completed.

4. Pour oil in a wok or deep saucepan to a depth of 3 inches. Heat to 370° F. Add one or two spring rolls at a time and cook for 2 minutes on the first side. Turn and cook for 1 minute on the other side. Drain on paper towels. Serve in a lettuce leaf.

Serves 8.

YAM AND TANGERINE CASSEROLE

The spectacular orange of the yams and tangerines is not only a colorful addition to the dinner plate but contributes bountiful amounts of vitamins A and C.

> 3 pounds yams
> 3 tangerines
> 4 tablespoons butter
> ¼ cup brown sugar
> ½ teaspoon kosher salt
> ¼ teaspoon nutmeg
> ¼ teaspoon cinnamon

1. Preheat oven to 375° F. Wash yams. Pierce in several places and put into preheated oven for 50 to 60 minutes depending on size. They are done when a knife inserted into center meets no resistance.

2. While yams are baking, peel tangerines, pull apart sections, remove seeds, and discard seeds and peel.

3. Cut yams in half and scoop out interior. Place into a food mill set over a 2-quart mixing bowl. Purée through food mill. Add seeded tangerine sections and purée with yams.

4. Stir in butter, sugar, salt, nutmeg, and cinnamon. If not served immediately, place combination in an ovenproof serving dish and cover with aluminum foil. At serving time reheat in a 350° F oven for 35 minutes until warmed through.

Serves 8.

WINTER VEGETABLE PÂTÉ

The combination of these readily available vegetables makes this beautiful tricolor pâté simple to prepare in any season.

> Oil for preparing pan
> 1 pound carrots
> 1 pound cauliflower
> 3 large potatoes
> 5 tablespoons butter
> 2 bunches spinach
> 6 eggs
> 1¼ teaspoon kosher salt
> 1 teaspoon pepper
> ½ teaspoon nutmeg
> 2 tablespoons brown sugar
> 1 tablespoon fresh or 1 teaspoon dried dill weed
> ¼ cup Parmesan cheese

1. Preheat oven to 350° F. Lightly oil a 5- by 9-inch loaf pan.

2. Peel and cut carrots into 2-inch lengths. Chop cauliflower into 2-inch sections. Peel and cube potatoes into 2-inch pieces.

3. Using a 10-inch skillet, heat 1 tablespoon butter. Add carrots and one third of the potatoes. Cook for 5 minutes over medium heat. Add ¼ cup water. Cover tightly and steam for 20 to 25 minutes. Drain liquid and reserve vegetables.

4. Heat another tablespoon of butter in skillet. Add cauliflower and the second third of potatoes. Heat for 5 minutes over medium heat. Add ¼ cup of water. Cover tightly and steam for 20 to 25 minutes. Drain liquid and reserve vegetables separately from carrot mixture.

5. Place last third of potatoes in skillet over medium heat. Add ¼ cup water. Cover tightly and steam for 10 minutes. Wash spinach but do not pat dry. Chop coarsely. Place spinach in skillet with potatoes and steam, stirring occasionally, until spinach is wilted (about 10 minutes).

6. In a food mill placed over a 2-quart mixing bowl, purée cauliflower-potato mixture with 2 eggs, ½ teaspoon salt, ¼ teaspoon pepper, 3 tablespoons butter, and nutmeg. Reserve.

7. Place food mill over a second bowl and purée carrot-potato mixture. Stir in 2 eggs, brown sugar, ½ teaspoon salt, ¼ teaspoon pepper, and dill. Pour into prepared loaf pan to cover the bottom. Carefully pour cauliflower mixture over carrot mixture.

8. Place food mill over a third bowl. Purée spinach-potato mixture. Stir in cheese and remaining 2 eggs, ¼ teaspoon salt, and ½ teaspoon pepper. Carefully pour spinach mixture over cauliflower mixture. Place loaf pan in a 9- by 12-inch baking pan. Fill baking pan with hot water to a depth of 2 inches. (This will allow loaf to have the texture of custard.) Place combined pans in preheated oven and bake for 55 minutes. The pâté is done when a knife inserted in center remains clean when removed.

9. Cool for 10 minutes. Slip knife around edges of loaf. Place serving dish over loaf and invert to remove loaf from pan.

Serves 12.

GRITS SOUFFLÉ

Grits are the dried and ground kernels of white corn, or hominy, and are a staple of many breakfasts. Follow directions for regular grits or use the instructions below for quick-cooking grits. Serve with Pumpkin Chile Verde (see page 114).

> *Butter for greasing dish*
> 1 *cup quick-cooking grits*
> 5 *cloves garlic, minced*
> ¾ *pound Cheddar cheese, shredded*
> 1 *teaspoon kosher salt*
> ¼ *teaspoon white pepper*
> 2 *eggs*

1. Preheat oven to 325° F. Butter a 1½-quart soufflé dish.

2. Bring 4 cups water to boil in a 1½-quart saucepan. Slowly stir in grits. Cover and cook for 5 to 6 minutes.

3. When grits are cooked, add garlic, cheese, salt, pepper, and eggs. Stir and pour into prepared soufflé dish. Bake for 45 to 55 minutes.

Serves 8.

Puréed carrots layered with calcium-rich broccoli and cauliflower make an attractive do-ahead side dish. Serve Winter Vegetable Pâté on crackers or bread as an appetizer or late-night snack.

WINTER BREADS

Nothing is quite as cozy as a warm kitchen and the seductive smell of bread baking. Winter is the time to experiment with whole grains, longer techniques, and breakfast pastries.

CARROT AND ORANGE BREAD

Whether this quick bread is served for breakfast or for afternoon tea, the orange adds a refreshing and nutritious touch.

> Butter and flour for
> preparing pan
> 1 orange
> 3 carrots
> 1 cup brown sugar
> ¾ cup oil
> 2 eggs
> 1 cup whole wheat flour
> 2½ cups unbleached flour
> 1 tablespoon cinnamon
> 2 teaspoons baking powder
> 1 teaspoon kosher salt
> ½ teaspoon mace
> ½ teaspoon vanilla extract
> ½ cup raisins (optional)

1. Preheat oven to 375° F. Butter and flour a 5- by 9-inch loaf pan.

2. Peel orange and discard bitter white membrane; finely chop both orange and rind. Peel and shred carrots. In a large mixing bowl, mix sugar, oil, and eggs. Sift flours, cinnamon, baking powder, salt, and mace. Add orange and vanilla to sugar mixture. Stir in flour mixture, the carrots, and raisins (if used). Pour into prepared pan and bake for 1¼ hours. Slice bread and serve with butter or cream cheese.

Makes 1 large loaf.

WHOLE WHEAT CROISSANTS

Simple to prepare in stages, these croissants require only a few minutes at each step. Wrapped in an airtight container, the dough or baked croissants can be frozen for one month so that you can have fresh croissants whenever you want.

> 1 package active dry yeast
> 1½ tablespoons honey
> ½ cup water, heated to 100° F
> ½ cup milk
> 2 tablespoons corn oil
> 1 cup whole wheat flour
> ½ tablespoon kosher salt
> 1⅓ cups bread flour
> 7 ounces unsalted butter, room
> temperature
> 3 tablespoons flour plus flour
> for dusting work surface
> 1 egg mixed with 1 tablespoon
> water, for glaze

1. Place yeast, honey, and the water in a 4-quart mixing bowl. Yeast is active or proofed when it bubbles gently after 10 to 15 minutes.

2. Add milk and oil. Stir to combine.

3. Stir in whole wheat flour and salt. Mix well. Add enough bread flour to form a soft dough. It may be easier to incorporate the last cup of bread flour on work surface rather than in mixing bowl. Knead only until flour is mixed into dough. Place dough in 3-quart mixing bowl; cover with plastic wrap and chill for 2 hours.

4. While dough is chilling, mix butter with 3 tablespoons flour. Wrap in plastic and chill 20 minutes or leave at room temperature if room is cooler than 65° F.

5. Remove chilled dough from refrigerator and place on lightly floured work surface. Roll dough into a rectangle approximately 8 inches by 16 inches. Place pieces of butter over two thirds of the dough. Fold unbuttered third of dough over adjacent buttered third, and remaining third onto both layers to form three layers. This process is similar to folding a business letter. Press edges together to seal in butter. Wrap dough in foil and return to refrigerator for 20 to 30 minutes.

6. Turn dough so that it is lengthwise on the work surface. Roll dough again to appproximately 8 inches by 16 inches. Fold into thirds as if folding a letter. Repeat the folding and rolling three more times, chilling dough for 20 minutes after each series of folds. It may be necessary to flour board lightly again between rolling and folding. Brush excess flour from dough before folding.

7. Wrap dough airtight and chill for 4 hours or longer. Dough may be frozen to use later.

8. To shape croissants, roll dough to a square about 15 inches by 15 inches. Cut dough in half across width and in thirds across length to make six rectangles about 5 inches by 7 inches. Cut each rectangle along the diagonal to make 12 triangle-shaped pieces of dough. Gently pull the narrow ends to make a isosceles triangle. Starting at wide end, slowly roll each triangle into a crescent shape. Tuck tip of croissant under itself. Place rolled crescents on a parchment-lined baking sheet to rise for 1 hour in a cool place.

9. Preheat oven to 400° F 30 minutes before rising is through. Brush tops of each crescent with beaten egg glaze. Cook in preheated oven for 18 minutes. Cool on a wire rack a few minutes before serving. Wrap croissants to be frozen in an airtight container. Reheat in 350° F oven for 10 minutes.

Makes 1 dozen croissants.

Cinnamon Croissants Combine 4 tablespoons melted butter and ¼ cup sugar mixed with 2 teaspoons cinnamon. Just before rolling into crescent shapes, brush with melted butter and cinnamon-sugar.

Blue Cheese and Almond Croissants Combine 2 ounces blue cheese with 4 tablespoons softened butter. Just before rolling into crescent shapes, spread with blue cheese-butter mixture, then continue as directed in step 8. Sprinkle with ¼ cup sliced, toasted almonds before baking.

NORA SHAUGHNESSY'S POTATO PECAN ROLLS

The potato in this recipe helps to create a lighter-than-air dough that can also be used for dinner rolls.

- 1 large potato, peeled
- ¼ cup water
- 1 package active dry yeast
- 1 tablespoon honey
- 1 egg
- ¼ cup milk
- 10 tablespoons brown sugar
- 2 teaspoons kosher salt
- ½ cup whole wheat flour
- 2 cups unbleached flour plus flour for kneading and dusting
- ½ tablespoon cinnamon
- ½ tablespoon cocoa
- 3 tablespoons butter
- 1 tablespoon water
- ½ cup chopped pecans

1. Place raw peeled potato in small saucepan and cover with water. Bring to a boil and reduce heat to a simmer. Cook for 20 to 25 minutes. Reserve ½ cup potato water and let it cool to 100° F. Mash potato.

2. Mix the ¼ cup water, yeast, and honey in small bowl.

3. In large bowl or bowl of a heavy-duty mixer, stir together potato water, yeast-honey mixture, egg, milk, 2 tablespoons brown sugar, salt, whole wheat flour, 2 cups unbleached flour, and mashed potatoes.

4. Beat vigorously to create a smooth dough (about 5 to 10 minutes). Add flour as necessary. Place dough on lightly floured work surface and knead for 5 minutes until dough is smooth and elastic. Place in a lightly oiled bowl, cover, and let rise in a cool place for 1 hour.

5. Heat remaining brown sugar, cinnamon, cocoa, butter, and water in small saucepan. Stir to melt sugar. Cool. Stir in pecans.

6. Punch down dough by kneading gently on lightly floured work surface. Roll to a rectangle approximately 10 inches by 16 inches by ½ inch thick. Spread pecan mixture on sheet of dough, leaving a 1-inch border of dough. Roll up from narrow end, jelly-roll fashion. Brush bottom edge with water. Press gently to seal.

7. Cut roll into eight sections approximately 2 inches wide. Place pieces, cut side down, in a 9- by 12-inch rectangular baking pan. Cover loosely with a towel and let rise for 40 minutes. Preheat oven to 375° F.

8. Bake for 22 to 24 minutes. Turn upside down onto a serving dish. Let cool for 5 minutes before serving.

Makes 8 large rolls.

Dinner Rolls Prepare dough as directed up to step 4. Preheat oven. Omit filling ingredients with the exception of chopped pecans. Punch down dough, adding in chopped pecans. Shape into eight balls. Place on baking sheet and let rise, loosely covered, for 35 minutes. Bake for 22 minutes.

Serve Nora Shaughnessy's Potato Pecan Rolls with a brisk cup of Irish tea for a special breakfast or as a treat to fight back the gloom of a chilly afternoon.

PANFORTE

Panforte is a cross between a dessert and a candy. It can be served in tiny pieces accompanied by a cup of espresso after dinner. It also makes an excellent present for those on your gift list who love sweets.

> ½ *pound whole almonds*
> ½ *pound whole filberts*
> 6 *ounces dried figs*
> 5 *ounces raisins*
> 5 *ounces golden raisins*
>   *Rind of whole orange*
>   *Rind of whole lemon*
> ½ *cup flour*
> ¼ *cup cocoa*
> 2 *teaspoons cinnamon*
> ⅛ *teaspoon white pepper*
> ⅛ *teaspoon mace*
> ¾ *cup honey*
> ½ *cup sugar*
>   *Juice from whole orange*
> ½ *cup confectioners' sugar*

1. Preheat oven to 350° F. Toast almonds and filberts on baking sheet for 10 to 15 minutes. Remove from oven and cool. Reduce oven temperature to 300° F. Line an 8- by 8-inch baking pan with aluminum foil.

2. *If using a food processor:* Place figs, raisins, golden raisins, and orange and lemon rinds into food processor. Mix ingredients and process to purée. *If processing manually:* On a cutting board, finely chop figs, raisins, golden raisins, orange and lemon rinds to a paste. Place mixture into a mixing bowl and stir to combine.

3. Sift together flour, cocoa, cinnamon, pepper, and mace. Add to dried fruit purée or mixture.

4. In a 1-quart saucepan, heat honey, sugar, and orange juice until sugar dissolves. Carefully pour hot liquid into dried fruit and flour mixture. Add toasted nuts and stir to combine. Place fruit and nut mixture into prepared baking pan. Bake in preheated oven 50 to 55 minutes.

Panforte also makes a special holiday gift. Quarter and wrap each section in colorful cellophane and deliver on a pretty plate or together with a pound of espresso-ground coffee.

WINTER DESSERTS

Sweet things are not necessarily bad for you. Desserts can bring a much-needed vitamin balance to the winter diet. Citrus fruits, offering essential vitamin C, are at their peak in winter months. Figs, raisins, prunes, pears, and apples, as well as dried apricots, are also plentiful. And of course nuts, such as roasted chestnuts, have long been a traditional part of the approaching winter holidays. Decorate a winter table with a centerpiece of apples, oranges, pears, and walnuts. After dinner, pass out knives and nutcrackers, and let diners choose their preferred dessert from this fruit "bouquet." These simple foods become a festive finale.

120

5. Cool in pan 10 minutes. While panforte cools, dust a 12-inch square of foil with ¼ cup confectioners' sugar. Turn panforte upside down onto coated foil and peel back foil used to line pan. Dust top with remaining ¼ cup confectioners' sugar. Cool completely.

6. Cut into 1-inch squares and serve immediately. Cut into quarters, cover in plastic wrap, and tie with ribbon to give as a gift.

Makes 32 bite-sized pieces or 4 squares for gift giving.

BANANAS EN PAPILLOTES

These bananas are baked *en papillote*—steamed in paper. A simpler substitute for the paper is aluminum foil, tightly sealed so that no juices escape. The light flavor is refreshing after a hearty winter meal.

> *1 vanilla bean*
> *3 bananas*
> *3 oranges*
> *6 tablespoons orange-flavored liqueur or orange juice*
> *2 tablespoons vanilla yogurt*

1. Cut vanilla bean into six pieces. Preheat oven to 400° F.

2. Slice bananas in half crosswise and then each piece in half lengthwise. Peel, section, and seed oranges. Discard peel and seeds.

3. Cut six 12-inch squares of aluminum foil. Place two lengths of banana, three orange sections, and one piece of vanilla bean on each piece of foil. Pour 1 tablespoon liqueur and place 1 teaspoon yogurt on top of each pile of fruit.

4. Tightly seal foil and place each package on a baking sheet. Bake for 6 to 7 minutes. Warm serving plates in oven for last minute.

5. Open packages. Remove foil and place fruit on warmed serving plates. Serve immediately.

Serves 6.

JOHN'S CINNAMON BUTTERMILK CAKE

Fresh fruit complements the simple sweetness of this cake. Instant buttermilk or 1 teaspoon distilled vinegar added to 1 cup milk is an adequate substitute for buttermilk.

> *Butter and flour for preparing pan*
> *½ cup butter*
> *½ cup sugar*
> *½ cup brown sugar*
> *1 egg*
> *2 teaspoons vanilla extract*
> *2 cups cake flour*
> *1 teaspoon baking soda*
> *½ teaspoon kosher salt*
> *1 cup buttermilk*
> *½ tablespoon cinnamon*
> *¼ cup sugar*

1. Preheat oven to 375° F. Butter and flour an 8- by 8-inch square pan or an 8-inch round pan.

2. In a 3-quart mixing bowl, cream butter, ½ cup sugar, and ½ cup brown sugar until light and fluffy. Add egg and vanilla. Sift flour, baking soda, and salt. Mix one third of the flour into sugar-egg mixture. Stir in one half of the buttermilk. Add another third of the sifted flour, then the remaining buttermilk, and finally the remaining one third flour. Mix cinnamon with the ¼ cup sugar. Pour batter into prepared pan and sprinkle with cinnamon-sugar mixture. Bake for 45 minutes in square pan or 55 minutes in round pan.

Makes one cake.

Orange Buttermilk Cake To basic batter, add minced rind of one orange. Bake cake as directed. For a glaze topping, heat together juice of the orange, ¼ cup sugar, and 2 tablespoons butter. Pour mixture over cake hot from the oven.

Walnut Cake To basic batter, add ½ teaspoon finely chopped lemon rind, 1 teaspoon almond extract, and 1 cup toasted walnuts. Bake as directed above. Dust with confectioners' sugar before serving.

PEAR TATIN TART

Use the oil pastry recipe from the Cherry–Nectarine Pie (see page 67) or a purchased pie shell for this delicious tart. Serve it warm from the oven with ice cream or Almond Crème Fraîche on the side.

> *4 pears*
> *¼ cup unsalted butter*
> *½ cup sugar*
> *¼ cup honey*
> *½ lemon, juiced*
> *Oil pastry from Cherry–Nectarine Pie (see page 67)*

Almond Crème Fraîche

> *1 cup crème fraîche*
> *1 tablespoon almond liqueur or 1 teaspoon almond extract*
> *4 tablespoons almonds, toasted and chopped*

1. Preheat oven to 400° F.

2. Peel pears. Remove stem. Cut in half lengthwise and core with melon ball cutter or sharp knife.

3. In an 8-inch ovenproof pan, melt butter. Add sugar, honey, and lemon juice. Stir to mix ingredients. Cook about 5 minutes over low heat until translucent.

4. Add pears, core side up, stem end toward center. Cook 30 minutes on stove top over medium heat.

5. Roll pastry into an 8-inch circle and place it in pan, over pears. Bake immediately in preheated oven until crust is lightly browned (25 minutes).

6. Let tart cool for 15 minutes on a cooling rack. Place a large serving dish over pan and invert to unmold tart. Do not let tart cool completely before removing from baking pan or sugar will cause it to stick to pan. Cut in wedges to serve.

Serves 6.

Almond Crème Fraîche Stir gently to combine all ingredients. Chill until served.

All guests will be thankful for this meal. This vegetarian version of the traditional holiday feast is a lovely tribute to the bounty of winter's harvest.

menu

HOLIDAY FEAST

Whole-Grain Bread

Pear and Broccoli Soup

Blue Cheese Crackers

Tunisian Stew

Wild Mushroom Ragout

Pumpkin Mousse

Parisian Compote

Beverage Suggestion:
Sparkling Apple Cider

A festive family-style dinner is a good way to introduce nonvegetarian friends to the variety of a menu without meat. Here is a colorful array of elegant foods that can be prepared in several stages. All recipes serve eight.

NUTRIENT BREAKDOWN	
Calories	1,980
(Without dessert	1,220)
Protein	30 gm
Fiber	11 gm
Cholesterol	329 gm
Vitamin C	265 mg
Calcium	417 mg
Sodium	2,900 mg

WHOLE-GRAIN BREAD

Start this recipe three days before baking by rinsing and soaking the wheat berries. Without the long soaking, wheat berries would be too hard to eat. They should just begin to sprout when they are mixed into dough. Wheat berries may be substituted with ¾ cup whole wheat flour to create a different type of bread.

> 1 cup wheat berries
> 1 package active dry yeast
> 2 cups warm water
> 2 tablespoons honey
> ¼ cup powdered milk
> 3 tablespoons oil
> 1 tablespoon kosher salt
> ¼ cup soy flour
> ¼ cup brown rice flour or rice cream
> ¼ cup cornmeal
> 1 cup whole wheat flour
> 4½ to 5 cups unbleached flour
> 1 egg
> 2 tablespoons water

1. Three days before baking place wheat berries in a small bowl and cover with boiling water. Let rest overnight. On day 2 drain berries and cover with boiling water again. On day 3 drain and pat dry.

2. In a large mixing bowl, dissolve yeast in ½ cup of the warm water (not to exceed 100° F). Add honey and let rest 10 minutes. Add remaining 1½ cups water, powdered milk, oil, salt, soy flour, rice flour, cornmeal, whole wheat flour, and wheat berries. Stir vigorously for 5 minutes. Slowly stir in unbleached flour until dough holds its shape and does not stick to sides of bowl. If dough is too difficult to stir, lightly flour work surface and knead in the last of the flour. Dough should be supple and elastic and not stick to your hands. Place in a lightly oiled mixing bowl, cover with plastic wrap, and let rise in a cool place until dough has doubled (about 1 hour).

3. After rising, punch down dough and cut in half. Shape dough into 2 loaves to fit 4½- by 8½-inch loaf pans. Let rise for 45 minutes. At the end of this second rising, preheat oven to 375° F.

4. Beat egg with the 2 tablespoons water in a small bowl. Brush over tops of loaves. Place in oven and bake for 55 to 60 minutes. Remove from pans and place on racks to cool. Loaves are done when bottoms sound hollow when tapped.

Makes 2 loaves.

PEAR AND BROCCOLI SOUP

Any pear may be used for this soup, but the red Bartlett pears of winter are particularly good. Broccoli adds necessary nutrients and color. Remember to reserve some of the florets to garnish the puréed base.

> 2 heads broccoli
> 6 red Bartlett pears
> 4 tablespoons butter
> 2 onions, finely diced
> 3 cloves garlic, minced
> 8 cups Vegetable Broth (see page 15)
> 1 tablespoon kosher salt
> 1¼ teaspoon rosemary
> Juice of 1½ lemons

1. Cut broccoli florets from stem and reserve 1½ cups for garnish. Chop remaining broccoli florets. Peel broccoli stems and cut into 1-inch cubes. Peel and core 4 pears and cut into 1-inch cubes.

2. Heat butter in a 3-quart saucepan. Add onion and garlic. Cook for 5 minutes, until lightly colored. Add chopped broccoli florets, stems, and cubed pears. Stir to combine and add Vegetable Broth.

3. Bring mixture to a boil and reduce heat. Add salt and rosemary. Simmer for 30 minutes.

4. Wash and quarter the remaining pears, leaving the skin on, and cut into 1-inch cubes. When soup is done, remove from heat and place one half in a food processor. Purée. Remove to a bowl and reserve. Purée the second half. Return to the saucepan. Add lemon juice, florets, and unpeeled pear cubes. Cook until broccoli florets are tender but still remain bright green, another 6 to 8 minutes.

BLUE CHEESE CRACKERS

You'll need a food processor to prepare this dough. The crackers are best eaten just out of the oven. The dough can be prepared ahead of time, frozen, sliced at serving time, and popped into the oven as guests arrive. The secret of their crispness is in thinly slicing the rounds of dough.

1 cup flour
½ teaspoon kosher salt
2 cloves garlic
⅛ teaspoon cayenne pepper
2 tablespoons Parmesan cheese
4 ounces blue cheese
6 tablespoons cold butter
6 tablespoons water
1 egg
¼ cup finely chopped almonds

1. Place flour, salt, garlic, cayenne, and Parmesan in a food processor. Turn on and off to combine. Add blue cheese and butter. Turn on and off to combine. Add 3 to 4 tablespoons of the water gradually, with machine running. Stop machine when dough holds together.

2. Roll dough into a cylinder about 1½ inches in diameter, and wrap it in aluminum foil. Chill for 2 hours, or freeze if serving at another time.

3. Preheat oven to 400° F when ready to bake. Beat egg with 2 tablespoons of the water to form an egg wash. Brush half the egg wash onto the exterior of the cylinder of dough. Roll in almonds. Slice into rounds of dough about ¼ inch thick. Place on a parchment-lined baking sheet. Brush circles with remaining egg wash.

4. Bake for 12 to 14 minutes. Cool on a baking rack.

TUNISIAN STEW

This lavish and colorful stew is served with couscous, a Middle Eastern steamed wheat. Both the grain and the stew may be prepared well ahead of the guests' arrival and simply reheated at the last minute. Traditionally, the stew cooks in the bottom of a special *couscousière* surrounding a whole chicken, while the grains steam over it. You may prepare the stew in one pan and cook the wheat grains separately. If you prefer to use instant couscous, just follow the instructions on the package and begin this recipe at step 2.

4 cups couscous
½ cup butter
3 tablespoon kosher salt
1 pumpkin (2½ lb)
6 small boiling potatoes
6 carrots
4 tablespoons oil
4 onions, finely diced
2 cloves garlic, minced
2 teaspoons black pepper
2 teaspoons cayenne or red pepper
1 teaspoon saffron
1 teaspoon turmeric
2 tablespoons fresh ginger
2 tablespoons cinnamon
6 cups water
3 zucchini
3 yellow zucchini
12 ounces garbanzo beans, cooked
6 ounces raisins

Spicy Harissa

½ teaspoon cumin seed
¼ teaspoon coriander seed
1 clove garlic, minced
½ cup Vegetable Broth (see page 15)
1 tablespoon olive oil
½ teaspoon parsley
½ teaspoon cilantro
⅛ teaspoon cayenne pepper
¼ teaspoon kosher salt

1. Rinse couscous under running water. Let soak in 8 cups of water for 30 minutes. Place couscous on a baking sheet or tray, and pat dry with paper towels. Rub grains together to remove any lumps. Line a colander or deep steamer with cheesecloth, add soaked couscous, place colander over a 4-quart pot of boiling water, and steam uncovered for 30 minutes. If colander and pan do not fit together tightly, you may have to tie cheesecloth around the bottom of the colander to form a seal. The goal is to have the grains swell as large as possible without becoming lumpy or soggy. When couscous is cooked, place on a platter and spread out. Toss with 2 tablespoons of the butter and 1 teaspoon of the salt. Stir to remove any lumps. Serve immediately. If preparing ahead, cover loosely with foil and refrigerate.

2. *To prepare stew:* Peel pumpkin, remove and discard seeds, and cut meat into 2-inch pieces. Peel potatoes and carrots and cut into 2-inch pieces.

3. In a large stockpot, heat 4 tablespoons each of butter and oil. Add onions and garlic. Sauté for 5 minutes, and add remaining salt, pepper, cayenne, saffron, turmeric, ginger, and cinnamon. Cook 2 to 3 minutes, and add pumpkin, potatoes, and carrots. Add the water and bring to a boil. Reduce heat and simmer for 15 minutes. Refrigerate if you are not serving immediately.

4. To serve, steam couscous for 20 minutes to reheat. Bring stew to boil and reduce heat to a simmer. Cube all zucchini into 1½-inch sections, and add with garbanzo beans and raisins to stew. Continue cooking for 5 to 8 minutes.

5. Put couscous into a large shallow bowl or platter, and toss with the remaining 2 tablespoons butter to remove any lumps. Place stew in the center of the couscous. Serve with Spicy Harissa as a condiment.

Spicy Harissa Toast cumin and coriander seeds in a small skillet over medium heat. Place all the ingredients in blender and purée. Store in refrigerator until needed. Serve as a condiment.

Makes ½ cup.

WILD MUSHROOM RAGOUT

The intensity of this dish will depend on the combination of various mushrooms. If the more unusual mushrooms are not available, use 2 pounds of domestic mushrooms and the optional dried mushrooms.

- ½ ounce dried mushrooms (optional)
- 1½ cup boiling water, for the dried mushrooms
- 1 pound domestic mushrooms
- 1 pound assorted wild mushrooms (chanterelle, boletus, hedgehog, oyster, and shiitake)
- 4 tablespoons butter
- 2 medium onions, finely chopped
- 4 cloves garlic, finely chopped
- 2 teaspoons kosher salt
- ¼ teaspoon white pepper
- ⅛ teaspoon nutmeg
- ¼ cup minced chives, for garnish

1. If adding dried mushrooms, place in small bowl and cover with the water for 20 minutes. Quarter domestic mushrooms, if large, and slice wild mushrooms about ½ inch thick.

2. Heat butter in a 2-quart saucepan. Add onions and garlic, and cook over medium heat until onions are translucent (about 5 minutes). Add fresh mushrooms. Drain dried mushrooms, slice if whole, and add. Season mixture with salt, pepper, and nutmeg. Reduce heat to low and cook for 25 minutes. Sprinkle with chives at serving time.

PUMPKIN MOUSSE

Buy a pumpkin on sale after Halloween, and save it for this dessert. Serve mousse from a stemmed goblet or from the Walnut Crumb Crust described here.

- 1 pumpkin (3 lb)
- 1 package unflavored gelatin
- 2 tablespoons water
- 1 tablespoon butter
- ½ cup brown sugar
- 4 tablespoons honey
- 1 tablespoon cinnamon
- 1 teaspoon nutmeg
- ¼ teaspoon cloves
- ¼ teaspoon allspice
- ¼ teaspoon kosher salt
- 3 tablespoons dark rum or orange juice
- 1 cup heavy cream
- ½ cup heavy cream, for garnish (optional)
- 2 tablespoons confectioners' sugar, for garnish (optional)

Walnut Crumb Crust

- 1 cup pulverized vanilla-cookie crumbs
- 3 tablespoons melted butter
- ⅓ cup pulverized walnuts
- ½ teaspoon cinnamon
- ⅛ teaspoon nutmeg

Glacéed Walnuts

- 8 whole walnuts, shelled
- 1 tablespoon butter
- ¼ cup sugar
- 2 tablespoons water

1. Peel and seed pumpkin and cut into 2-inch pieces. Place in a 4-quart saucepan and cover with water. Bring to boil and cook until tender when pierced with the tip of a knife (about 30 minutes). Dissolve gelatin in 2 tablespoons water.

2. Drain pumpkin in a colander, then place in blender or food processor. Add butter, brown sugar, honey, cinnamon, nutmeg, cloves, allspice, salt, and rum. Purée. Stir in dissolved gelatin. Cool to room temperature.

3. Whip the 1 cup of cream so that it forms soft peaks. Fold into pumpkin mixture. Pour into serving glasses or Walnut Crumb Crust, and chill for 5 to 6 hours. Whip optional cream with confectioners' sugar. Garnish with Glacéed Walnuts.

Walnut Crumb Crust Combine all the ingredients in a 1-quart mixing bowl. Press into a 9-inch springform pan and chill for 30 minutes.

Glacéed Walnuts Toast walnuts as described on page 108. Lightly butter baking sheet. In a 1-quart saucepan, combine sugar with water. Stir to dissolve sugar. Cook until light brown, at about 250° F on a candy thermometer. Carefully add walnuts, taking care not to splash hot sugar syrup. Stir to coat nuts. Place individual nuts on prepared baking sheet to cool. Store in an airtight tin.

PARISIAN COMPOTE

Quince are the "golden apples" of Greek mythology given by Paris to the goddess Aphrodite as a symbol of love. Try their tart flavor in recipes otherwise made with apples or pears.

- 3 pears
- 3 quince or Golden Delicious apples
- 1 cup water
- ½ cup white wine
- ½ cup sugar
- 2 tablespoons honey
- ½ vanilla bean
- 1 stick cinnamon
- 16 walnut halves, toasted, for garnish

1. Peel and quarter pears and quince. In a 2-quart saucepan, combine the water, wine, sugar, and honey.

2. Bring mixture to boil and stir to dissolve sugar. Add vanilla bean, cinnamon stick, and quince. Reduce heat to simmer and cook for 18 minutes.

3. Add pears and continue cooking for 15 minutes more. Using slotted spoon, remove fruit to a serving dish, and discard vanilla bean and cinnamon stick. Boil juices until reduced by half. Pour liquid over fruit. Garnish with walnut halves.

INDEX

Note: Page numbers in italics refer to illustrations separated from recipe text. Recipe titles appear under food categories only. Individual food entries refer to charts or discussions in text.

U.S. MEASURE AND METRIC MEASURE CONVERSION CHART

Formulas for Exact Measures

Rounded Measures for Quick Reference

	Symbol	When you know:	Multiply by:	To find:			
Mass (Weight)	oz	ounces	28.35	grams	1 oz		= 30 g
	lb	pounds	0.45	kilograms	4 oz		= 115 g
	g	grams	0.035	ounces	8 oz		= 225 g
	kg	kilograms	2.2	pounds	16 oz	= 1 lb	= 450 g
					32 oz	= 2 lb	= 900 g
					36 oz	= 2¼ lb	= 1,000 g (1 kg)
Volume	tsp	teaspoons	5.0	milliliters	¼ tsp	= ¹⁄₂₄ oz	= 1 ml
	tbsp	tablespoons	15.0	milliliters	½ tsp	= ¹⁄₁₂ oz	= 2 ml
	fl oz	fluid ounces	29.57	milliliters	1 tsp	= ⅙ oz	= 5 ml
	c	cups	0.24	liters	1 tbsp	= ½ oz	= 15 ml
	pt	pints	0.47	liters	1 c	= 8 oz	= 250 ml
	qt	quarts	0.95	liters	2 c (1 pt)	= 16 oz	= 500 ml
	gal	gallons	3.785	liters	4 c (1 qt)	= 32 oz	= 1 l.
	ml	milliliters	0.034	fluid ounces	4 qt (1 gal)	= 128 oz	= 3¾ l.
Temperature	°F	Fahrenheit	5/9 (after subtracting 32)	Celsius	32° F	= 0° C	
	°C	Celsius	9/5 (then add 32)	Fahrenheit	68° F	= 20° C	
					212° F	= 100° C	